THE GOLD OF OPHIR

THE
GOLD
OF
OPHIR

TRAVELS, MYTHS, AND LEGENDS
IN THE NEW WORLD

CHOSEN AND WITH AN ESSAY BY
EDWARD DAHLBERG

E. P. DUTTON & CO., INC. | NEW YORK | 1972

For Coburn H. Britton:
with love,
oftentimes mistaken for dross in this world,
but the Gold of Ophir
between us.

CONTENTS

"They sacrifice on the tops of the mountains, and burn incense upon the hills, under oaks and poplars and fir-trees, because the shadow thereof is good."

—HOSEA

THE GOLD OF OPHIR

THE GOLD OF OPHIR

By EDWARD DAHLBERG

Now is the eventide of the historiographer; the news-historian gives his false public kneel to FACT, the Baal Peor of our pedants. What concerns me are the three Americas, and not a discourse of a truncated continent we name with putid ignorance the United States.

Alas, we know as little about our beginnings as the tapir that hides in the swampy growths when the morning appears. Our best ethnologists and explorers are no better known than the relics of Cholula. Their works, often merely titles, are cenotaphs. How common it is to epitaph a noble scholiast or poet by remarking, "I have heard of him."

Who may claim he has a dram of intelligence who is unfamiliar with the soil that nourishes his body and higher faculties? Worse, our earth by now is the avenging Erinyes of the North American people. Can it not be said that our veins are the great floods of the New World, the Amazon, the Rio Negro and the river Magdalene, and that our most virile thoughts are the ingredients of porphyry, feldspar, limestone, and gneiss? Pliny alleges that emerald clears one's sight. It is worth noticing that many cities in nether America lie at the foot of volcanoes and that the houses of the inhabitants are built of lava and rocks of igneous origin. The volcanic Cordilleras furnished the light for the Indian, just as Etna was the torch of Ceres, the goddess of grain.

For the most part, my concern is with the cormorant man who sought the cruel auriferous ore, gold, but most often found instead marcasite and death. The misfortune of Columbus we know; he says in one of his epistles that he made the voyages to the New World for lucre.

There have been numerous apologists for the conquistadors. Perhaps without exception they were bloodthirsty and avaricious. Las Casas indignantly stated that forty million Indians had been extirpated by the Spaniards. This is doubtless hyperbole, but that is of no moment, for it is hard to find fault with Las Casas' virtue.

Pedro de Alvarado, the lieutenant of Cortés, annihilated four to five million natives in the peninsula of Guatemala and Yucatán within a few years. On the day 4 Quat, according to the Quiché Maya calendar, Alvarado had a king and three caciques burned alive because they were unable to supply him with as much gold as he coveted. In a letter to Emperor Charles the Fifth, Cortés explains that he had only refrained from razing to the ground an entire village because the flames might attract the natives nearby who would come to the aid of the wretches. When a band of these red Indians, fearing that their tribe would perish at the hands of the Spanish adventurers, came to spy on their camp, Cortés cut off the hands of fifty of the Indians. De Soto lopped off the heads of Indian couriers because he was too fatigued to remove their iron collars. Gonzalo Pizarro threw numerous Incas to the dogs, which devoured them, because they were unable to tell him anything about a land of the cinnamon trees. Endeavoring to find out where the remains of Yahuarhuacac and a vast store of gold had been secretly buried so that the Spaniards would not trouble his remains to gratify their greed, Gonzalo Pizarro tortured many Incas until he discovered that the grave was at Xaquixaguana.

Fray Motolinia, a mild and good man, blamed the Spaniards for the ten plagues in Mexico. The worst, the monk said, was the gold mines where the Aztecan laborer had to toil until he perished. He was compelled to furnish all the materials for the mines and even his own food. Often he ran for thirty leagues with the little maize he had and died on the way. For half a league from Oaxaca, the principal mining town, the ground was so bleached with human bones that one could not go in that direction without stepping upon skeletons. The Indian was the mule; he was forced to walk one hundred and thirty leagues, his naked back loaded with artillery or an anchor weighing seventy-five pounds. Had the poor Aztec no food, he went to the oratory to look for a slain victim that had been offered to an idol, and after the priests and their followers had feasted upon the flesh of the captive, he ate what was left.

Another plague was the taxes; the Indian had to sell his children and land to meet this robbing. Often having nothing except his drawers or a loincloth, he took his own life.

Human flesh has been for sale in all ages. Columbus captured Indians and kept them as slaves. Las Casas, overwhelmed by the frightful plight of the Indians, recommended that Negroes be imported to Mexico to take the place of red bondsmen. Las Casas agreed that each Spaniard be allowed to import from Africa a dozen Negroes as slaves. Africans were heavily engaged in this bitter marketing of black flesh which they exported to America.

Another plague was the Spanish overseer and his black servant. Too lazy to collect whatever he could from the Aztec workmen, he sent his Negro vassal to extort maize and land, and the black man was more ferocious with the Indians than his master.

Errors, rituals, and greed drive men to their Odyssean destinies. An apocalyptic cutthroat, the Spaniard dissembled, cheated, robbed and murdered whilst he paid the most humble homage to the Holy Ghost. That he was a true believer cannot be misdoubted, but his guile was no less genuine.

Commonly the Levantine freebooter and voyager was only by mischance a discoverer. The Portuguese were so indifferent to the *sertao*, the forests far from the Atlantic skirting Brazil, that they lived along the coasts like sea-crabs. When Columbus came to Hispaniola (Haiti), he was crestfallen; he saw a few huts made of reeds and covered with palm leaves and woven grasses and scattered villagers. Where were the ginger, pepper and the spices of the Moluccas? He found a little gold, mastic, and cinnamon, but this was no pelf for his sovereigns Ferdinand and Isabella. Of course, the simple, rural manners of the people astonished him. He was delighted with the albic, glabrous skin of the maidens at Isabella and Navidad who wore nothing except gourds and seashells to cover their privy members. How enchanting it was to learn that these timorous natives did not covet property, had no martial passions, and prized broken glass more than gold.

The Spaniard mapped the headlands, estuaries, morasses, and vales the best he could, giving the appellations of saints to riverine hamlets and ranges of basaltic hills to conceal his chagrin and cupidity.

Columbus, a man of far more refinement than rough Balboa, was no less greedy. Neither knew what he was doing. Columbus never realized he had come to the New World. Although Balboa fell upon his knees when he saw the South Sea from the peak of Darien, it had not occurred to him that there was another ocean. Balboa viewed this infinite dropsy, an unknown ocean, with religious awe; for man is the only animal on earth with beliefs in the supernatural. No one can be more intelligent than Homer who is always telling us about prodigies, the anthropaghagous Polyphemi, the Elysian Fields, and moly, which the bard says is a plant that cures protean men of their distempered humors, and unbearable seasons of phlegm. Dioscorides informs us that moly is only a species of garlic.

How rapturous is one when he hears that in Huancavelica of Peru water flowing hot out of a fountain turns into rocks, or that at Luguna in the Canaries the roofs and walls of the houses are covered with houseleeks. Yet this is a source of rituals; Pythagoras states that one should fasten leeks to his door to avert evil. The Greeks of old did the same to avoid disappointment, disease or death. Jane Harrison relates that before the victim, the *pharmakos*, is slain, he is beaten with leeks.

Were not all races people-eaters we would think men as naïve and simple as the penguin. Though we are repulsed by the Spaniard's cruelty we also admire his extraordinary fortitude. Orellana and his soldiers were looking for the lands of the cinnamons. They had been floating in a bark upon a massive river, not knowing in what direction they were going. After they had consumed a thousand dogs, they had nothing to eat but palm shoots, fruit stones, fungi, or their belts and shoes cooked with herbs. One day they imagined they were close to the Atlantic because they *felt* the pulse of the great river. They had no compass or loadstone and none of them was a sailor. Orellana and his men had not intended to undergo miserable deprivations, the wildest rains, and thick tempests, even for cinnamons, and certainly not just to discover a body of water, now called the Amazon, and then known as the Orellana or the Maranon.

Man is always starving; there is almost no sorrow he cannot abide; for the whole earth is a groaning brute, and the cause of his endless aches is that the ground and the seas suffer too. What he cannot endure is his inanition, his Guinea calms; his most severe ill is his torpor and this is as periodic as the scab which occurs after the rising of the Pleiad.

Mischance is a deity; Pluto, our eternal darkness, lay in the arms of Tyche, who is Chance. In the *Iliads* it is told that Paeon the physician healed Pluto after he had been wounded by Hercules. What a rare myth, for it suggests that death is not death, and that the deceased can be hurt. Nearly every discovery of the Spaniard was a mistake. All discoveries and sovereign ideas are accidental.

America is a great, negative continent. Almost every conquistador reaped the penury and death which he sought, since men are automatic, and know not what they do, but must perforce do it. When the Spaniard referred to this land as *terra incognita*, he was describing his own darkling nature, that Orphic cave. The men who went with Champlain encountered snowy mishaps, sleet, blizzards, and the hardest terrain. They explored the St. Lawrence and its perfidious rapids, and Champlain pondered the fierce weather in his own soul, saying that the New World was a *terra damnata*.

The rites of the sundry nations are more similar than not. The

Inca offered maize, coca, shells (*mullu* in their language), and old shoes to hills, gullies, and to the junction of rivers or paths. Hecate was the Greek goddess of the crossroads, and Lares guarded the roads that meet. In Guatemala the natives, informing Pedro de Alvarado, their ferocious enemy, that they were at war with him, sacrificed a woman and a dog and placed them betwixt two mountain passes that merged.

All people have legends about the beginnings of the world and how each nation sprung from dust, plants, or the seas. The inhabitants of Hispaniola thought that mountains, streams, and the prodigious waters flowed out of a gourd. Nearly everyone throughout the globe is familiar with the great deluge. After the Peruvian flood the survivors were said to have come out of a cleft at Paritambo. Ravines were venerated by the Inca, and a chasm, known as a *magera,* in the *Prologemena,* was a sanctified place to the Greeks. Porphyry, in his commentary on the thirteenth book of the *Odyssey* writes: "Ceres educated Proserpine with her Nymphs in a cave" and ". . . the ancients made a cavern to be a symbol of the world [and] Saturn fabricated a cavern in the ocean itself and concealed his children." Empedocles held a similar belief in crevices. The women, during the festival of Demeter, dropped a pig into a cave.

The Indians were no less pious than those who peopled Latium under the dominion of Saturn. The Romans paid devout observance to ovens, hinges, doors; Hera for the Greeks was a log, and Terminus, the god who divided Roman land between neighbors, was a stone or a bole. The idols of the Aztecs were wrought of basalt, terra-cotta, or flint, and the eyes of their demons were composed of grains of maize or beans, and the teeth of glass or hyalite.

Quetzalcoatl, Mexican god of wind, who first appeared on the coasts of Panuco, taught the people to pierce their sinning tongues and ears with the thorny maguey leaves until the blood flowed. Their idols were covered with reeds dabbled in human gore. He instructed them in the rites of sacrifice and penance. Styx is the darksome underworld of our wicked imaginings; the

Inca believed that bad people who died were tormented by demons called *supay*. The Greeks assuaged the ghosts, bringing them victims and grains; the deceased fattened on their sorrows. Whoever is glutted with the pains of his foul acts feeds on the dole of the dead, and they in turn provide him with the festal meal of remorse.

The Aztec priest wore the skin of the slave he had offered to his idol in the *teocalli*, the temple, and the Greek hierophant put on the same garb, certain that this integument had "medicinal properties." The Greeks had many braziers and so had the Mexicans who used incense, *copal*. Jane Harrison thinks that brimstone was a sort of incense which was supposed to cleanse the sinner. We are acquainted with the Christian injunction, purge me with hyssop, and we may well wonder if the Mexican did not share the same faith in the purgative virtues of *copal*.

Many nations deify the shades; Demeter protected the tombs, and the Indian paid such reverence to the deceased that he imagined any conic hillock "covered with bushes, molina . . . and cactus" was a sacral tumulus. A petty king at Hispaniola placed the ashes of his deceased son in a bitter gourd which he hung from a balsam tree. Father Sahagun, referring to Aztec sensibilities, says, "When one dies they are wont to say he is now a *teotl* [god]." When a girl was inhumed in Mexico the mourners placed a besom alongside her, signifying her devotion to her parental household and her purity, and laid roses and maize cakes on the stone that covered her. Indians of Brazil thought it inhuman to allow the worms to feed upon their beloved ones, and so they ate them and believed they were their living sepulchers. The same people interred in a coca orchard or in their homes. The American dumps his kindred in a morose factory cemetery, and allows them to starve; of course, it's a superstition to imagine we can feed the dead, but there is much feeling in it.

Spleen is common to all human kind. An Indian of Brazil who was vexed ate dirt. When a captive was taken, these Indians held a festival of insults; they heaped invectives upon him while playing flutes made of the bones of human legs. A similar feast of vituperation obtained in Greece; the victim was beaten and treated with every form of insolence before he was slain to honor Zeus.

Vestals were esteemed by Romans and the autochthonous Americans. Romulus lamented the rape of the Sabine virgins. Ovid states that in the Golden Age of Latium maidens were taught by Pallas to card the wool and to unload the distaffs. The Latin poet says that the eldest vestal burned the calves in the fire that their ashes might purify the people on the day of Pales. Mexican girls of unspotted virtue fed the idols with meat and loaves shaped like human hands and feet; they sprinkled incense upon the altars, swept the "fane" with feathers, and busied themselves spinning, weaving, and making blankets. Anyone who violated an Aztec nun was punished with death.

Who is civilized and who barbaric? The Indian priests lay on the ground in the *teocalli* with no covering except a loincloth. They abstained from food for many days, did not touch salt or garlic, and had no sexual commerce with women. Martin de Valencia, a Christian zealot, could not humiliate himself enough, and who can? He was restless and loathed his cell because it did not resemble a maggoty grave. Unable to endure his seclusion, and inconsolable after prayer and fasting, he began to regard the trees surrounding him as demons. Beside himself, he threw ashes into his broth, and still he could not overcome that inward dryness that is a feral affliction to a contemplative man.

Motolinia, the highly intelligent padre, living two millennia after Aristotle wrote his book, more of a fable than the natural history of animals, believed that griffins, having the heads and wings of eagles, and the bodies and hindquarters of lions, dwelt on the ridge of the volcanic Popocatepetl. Man has and always will be the irrational brute with hands. The Franciscan monks at Santo Domingo, doing all they could to extirpate the larvae of ants, and failing in their efforts, selected St. Saturnin as their defender, and shortly thereafter these pismires disappeared. Women who were pregnant and whose lives were in jeopardy were said to survive after they had touched the cord of St. Francis. In Ovid's *Fasti* the invocation is: ". . . ye ants, O spare the sown grain."

It is trite to assume that the Indian was savage, no better, as the French who came to Canada said, than a wild weed. The Indian was quick to learn languages, and to discern Occidental cant. Often the natives of New Spain were exhorted to renounce their concubines, and on one occasion when so admonished they replied that the Spaniards had many wives. Upon being advised the Spaniard kept these women as servants, the Indians retorted that they retained them so that they might weave their mantles and take care of the fields. Observing the religious Spaniards kneeling to the Rood, they asked why they had no better sense than to worship a tree.

The Incas had a Genesis, more promising as a legend than the Gilgamesh epic, but not as psalmodic as the Old Testament or the Gospels. It is revealed that at Tishuanaco, Pachacamac the Creator raised up divers nations wrought of clay. Pausanias claims that he saw the original primate of the Greeks made of penguid marl by Prometheus. It is fabled that the first red inhabitants were turned into stones because they were disobedient. Lot's wife was translated into a column of salt for hankering after Sodom. Only foolish persons are homesick for their past, and long before they are old they are in their swaddling clothes.

The Indians of Callao held that the sun and the moon were born in the waters of Lake Titicaca, and the Arcadians assured the Greeks they were older than the moon. Zeus is a god of thunder and lightning; he is also Helios the sun, and these two planets and the elements were worshipped by the Indians. Isis, the Ancient One, is the moon and Osiris, her consort, the sun, in Egyptian theogony. Quetzalcoatl, we know, is the wind, and Agamemnon, though rancorous, is highly intelligent, but that does not prevent him from sacrificing his daughter to appease Artemis and the Winds. And Socrates, deemed the wisest of men by the Pythian oracle, says: "Do you mean that I do not believe in the godhead of the sun or moon, which is the common creed of all men?"

Greeks and Incas paid the strictest attention to youths: boys from eleven to fourteen years of age went to the sacred hill of Huanacauri; Inca girls who were in the procession carried vases of *chicha*, boiled maize, to the foot of this mount where sacrifices were made. In the month Capac Raymi, Christoval de Molina tells us, they held their principal feasts; at this time the youths were given breeches, the toga of virilia, shoes made of reeds and of the color of saffron, and slings. After the fasting and the orisons were over, the parents and their near relations flogged them to make sure they bore them the proper filial regard and did not forget their ancestral valor.

Then they marched to the square of Cuzco, the holy city of the Incas, where the embalmed lords and the *huacas*, the idols, were exhibited, and the youths were once more whipped. Aristophanes, dismayed by the truculence of the epheboi, who crossed their legs wantonly, and sat in an impudent and lickerish manner, and who had small respect for their elders, speaks of former times when no boy would ever anoint himself below his navel.

Without some degree of shame, insolence is rife and modesty is considered provincial. The populace given to rabble habits and practices is as phlegmatic as the sloth who moves on its belly, never standing on its feet. In an age of male and female sluts, the attitude of the people is ignominious. It is fabled that Venus assigns a civil attire for men and women, but today there is an addle show of virility which indicates that sexual love has sharply abated. When virgins and boys are garbed to show their shame, and the hunkers are accented, the pudenda of the nation is flaccid.

The Chichimecas were naked giants and as uncultivated as the man-eating Polyphemi. Polite nations of the world were attired with appropriate modesty. Backward Indians ranged the plains, or *ilanos*, without any clothing except leaves or gourds to cover their private parts. The rude Canadian Indians, as it is disclosed in the Jesuit Relations, wore only the bark of a tree to hide their privy members. The Chichimecas, who inhabited Mexico before the arrival of the Aztecs, were naked giants who plucked up trees as if they were lettuce. They were uncouth, ill-languaged, had no houses, and like Cyclops knew nothing of the grain of Ceres, for they did not till the soil, and ate roots, vipers, and jaguars.

According to Torquemada, Xiuhtlato told the people how to make bread of maize; and South American Indians used cassava and the root of the Yucca for bread. Before the Greeks learned how to bake loaves they ate seeds and laid pots of uncooked porridge on the altars of Zeus. The Egyptians used swamp roots for bread.

Nations close to plants, herbs, and rocks do not despise poverty, the modern stigma, or the five Christly wounds in the body of the poor. Ovid says that in rustic Latium the altars were loaded with savin and crackling laurels. Nor did Demeter disdain grains of salt, spelt, or a few violets. The Inca having no coca, maize, or shells to pay his homage to a river or mountain, offered a stone, green weeds, or a blade of grass to win good tidings from a flux of water or a summit. The other day I discovered that wild thyme flourishes in barren hills, and was pierced by this bit of natural history. Who could believe Shakespearean poesy thrived in sterile land?

The natives of Central America were content with the bare ground for a pallet, a piece of wood for a pillow, and regarded a tree in the forest as their summer house. Penury is a caitiff god that brings much woe to men, which is the price of understanding. However, Plutus, an arrogant and greedy deity, eats up the populace and its legends. Without fables the people wax mad and are as poisonous as henbane that grows near dunghills and highways, the rabble altars of the North American.

The Indians and Greeks observed human sacrifices. Motolinia says that when the corn was palm-high, a boy and a girl about the age of three or four were killed. After the stalks of maize were knee-high, four children were slaughtered to appease the water god, Tlaloc, and to make sure there would be no want of rain. It

is not what happens that causes men to cower so much as that
which may occur. His fears are the origin of his theogony.
Animal uneasiness is man's clearest understanding, and no one
should dismiss his qualms or misgivings. There was also a merchant festival; during this ceremony a woman was clothed as the
goddess of salt, and after the throng had danced all night she was
sacrificed the following morning.

Mexican children were docile, and were adored by their parents who slashed their throats to assuage a demon because they
could not bear to rip out their hearts. Not always capable of
murdering hundreds of slaves that they felt necessary to quiet the
idols, they made an unction of spiders, scorpions, palmers, sala-
manders, and vipers which they burned and mixed with a seed.
Of this they concocted a beverage that was so intoxicating that
they were senseless enough to murder about four hundred captives in the temple of Camaztli. Manetho asserts that in the dog
days the Egyptians burned a man alive, expecting that this would
bring rain. The Greeks observed a harvest festival, the Thargelia;
during a plague or famine they selected a captive, struck him
with leeks and dried figs, and then burned him in order to save
the stricken city.

Those who are repulsed by such horrid rites must ask themselves whether there is any difference between human sacrifice
and modern war. The youths of the country are also captives,
enslaved soldiers sent to remote lands to be slaughtered to sanc-
tify the new merchant god named Petrol.

There is not a nation in this piacular earth that does not require
dittany, a sharp hot herb, the juice of which taken with wine is
said by Dioscorides to be a remedy against serpents. Every man
has adders in his soul. The saint, the savage, and the divine
lawgiver go into the wilderness or to the mountains to expel their
satan who has a thousand gluttonous mouths in his body.

How men make civilization smell sweet as fennel is an enigma.
Men are too protean to be just; no one can weigh his acts in Job's
Balance without cringing. Nor is there an enlightened legislator
who, if given absolute power over his subjects, will not become

the hierophantic assassin in order to establish a penitentiary Utopia.

Mention should be made of the gold of Ophir. The ships of Tarshish are a proverb unto this day. We first came upon the former name in Genesis where it is told that Solomon sent out a fleet to fetch the gold of Ophir. That Ophir was any particular nation José de Acosta doubts. St. Jerome asserts that Tarshish had many significances; it may mean Crisolite, Jacinth or a region of the East Indies. Ophir was thought to have the finest gold. The Spaniards, as de Acosta relates, sailing for Peru supposed they were bound for Ophir. Peter Martyr, the first historian of America, believed that Columbus had located the Antipodes. He writes in an *epistola* that Columbus, touching the shores of the New World, was sure he had reached a parcel of the earth near the Ganges. It was also assumed by Columbus that he had arrived at Marco Polo's Cipango (Japan) or Cathay.

New Ground was a kind of imaginary savannah loaded with angelic miasma. The Atlantic, called the Sea of Darkness, was considered a vasty, bottomless gulf. It had been rumored that on an early date the Carthaginians had made voyages to the Canaries which Pliny alluded to as the Fortunate or the Purple Islands. Homer was acquainted with these blessed isles he imagined were Elysium.

Nobody knows who was the first to have broken the Pillars of Hercules and ventured into the pelagic deep. There were various legends, but no historical annals. When a fable becomes a humdrum fact, man is the worse for it.

The Canaries consist of seven islands, the most fertile of which is Tenerife; the western slope of Tenerife is verdurous and zephyry, whilst the eastern loins of this smoking peak are more sterile than lava. But we are discussing the phonolites, the acoriae, the mica slate, and quartz of the intellect, or, if you will, the soul. One part of the human spirit includes palm trees, mangroves, oaks, laurels, arbutus, and the other watery mists, the salt marshes of Avernus and the mire of grievous Cocytus.

It can be affirmed that the winged caravels that broke the Pillars and furrowed Oceanus, going past Gades (Cadiz) knew whither they were going, but that the Admiral of the Ocean Seas did not. With no compass or loadstone that always points north, his pilot sat in the prow of the carrack depending upon the stars, parches of seaweeds, or the flight of a frigate bird to determine his course.

Fifteen hundred years after Pliny had described the loadstone, the seafarer had no intelligence of its useful properties. Two years following Columbus' discovery, ships going to Hispaniola carried mariners and astrologers to assist the captain.

Not Columbus, but the Jews, banished from Spain by the Inquisition, were the eminent hydrographers of the time. The unfortunate Jews who remained in Spain were robbed of their money and jewels in order to build pinnaces and furnish the men for the second voyage of Columbus. The purblind voyagers relied upon ancient cartographers, Strabo, Ptolemy, and Eratosthenes. Aristotle believed that the Burning Zone was uninhabitable, and St. Augustine thought there were no human beings beyond the Tropic of Cancer.

Late as the seventeenth century, José de Acosta, the Jesuit who lived in the equatorial zone, disclosed that when the sun entered into the Aries, the weather was extremely cold, and that Potosí, renowned for its gold and silver mines, was environed with caustic winds and void of grass or herbs.

The ancients, with what prescience we should not diminish or fleer at, had the utmost reluctance to go past the Pillars, and venture into Oceanus. Pindar the poet, having similar prophetic qualms, warned the Greeks: "That it is not lawful, neither for wise men nor for fools, to know what is beyond the Strait of Gibraltar."

Had Terra Incognita risen from the seas long after Asia, Africa, or Europe? Humboldt misdoubted that. Why then was the New Continent meagerly peopled, and why had they no domestic animals? There were the forest hen, but no poultry as we know it, the sloth, the ant-eating tapir, the llama, the Peruvian sheep, the peccary that has an evil-smelling gland, described by the first explorers as a navel; and the *manatí*, the beef of the Indians, which feeds on mangrove leaves, but lives in estuaries and saline rivers.

Columbus shipped horses to America and De Soto brought sows. Turquoise was here, but no jade, though jade hatchets have been found in the plains and in the Andes. There were remnants of gigantic cetaceous animals, the bones of a species of elephant; in Uruguay the bones of the megatherium were discovered.

Indian rituals were astounding in many respects, but agriculture was primitive, and there was almost no poetry, and no alphabet. Diodorus Siculus alleges that the Atlantides were ignorant of the use of corn because they were separated from the human race long before it was cultivated.

Our knowledge of the triune Americas is still as nebulous as the origin of the Guanches; the remnants of that people consist of a few mummies and one hundred and fifty words. The Guanches at Tenerife were no more than eighty leagues from Africa, and yet they had no flax or corn, and they plowed the ground with a goat's horn. Their humble aliment was an undomesticated grain, *goffo*, a word in their extinct language, which after it had been washed and toasted was bruised in a hand mill like the ones employed in Spain for grinding the grease of bullocks. Does not this custom smack of a remark made by Sancho Panza?

Humboldt states that one-fourth of the extraordinary altitude of the Cordilleras is a region of snow. Would that our humid Occidental civilization afforded us a hard wintry metaphysic or a kind sensual poesy. Man without freezing steppes in his nature will have no equinoctial sun in his conceptions either. Since man is less than zero, he imagines his quest is a plus. Did he not suppose so, he would have a caitiff portion and the destiny of a hemp seed. The thinker is a restless ontological mariner, seeking the Moluccas, Terra Incognita, and other planets, to find himself. For neither man nor the volcano of Gotopaxi has august heights except at a distance.

It is said that after Ynca Yupangui expired, a thousand of his servants were murdered and inhumed with him so that they could attend to his wants in the underworld of the *manes*. How can one account for the Inca so civil in other ways? No North American has equaled the Inca architect. Without knowledge of mortar or cement, the titanic rocks of his temples were joined together with such miraculous skill that the walls of the edifices were as seamless as the coat of Christ. Compared with the pyramids of Cholula and the chapels of the Inca, what are we to think of the Mammon Towers in our concrete Acheron.

The Mexican and the Inca were remarkable lapidaries and goldsmiths; each Aztec and Inca cut the stones and the timber for his house; he was a weaver, shoemaker, carpenter, mason, and tailor. The artisan in the United States has almost vanished. The machine will never replace the genius of the hand.

The paralysis of the Promethean will is the result of mechanical vehicles. The machine has turned the American into the most epicene and lonely automaton in the world. Solitude was not the malaise of the Indians who dwelt together in communal tribes. Even the Zamura vultures in Mexico roost in a flock of forty to fifty on coca trees. The titanic steel furnace is the chimera that breathes forth noisome flames, but not the volcanic fire that attracted Empedocles and Pliny.

The North American mammalian thinker, having no place in the cruel iron cities, will be forced to migrate to the two Americas below him, for the naphtha that flows out of the primitive rocks in the peninsula of Araya may yet feed the lamp of Pallas Minerva.

FROM

DE ORBE NOVO

THE EIGHT DECADES
OF PETER MARTYR D'ANGHERA

TRANSLATED BY
FRANCIS AUGUSTUS MacNUTT

BOOK I

PETER MARTYR, APOSTOLIC PROTONOTARY
AND ROYAL COUNSELLOR
TO THE VISCOUNT ASCANIO SFORZA,
CARDINAL VICE-CHANCELLOR

It was a gentle custom of the ancients to number amongst the gods those heroes by whose genius and greatness of soul unknown lands were discovered. Since we, however, only render homage to one God in Three Persons, and consequently may not adore the discoverers of new lands, it remains for us to offer them our admiration. Likewise should we admire the sovereigns under whose inspiration and auspices the intentions of the discoverers were realised; let us praise the one and the other, and exalt them according to their merits.

Attend now to what is told concerning the recently discovered islands in the Western ocean. Since you have expressed in your letters a desire for information I will, to avoid doing injustice to any one, recount the events from their beginnings.

A certain Christopher Columbus, a Genoese, proposed to the Catholic King and Queen, Ferdinand and Isabella, to discover the islands which touch the Indies, by sailing from the western extremity of this country. He asked for ships and whatever was necessary to navigation, promising not only to propagate the Christian religion, but also certainly to bring back pearls, spices and gold beyond anything ever imagined. He succeeded in persuading them and, in response to his demands, they provided him

From *De Orbe Novo*, The eight Decades of Peter Martyr D'Anghera, Translated from the Latin with Notes and Introduction by Francis Augustus MacNutt, G. P. Putnam's Sons, New York and London, The Knickerbocker Press, 1912, Volume One, pp. 57–149. (Footnotes partially deleted.)

at the expense of the royal treasury with three ships;[1] the first
having a covered deck, the other two being merchantmen without decks, of the kind called by the Spaniards *caravels*. When
everything was ready Columbus sailed from the coast of Spain,
about the calends of September in the year 1492, taking with him
about 220 Spaniards.[2]

The Fortunate Isles, or, as the Spaniards call them, the Canaries, were long since discovered in the middle of the ocean.
They are distant from Cadiz about three hundred leagues; for,
according to the masters of the art of navigation, each marine
league is equal to four thousand paces.[3] In ancient times these
islands were called Fortunate, because of the mild temperature
they enjoyed. The islanders suffered neither from the heat of
summer nor the rigours of winter: some authors consider that the
real Fortunate Isles correspond to the archipelago which the
Portuguese have named Cape Verde. If they are at present called
the Canaries, it is because they are inhabited by men who are
naked and have no religion. They lie to the south and are outside
European climates. Columbus stopped there to replenish his
supply of provisions and water, and to rest his crew before starting on the difficult part of his enterprise.

Since we are speaking of the Canaries, it may not be thought
uninteresting to recall how they were discovered and civilised.
During many centuries they were unknown or rather forgotten.

---

[1] This statement is not absolutely exact, as the funds came from various
sources. Columbus, assisted by the Pinzon brothers of Palos, furnished one-
eighth of the amount, or the cost of one vessel. Two vessels were supplied
by the town of Palos, in response to a royal order; the town owing such
service to the crown. The ready money required was advanced by Sant-
angel, receiver of the ecclesiastical revenues of Aragon.

[2] From Palos on August 3d, 1492. The inscription on the floor of Seville
Cathedral reads: *con tres galeras y 90 personas*. It follows that Peter Martyr's
figures are exaggerated, for only Oviedo amongst early authorities exceeds
the number ninety, and he numbers the united crews at 120 men.

[3] According to the computations of Columbus, four miles were equal to
one marine league; the Italian mile, assumed to have been used by him, was
equal to 1842 English feet. Fifty-six and two-thirds miles were equal to a
degree.

It was about the year 1405 that a Frenchman called Bethencourt rediscovered the seven Canaries. They were conceded to him in gift by the Queen Katherine, who was Regent during the minority of her son John. Bethencourt lived several years in the archipelago, where he took possession of the two islands of Lancerote and Fuerteventura, and civilised their inhabitants. Upon his death, his heir sold these two islands to the Spaniards. Afterwards Ferdinando Pedraria and his wife landed upon two other of the Canaries, Ferro and Gomera. Within our own times the Grand Canary was conquered by Pedro de Vera, a Spanish nobleman from Xeres; Palma and Teneriffe were conquered by Alonzo de Lugo, but at the cost of the royal treasury. The islands of Gomera and Ferro were conquered by the same Lugo, but not without difficulty; for the natives, although they lived naked in the woods and had no other arms than sticks and stones, surprised his soldiers one day and killed about four hundred of them. He finally succeeded in subduing them, and to-day the whole archipelago recognises the Spanish authority.

Upon leaving these islands and heading straight to the west, with a slight deviation to the south-west, Columbus sailed thirty-three successive days without seeing anything but sea and sky. His companions began to murmur in secret, for at first they concealed their discontent, but soon, openly, desiring to get rid of their leader, whom they even planned to throw into the sea. They considered that they had been deceived by this Genoese, who was leading them to some place from whence they could never return. After the thirtieth day they angrily demanded that he should turn back and go no farther; Columbus, by using gentle words holding out promises and flattering their hopes, sought to gain time, and he succeeded in calming their fears; finally also reminding them that if they refused him their obedience or attempted violence against him, they would be accused of treason by their sovereigns. To their great joy, the much-desired land was finally discovered.[4] During his first voyage Columbus visited

[4] Land was discovered on the morning of October 12th, Julian calendar. Efforts to identify the island on which Columbus first landed have been

six islands, two of which were of extraordinary magnitude; one of these he named Hispaniola, and the other Juana,[5] though he was not positive that the latter was an island. While sailing along the coasts of these islands, in the month of November, the Spaniards heard nightingales singing in the dense forests, and they discovered great rivers of fresh water, and natural harbours sufficient for the largest fleets. Columbus reconnoitred the coast of Juana in a straight line towards the north-west for no less than eight hundred thousand paces or eighty leagues, which led him to believe that it was a continent, since as far as the eye could reach, no signs of any limits to the island were perceptible. He decided to return,[6] also because of the tumultuous sea, for the coast of Juana towards the north is very broken, and at that winter season, the north winds were dangerous to his ships. Laying his course eastwards, he held towards an island which he believed to be the island of Ophir; examination of the maps, however, shows that it was the Antilles and neighbouring islands. He named this island Hispaniola. Having decided to land, Columbus put in towards shore, when the largest of his ships struck a concealed rock and was wrecked. Fortunately the reef stood high in the water, which saved the crew from drowning; the other two boats quickly approached, and all the sailors were taken safely on board.

It was at this place that the Spaniards, on landing, first beheld the islanders. Upon seeing strangers approaching, the natives collected and fled into the depths of the forests like timid hares

---

numerous. The natives called it Guanahani and Columbus named it San Salvador. Muñoz believed it to be the present Watling's Island; Humboldt and Washington Irving thought Cat Island more likely, while Navarrete identified it as Grand Turk. Captain G. V. Fox, U.S.N., published in Appendix 18 to the Report for 1880 the conclusions he had reached after exhaustive examinations conducted in the Bahamas, with which islands and their seas long service had made him familiar. He selected Samana or Atwood Cay as the first land discovered.

[5] In honour of the Infante Don Juan, heir to the Castilian crown. It has, however, always borne its native name of Cuba.

[6] But for this infelicitous change in his course, Columbus must have discovered the coast of Mexico.

pursued by hounds. The Spaniards followed them, but only succeeded in capturing one woman, whom they took on board their ships, where they gave her plenty of food and wine and clothes (for both sexes lived absolutely naked and in a state of nature); afterwards this woman, who knew where the fugitives were concealed, returned to her people, to whom she showed her ornaments, praising the liberality of the Spaniards; upon which they all returned to the coast, convinced that the newcomers were descended from heaven. They swam out to the ships, bringing gold, of which they had a small quantity, which they exchanged gladly for trifles of glass or pottery. For a needle, a bell, a fragment of mirror, or any such thing, they gladly gave in exchange whatever gold was asked of them, or all that they had about them. As soon as more intimate relations were established and the Spaniards came to understand the local customs, they gathered by signs and by conjectures that the islanders were governed by kings. When they landed from their ships they were received with great honour by these kings and by all the natives, making every demonstration of homage of which they were capable. At sunset, the hour of the Angelus, the Spaniards knelt according to Christian custom, and their example was immediately followed by the natives. The latter likewise adored the Cross as they saw the Christians doing.[7]

These people also brought off the men from the wrecked ship, as well as all it contained, transporting everything in barques which they called canoes. They did this with as much alacrity and joy as though they were saving their own relatives; and certainly amongst ourselves greater charity could not have been displayed.

Their canoes are constructed out of single tree-trunks, which they dig out with tools of sharpened stone. They are very long

[7] The first report Columbus made to the Catholic sovereigns was most flattering to the American aborigines. *Certifico a vuestras altezas que en el mundo creo que no hay mejor gente ni mejor tierra: ellos aman a sus projimos como a si mismo.* Like most generalisations, these were found, upon closer acquaintance with native character and customs, to be too comprehensive as well as inaccurate.

and narrow, and are made of a single piece of wood. It is alleged that some have been seen capable of carrying eighty rowers. It has been nowhere discovered that iron is used by the natives of Hispaniola. Their houses are most ingeniously constructed, and all the objects they manufacture for their own use excited the admiration of the Spaniards. It is positive that they make their tools out of very hard stones found in the streams, and which they polish.

The Spaniards learned that there were other islands not far distant, inhabited by fierce peoples who live on human flesh; this explained why the natives of Hispaniola fled so promptly on their arrival. They told the Spaniards later that they had taken them for the cannibals, which is the name they give to these barbarians. They also call them *Caraibes*. The islands inhabited by these monsters lie towards the south, and about half-way to the other islands. The inhabitants of Hispaniola, who are a mild people, complained that they were exposed to frequent attacks from the cannibals who landed amongst them and pursued them through the forests like hunters chasing wild beasts. The cannibals captured children, whom they castrated, just as we do chickens and pigs we wish to fatten for the table, and when they were grown and became fat they ate them. Older persons, who fell into their power, were killed and cut into pieces for food; they also ate the intestines and the extremities, which they salted, just as we do hams. They did not eat women, as this would be considered a crime and an infamy. If they captured any women, they kept them and cared for them, in order that they might produce children; just as we do with hens, sheep, mares, and other animals. Old women, when captured, were made slaves. The inhabitants of these islands (which, from now on we may consider ours), women and men, have no other means of escaping capture by the cannibals, than by flight. Although they use wooden arrows with sharpened points, they are aware that these arms are of little use against the fury and violence of their enemies, and they all admit that ten cannibals could easily overcome a hundred of their own men in a pitched battle.

Although these people adore the heavens and the stars, their religion is not yet sufficiently understood; as for their other customs, the brief time the Spaniards stopped there and the want of interpreters did not allow full information to be obtained. They eat roots which in size and form resemble our turnips, but which in taste are similar to our tender chestnuts. These they call *ages*. Another root which they eat they call *yucca;* and of this they make bread. They eat the ages either roasted or boiled, or made into bread. They cut the yucca, which is very juicy, into pieces, mashing and kneading it and then baking it in the form of cakes. It is a singular thing that they consider the juice of the yucca to be more poisonous than that of the aconite, and upon drinking it, death immediately follows. On the other hand, bread made from this paste is very appetising and wholesome: all the Spaniards have tried it. The islanders also easily make bread with a kind of millet, similar to that which exists plenteously amongst the Milanese and Andalusians. This millet is a little more than a palm in length, ending in a point, and is about the thickness of the upper part of a man's arm. The grains are about the form and size of peas. While they are growing, they are white, but become black when ripe. When ground they are whiter than snow. This kind of grain is called *maiz*.

The islanders set some value on gold and wear it in the form of fine leaves, fixed in the lobes of their ears and their nostrils. As soon as our compatriots were certain that they had no commercial relations with other peoples and no other coasts than those of their own islands, they asked them by signs whence they procured the gold. As nearly as could be conjectured, the natives obtain gold from the sands of the rivers which flow down from the high mountains. This process was not a difficult one. Before beating it into leaves, they form it into ingots; but none was found in that part of the island where the Spaniards had landed. It was shortly afterwards discovered, for when the Spaniards left that locality and landed at another point to obtain fresh water and to fish, they discovered a river of which the stones contained flakes of gold.

With the exception of three kinds of rabbits, no quadruped is found in these islands. There are serpents, but they are not dangerous. Wild geese, turtle-doves, ducks of a larger size than ours, with plumage as white as that of a swan, and red heads, exist. The Spaniards brought back with them some forty parrots, some green, others yellow, and some having vermilion collars like the parrakeets of India, as described by Pliny; and all of them have the most brilliant plumage. Their wings are green or yellow, but mixed with bluish or purple feathers, presenting a variety which enchants the eye. I have wished, most illustrious Prince, to give you these details about the parrots; and although the opinion of Columbus[8] seems to be contradictory to the theories of the ancients concerning the size of the globe and its circumnavigation, the birds and many other objects brought thence seem to indicate that these islands do belong, be it by proximity or by their products, to India; particularly when one recalls what Aristotle, at the end of his treatise *De Cœlo et Mundo*, and Seneca, and other learned cosmographers have always affirmed, that India was only separated from the west coast of Spain by a very small expanse of sea.

Mastic, aloes, cotton, and similar products flourish in abundance. Silky kinds of cotton grow upon trees as in China; also rough-coated berries of different colours more pungent to the taste than Caucasian pepper; and twigs cut from the trees, which in their form resemble cinnamon, but in taste, odour, and the outer bark, resemble ginger.

Happy at having discovered this unknown land, and to have found indications of a hitherto unknown continent, Columbus resolved to take advantage of favouring winds and the approach of spring to return to Europe; but he left thirty-eight of his companions under the protection of the king of whom I have spoken, in order that they might, during his absence, acquaint themselves with the country and its condition. After signing a

[8] Columbus died in the belief that the countries he had discovered formed part of the Indies. They were thus described officially by the Spanish sovereigns.

treaty of friendship with this king who was called by his enemies Guaccanarillo,[9] Columbus took all precautions for ensuring the health, the life, and the safety of the men whom he left behind. The king, touched with pity for these voluntary exiles, shed abundant tears, and promised to render them every assistance in his power. After mutual embraces, Columbus gave the order to depart for Spain. He took with him ten islanders,[10] thanks to whom all the words of their language have been written down with Latin characters. Thus they call the heavens *tueri*, a house *boa*, gold *cauni*, a virtuous man *taino*, nothing *nagani*. They pronounce all these names just as distinctly as we do Latin.

You are now acquainted with such details concerning this first voyage as it has seemed expedient to me to record. The King and Queen, who, above everything and even in their sleep, thought about the propagation of the Christian faith, hoping that these numerous and gentle peoples might be easily converted to our religion, experienced the liveliest emotions upon hearing these news. Columbus was received upon his return with the great honour he merited for what he had accomplished. They bade him sit in their presence, which for the Spanish sovereigns is regarded as a proof of the greatest friendship and the highest mark of gratitude. They commanded that henceforward Columbus should be called "*Præfectus Marinus*," or, in the Spanish tongue, *Amiral*. His brother Bartholomew, likewise very proficient in the art of navigation, was honoured by them with the title of Prefect of the Island of Hispaniola, which is in the vulgar tongue called *Adelantado*.[11] To make my meaning clear I shall henceforth employ these usual words of Admiral and Adelantado as well as the terms which are now commonly used in navigation. But let us return to our narrative.

It was thought, as Columbus had moreover declared in the

[9] Otherwise Guacanagari.

[10] One of these Indians died at sea on the voyage, and three others landed very ill at Palos; the remaining six were presented to Ferdinand and Isabella at Barcelona, and were afterwards baptised.

[11] This statement is premature; Bartholomew's appointment was made considerably later.

beginning, that in these islands would be found riches such as all struggle to obtain. There were two motives which determined the royal pair to plan a second expedition, for which they ordered seventeen ships to be equipped; three of these were vessels with covered decks, twelve were of the kind called caravels by the Spaniards, which had none, and two were larger caravels, of which the height of the masts made it possible to adapt decks. The equipment of this fleet was confided to Juan de Fonseca, Dean of Seville, a man of illustrious birth, of genius and initiative.[12] In obedience to his orders more than twelve hundred foot-soldiers, amongst whom were all sorts of labourers and numerous artisans, were commanded to embark. Some noblemen were found amongst the company. The Admiral took on board mares, sheep, cows and the corresponding males for the propagation of their species; nor did he forget vegetables, grain, barley, and similar seeds, not only for provisions but also for sowing; vines and young plants such as were wanting in that country were carefully taken. In fact the Spaniards have not found any tree in that island which was known to them except pines and palms; and even the palms were extraordinarily high, very hard, slender, and straight, owing, no doubt, to the fertility of the soil. Even the fruits they produce in abundance were unknown.

The Spaniards declare that there is not in the whole universe a more fertile region. The Admiral ordered his work people to take with them the tools of their trades, and in general everything necessary to build a new city. Won by the accounts of the Admiral and attracted by the love of novelty, some of the more intimate courtiers also decided to take part in this second voyage. They sailed from Cadiz with a favourable wind, the seventh day of the calends of October in the year of grace 1493.[13] On the calends they touched the Canaries. The last of the Canaries is

[12] The evil that has been attributed to Juan Fonseca, Bishop of Burgos, may exceed his dues, but the praise here and elsewhere given him by Peter Martyr is excessive and all but unique. That he cordially hated Columbus and after him Cortes, Las Casas and most of the men of action in the New World, is undeniable.

[13] The sailing date was Sept. 25, 1493.

called Ferro by the Spaniards. There is no potable water on it, save a kind of dew produced by one sole tree standing upon the most lofty point of the whole island; and from which it falls drop by drop into an artificial trough. From this island, Columbus put to sea the third day of the ides of October. We have learned this news a few days after his departure. You shall hear the rest later. Fare you well.

From the Court of Spain, the ides of November, 1493.

BOOK II

TO THE VISCOUNT ASCANIO SFORZA,
CARDINAL VICE-CHANCELLOR

You renew to me, Most Illustrious Prince, your desire to know all that treats of the Spanish discoveries in the New World. You have let me know that the details I have given you concerning the first voyage pleased you; listen now to the continuation of events.

Medina del Campo is a town of Ulterior Spain, as it is called in Italy, or of Old Castile, as it is called here. It is distant about four hundred miles from Cadiz. While the Court sojourned there the ninth day of the calends of April, messengers sent to the King and Queen informed them that twelve ships returning from the islands had arrived at Cadiz, after a happy voyage. The commander of the squadron did not wish to say more by the messengers to the King and Queen except that the Admiral had stopped with five ships and nine hundred men at Hispaniola, which he wished to explore. He wrote that he would give further details by word of mouth. The eve of the nones of April, this commander of the squadron, who was the brother of the nurse of the eldest royal prince's, arrived at Medina, being sent by Columbus. I questioned him and other trustworthy witnesses, and shall now repeat what they told me, hoping by so doing to render myself agreeable to you. What I learned from their mouths you shall now in turn learn from me.

The third day of the ides of October the Spaniards left the island of Ferro,[1] which is the most distant of the Canaries from

---

[1] The chronology throughout is erroneous. Columbus had sailed from Cadiz on September 25th, arriving at Gomera on October 5th.

Europe, and put out upon the high seas in seventeen ships. Twenty-one full days passed before they saw any land; driven by the north wind they were carried much farther to the south-west than on the first voyage, and thus they arrived at the archipelago of the cannibals, or the Caribs, which we only know from the descriptions given by the islanders. The first island they discovered was so thickly wooded that there was not an inch of bare or stony land. As the discovery took place on a Sunday, the Admiral wished to call the island Domingo.[2] It was supposed to be deserted, and he did not stop there. He calculated that they had covered 820 leagues in these twenty-one days. The ships had always been driven forward by the south-west wind. At some little distance from Domingo other islands were perceived, covered with trees, of which the trunks, roots, and leaves exhaled sweet odours. Those who landed to visit the island found neither men nor animals, except lizards of extraordinarily great size. This island they called Galana. From the summit of a promontory, a mountain was visible on the horizon and thirty miles distant from that mountain a river of important breadth descended into the plain. This was the first inhabited land[3] found since leaving the Canaries, but it was inhabited by those odious cannibals, of whom they had only heard by report, but have now learned to know, thanks to those interpreters whom the Admiral had taken to Spain on his first voyage.

While exploring the island, numerous villages, composed of twenty or thirty houses each, were discovered; in the centre is a public square, round which the houses are placed in a circle. And since I am speaking about these houses, it seems proper that I should describe them to you. It seems they are built entirely of wood in a circular form. The construction of the building is begun by planting in the earth very tall trunks of trees; by means of them, shorter beams are placed in the interior and support the

[2] The first island was discovered on November 3d, and was named La Deseada, or The Desired; five others, including Domingo and Maria Galante were discovered on the same date.

[3] The island of Guadeloupe, called by the natives Caracueira.

outer posts. The extremities of the higher ones are brought together in a point, after the fashion of a military tent. These frames they then cover with palm and other leaves, ingeniously interlaced, as a protection against rain. From the shorter beams in the interior they suspend knotted cords made of cotton or of certain roots similar to rushes, and on these they lay coverings.[4]

The island produces cotton such as the Spaniards call *algodon* and the Italians *bombasio*. The people sleep on these suspended beds or on straw spread upon the floor. There is a sort of court surrounded by houses where they assemble for games. They call their houses *boios*. The Spaniards noticed two wooden statues, almost shapeless, standing upon two interlaced serpents, which at first they took to be the gods of the islanders; but which they later learned were placed there merely for ornament. We have already remarked above that it is believed they adore the heavens; nevertheless, they make out of cotton-fabric certain masks, which resemble imaginary goblins they think they have seen in the night.

But let us return to our narrative. Upon the arrival of the Spaniards, the islanders, both men and women, abandoned their houses and fled. About thirty women and children whom they had captured in the neighbouring islands and kept either as slaves or to be eaten, took refuge with the Spaniards. In the houses were found pots of all kinds, jars and large earthen vessels, boxes and tools resembling ours. Birds were boiling in their pots, also geese mixed with bits of human flesh, while other parts of human bodies were fixed on spits, ready for roasting. Upon searching another house the Spaniards found arm and leg bones, which the cannibals carefully preserve for pointing their arrows; for they have no iron. All other bones, after the flesh is eaten, they throw aside. The Spaniards discovered the recently decapitated head of a young man still wet with blood. Exploring the interior of the island they discovered seven rivers,[5] without mentioning a much

[4] Hamacs, which are still commonly used in *tierra caliente* of the West Indies, Mexico, and Central America.

[5] In reality, these so-called rivers were unimportant mountain torrents.

larger watercourse similar to the Guadalquivir at Cordoba and larger than our Ticino, of which the banks were deliciously umbrageous. They gave the name of Guadaloupe to this island because of the resemblance one of its mountains bore to the Mount Guadaloupe, celebrated for its miraculous statue of the Virgin Immaculate. The natives call their island Caracueira, and it is the principal one inhabited by the Caribs. The Spaniards took from Guadaloupe seven parrots larger than pheasants, and totally unlike any other parrots in colour. Their entire breast and back are covered with purple plumes, and from their shoulders fall long feathers of the same colour as I have often remarked in Europe is the case with the capons peasants raise. The other feathers are of various colours,—green, bluish, purple, or yellow. Parrots are as numerous in all these islands as sparrows or other small birds are with us; and just as we keep magpies, thrushes, and similar birds to fatten them, so do these islanders also keep birds to eat, though their forests are full of parrots.

The female captives who had taken refuge with our people received by the Admiral's order some trifling presents, and were begged by signs to go and hunt for the cannibals, for they knew their place of concealment. In fact they went back to the men during the night, and the following morning returned with several cannibals who were attracted by the hope of receiving presents; but when they saw our men, these savages, whether because they were afraid or because they were conscious of their crimes, looked at one another, making a low murmur, and then, suddenly forming into a wedge-shaped group, they fled swiftly, like a flock of birds, into the shady valleys.

Having called together his men who had passed some days exploring the interior of the island, Columbus gave the signal for departure. He took no cannibal with him, but he ordered their boats, dug out of single tree-trunks, to be destroyed, and on the eve of the ides of November he weighed anchor and left Guadaloupe.

Desiring to see the men of his crew whom he had left the preceding year at Hispaniola to explore that country, Columbus passed daily by other islands which he discovered to the right and left. Straight ahead to the north appeared a large island. Those natives who had been brought to Spain on his first voyage, and those who had been delivered from captivity, declared that it was called Madanina, and that it was inhabited exclusively by women.[6] The Spaniards had, in fact, heard this island spoken of during their first voyage. It appeared that the cannibals went at certain epochs of the year to visit these women, as in ancient history the Thracians crossed to the island of Lesbos inhabited by the Amazons. When their children were weaned, they sent the boys to their fathers, but kept the girls, precisely as did the Amazons. It is claimed that these women know of vast caverns where they conceal themselves if any man tries to visit them at another than the established time. Should any one attempt to force his way into these caverns by violence or by trickery, they defend themselves with arrows, which they shoot with great precision. At least, this is the story as it is told, and I repeat it to you. The north wind renders this island unapproachable, and it can only be reached when the wind is in the south-west.

While still in view of Madanina at a distance of about forty miles, the Spaniards passed another island, which, according to the accounts of the natives, was very populous and rich in food-stuffs of all kinds. As this island was very mountainous they named it Montserrat. Amongst other details given by the islanders on board, and as far as could be ascertained from their signs and their gestures, the cannibals of Montserrat frequently set out on hunts to take captives for food, and in so doing go a distance of more than a thousand miles from their coasts. The next day the Spaniards discovered another island, and as it was of spherical form, Columbus named it Santa Maria Rotunda. In less time he passed by another island discovered next day, and which, without stopping, he dedicated to St. Martin, and the following day still a third island came into view. The Spaniards estimated its width from easy to west at fifty miles.

[6] This is the island of Martinique; the legend of its Amazons is purely fantastic.

It afterwards became known that these islands were of the most extraordinary beauty and fertility, and to this last one the name of the Blessed Virgin of Antigua was given. Sailing on past numerous islands which followed Antigua, Columbus arrived, forty miles farther on, at an island which surpassed all the others in size, and which the natives called Agay. The Admiral gave it the name of Santa Cruz. Here he ordered the anchor to be lowered, in order that he might replenish his supply of water, and he sent thirty men from his vessel to land and explore. These men found four dogs on the shore, and the same number of youths and women approached with hands extended, like supplicants. It was supposed they were begging for assistance or to be rescued from the hands of those abominable people. Whatever decision the Spaniards might take in regard to them, seemed better to them than their actual condition. The cannibals fled as they had done at Guadaloupe, and disappeared into the forests.

Two days were passed at Santa Cruz, where thirty of our Spaniards placed in an ambuscade saw, from the place where they were watching, a canoe in the distance coming towards them, in which there were eight men and as many women. At a given signal they fell upon the canoe; as they approached, the men and women let fly a volley of arrows with great rapidity and accuracy. Before the Spaniards had time to protect themselves with their shields, one of our men, a Galician, was killed by a woman, and another was seriously wounded by an arrow shot by that same woman. It was discovered that their poisoned arrows contained a kind of liquid which oozed out when the point broke. There was one woman amongst these savages whom, as nearly as could be conjectured, all the others seemed to obey, as though she was their queen. With her was her son, a fierce, robust young man, with ferocious eyes and a face like a lion's. Rather than further expose themselves to their arrows, our men chose to engage them in a hand to hand combat. Rowing stoutly, they pushed their barque against the canoe of the savages, which was overturned by the shock; the canoe sank, but the savages, throwing themselves into the water, continued while swimming to shoot their arrows

with the same rapidity. Climbing upon a rock level with the
water, they still fought with great bravery, though they were
finally captured, after one had been killed and the son of the
queen had received two wounds. When they were brought on
board the Admiral's ship, they no more changed their ferocious
and savage mood than do the lions of Africa, when they find
themselves caught in nets. There was no one who saw them who
did not shiver with horror, so infernal and repugnant was the
aspect nature and their own cruel character had given them. I
affirm this after what I have myself seen, and so likewise do all
those who went with me in Madrid to examine them.

I return to my narrative. Each day the Spaniards advanced
farther. They had covered a distance of five hundred miles.
Driven first by the south wind, then by the west wind, and
finally by the wind from the north-west, they found themselves
in a sea dotted with innumerable islands, strangely different one
from another; some were covered with forests and prairies and
offered delightful shade, while others, which were dry and
sterile, had very lofty and rocky mountains. The rocks of these
latter were of various colours, some purple, some violet, and some
entirely white. It is thought they contain metals and precious
stones.

The ships did not touch, as the weather was unfavourable, and
also because navigation amongst these islands is dangerous. Post-
poning until another time the exploration of these islands, which
because of their confused grouping could not be counted, the
Spaniards continued their voyage. Some lighter ships of the fleet
did, however, cruise amongst them, reconnoitring forty-six of
them, while the heavier ships, fearing the reefs, kept to the high
sea. This collection of islands is called an archipelago. Outside the
archipelago and directly across the course rises the island called
by the natives Burichena, which Columbus placed under the
patronage of San Juan.[7] A number of the captives rescued from
the hands of the cannibals declared they were natives of that

[7] Porto Rico.

island, which they said was populous and well cultivated; they explained that it had excellent ports, was covered with forests, and that its inhabitants hated the cannibals and were constantly at war with them. The inhabitants possessed no boats by which they could reach the coasts of the cannibals from their island; but whenever they were lucky in repulsing a cannibal invasion for the purpose of plundering, they cut their prisoners into small bits, roasted, and greedily ate them; for in war there is alternative good and bad fortune.

All this was recounted through the native interpreters who had been taken back to Spain on the first voyage. Not to lose time, the Spaniards passed by Burichena; nevertheless some sailors, who landed on the extreme western point of the island to take a supply of fresh water, found there a handsome house built in the fashion of the country, and surrounded by a dozen or more ordinary structures, all of which were abandoned by their owners. Whether the inhabitants betake themselves at that period of the year to the mountains to escape the heat, and then return to the lowlands when the temperature is fresher, or whether they had fled out of fear of the cannibals, is not precisely known. There is but one king for the whole of the island, and he is reverently obeyed. The south coast of this island, which the Spaniards followed, is two hundred miles long.

During the night two women and a young man, who had been rescued from the cannibals, sprang into the sea and swam to their native island. A few days later the Spaniards finally arrived at the much-desired Hispaniola, which is five hundred leagues from the nearest of the cannibal islands. Cruel fate had decreed the death of all those Spaniards who had been left there.

There is a coast region of Hispaniola which the natives call Xarama, and it was from Xarama that Columbus had set sail on his first voyage, when he was about to return to Spain, taking with him the ten interpreters of whom I spoke above, of whom only three survived; the others having succumbed to the change of climate, country, and food.

Hardly were the ships in sight of the coast of Xarama, which Columbus called Santa Reina, than the Admiral ordered one of these interpreters to be set at liberty, and two others managed to jump into the sea and swim to the shore. As Columbus did not yet know the sad fate of the thirty-eight men whom he had left on the island the preceding year, he was not concerned at this flight. When the Spaniards were near to the coast a long canoe with several rowers came out to meet them. In it was the brother of Guaccanarillo, that king with whom the Admiral had signed a treaty when he left Hispaniola, and to whose care he had urgently commended the sailors he had left behind. The brother brought to the Admiral, in the king's name, a present of two golden statues; he also spoke in his own language—as was later understood,—of the death of our compatriots; but as there was no interpreter, nobody at the time understood his words.

Upon arriving, however, at the blockhouse and the houses, which were surrounded by an entrenchment, they were all found reduced to ashes, while over the place a profound silence reigned. The Admiral and his companions were deeply moved by this discovery. Thinking and hoping that some of the men might still be alive, he ordered cannon and guns to be fired, that the noise of these formidable detonations echoing amongst the mountains and along the coasts might serve as a signal of his arrival to any of our men who might be hidden among the islanders or among wild beasts. It was in vain; for they were all dead.

The Admiral afterwards sent messengers to Guaccanarillo, who, as far as they could understand, related as follows: there are on the island, which is very large, a number of kings, who are more powerful than he; two of these, disturbed by the news of the arrival of the Spaniards, assembled considerable forces, attacked and killed our men and burned their entrenchments, houses, and possessions; Guaccanarillo had striven to save our men, and in the struggle had been wounded with an arrow, his leg being still bandaged with cotton; and for this reason he had not, despite his keen desire, been able to go to meet the Admiral.

There do exist several sovereigns on the island, some more powerful than the others; just as we read that the fabulous Æneas found Latium divided amongst several kings, Latinus, Mezentius, Turnus, and Tarchon, all near neighbours who fought over the territory. The islanders of Hispaniola, in my opinion, may be esteemed more fortunate than were the Latins, above all should they become converted to the true religion. They go naked, they know neither weights nor measures, nor that source of all misfortunes, money; living in a golden age, without laws, without lying judges, without books, satisfied with their life, and in no wise solicitous for the future. Nevertheless ambition and the desire to rule trouble even them, and they fight amongst themselves, so that even in the golden age there is never a moment without war; the maxim *Cede, non cedam,* has always prevailed amongst mortal men.

The following day the Admiral sent to Guaccanarillo a Sevillan called Melchior, who had once been sent by the King and the Queen to the sovereign Pontiff when they captured Malaga. Melchior found him in bed, feigning illness, and surrounded by the beds of his seven concubines. Upon removing the bandage [from his leg] Melchior discovered no trace of any wound, and this caused him to suspect that Guaccanarillo was the murderer of our compatriots. He concealed his suspicions, however, and obtained the king's assurance that he would come the following day to see the Admiral on board his ship, which he did. As soon as he came on board, and after saluting the Spaniards and distributing some gold among the officers, he turned to the women whom we had rescued from the cannibals and, glancing with half-opened eyes at one of them whom we called Catherine, he spoke to her very softly; after which, with the Admiral's permission, which he asked with great politeness and urbanity, he inspected the horses and other things he had never before seen, and then left.

Some persons advised Columbus to hold Guaccanarillo prisoner, to make him expiate in case it was proven that our compatriots had been assassinated by his orders; but the Admiral, deeming it inopportune to irritate the islanders, allowed him to depart.

The day after the morrow, the brother of the king, acting in his own name or in that of Guaccanarillo, came on board and won over the women, for the following night Catherine, in order to recover her own liberty and that of all her companions, yielded to the solicitation of Guaccanarillo or his brother, and accomplished a feat more heroic than that of the Roman Clelia, when she liberated the other virgins who had served with her as hostages, swam the Tiber and thus escaped from the power of Lars Porsena. Clelia crossed the river on a horse, while Catherine and several other women trusted only to their arms and swam for a distance of three miles in a sea by no means calm; for that, according to every one's opinion, was the distance between the ships and the coast. The sailors pursued them in light boats, guided by the same light from the shore which served for the women, of whom they captured three. It is believed that Catherine and four others escaped to Guaccanarillo, for at daybreak, men sent out by the Admiral announced that he and the women had fled together, taking all their goods with them; and this fact confirmed the suspicion that he had consented to the assassination of our men.

Melchior, whom I have mentioned, was then despatched with three hundred men to search for him. In the course of his march he came upon a winding gorge, overlooked by five lofty hills in such wise as to suggest the estuary of a large river. There was found a large harbour, safe and spacious, which they named Port Royal. The entrance of this harbour is crescent-shaped, and is so regularly formed that it is difficult to detect whether ships have entered from the right or the left; this can only be ascertained when they return to the entrance. Three large ships can enter abreast. The surrounding hills form the coasts, and afford shelter from the winds. In the middle of the harbour there rises a promontory covered with forests, which are full of parrots and many other birds which there build their nests and fill the air with sweet melodies. Two considerable rivers empty into this harbour.

In the course of their explorations of this country the Spaniards perceived in the distance a large house, which they approached, persuaded that it was the retreat of Guaccanarillo. They were met by a man with a wrinkled forehead and frowning brows, who was escorted by about a hundred warriors armed with bows and arrows, pointed lances and clubs. He advanced menacingly towards them. *"Tainos,"* the natives cried, that is to say, good men and not cannibals. In response to our amicable signs, they dropped their arms and modified their ferocious attitude. To each one was presented a hawk's bell, and they became so friendly that they fearlessly went on board the ships, sliding down the steep banks of the river, and overwhelmed our compatriots with gifts. Upon measuring the large house which was of spherical form, it was found to have a diameter of thirty-five long paces; surrounding it were thirty other ordinary houses. The ceilings were decked with branches of various colours most artfully plaited together. In reply to our inquiries about Guaccanarillo, the natives responded,—as far as could be understood, —that they were not subjects of his, but of a chief who was there present; they likewise declared they understood that Guaccanarillo had left the coast to take refuge in the mountains. After concluding a treaty of friendship with that cacique, such being the name given to their kings, the Spaniards returned to report what they had learned to the Admiral.

Columbus had meanwhile sent some officers with an escort of men to effect a reconnaissance farther in the interior; two of the most conspicuous of these were Hojeda and Corvalano, both young and courageous noblemen. One of them discovered three rivers, the other four, all of which had their sources in these same mountains. In the sands of these rivers gold was found, which the Indians, who acted as their escort, proceeded in their presence to collect in the following manner: they dug a hole in the sand about the depth of an arm, merely scooping the sand out of this trough with the right and left hands. They extracted the grains of gold, which they afterwards presented to the Spaniards. Some declared they saw grains as big as peas. I have seen with my own eyes a shapeless ingot similar to a round river stone, which was found by Hojeda, and was afterwards brought to Spain; it weighed nine ounces. Satisfied with this first examination they returned to report to the Admiral.

Columbus, as I have been told, had forbidden them to do more than examine and reconnoitre the country. The news spread that the king of the mountain country, where all these rivers rise, was call the Cacique Caunaboa, that is to say, the Lord of the Golden House; for in their language *boa* is the word for a house, *cauna* for gold, and *cacique* for king, as I have above written. Nowhere are better fresh-water fish to be found, nor more beautiful nor better in taste, and less dangerous. The waters of all these rivers are likewise very wholesome.

Melchior has told me that amongst the cannibals the days of the month of December are equal to the nights, but knowledge contradicts this observation. I well know that in this self-same month of December, some birds made their nests and others already hatched out their little ones; the heat was also considerable. When I inquired particularly concerning the elevation of the north star above the horizon, he answered me that in the land of the cannibals the Great Bear entirely disappeared beneath the arctic pole. There is nobody who came back from this second voyage whose testimony one may more safely accept than his; but had he possessed knowledge of astronomy he would have limited himself to saying that the day is about as long as the night. For in no place in the world does the night during the solstice precisely equal the day; and it is certain that on this voyage the Spaniards never reached the equator, for they constantly beheld on the horizon the polar star, which served them as guide. As for Melchior's companions, they were without knowledge or experience, therefore I offer you few particulars, and those only casually, as I have been able to collect them. I hope to narrate to you what I may be able to learn from others. Moreover Columbus, whose particular friend I am, has written me that he would recount me fully all that he has been fortunate enough to discover.[8]

The Admiral selected an elevation near the port as the site for a town;[9] and, within a few days, some houses and a church were built, as well as could be done in so short a time. And there, on the feast of the Three Kings (for when treating of this country one must speak of a new world, so distant is it and so devoid of civilisation and religion) the Holy Sacrifice was celebrated by thirteen priests.[10]

As the time when he had promised to send news to the King and Queen approached, and as the season was moreover favourable [for sailing], Columbus decided not to prolong his stay. He therefore ordered the twelve caravels, whose arrival we have announced, to sail, though he was much afflicted by the assassination of his comrades; because, but for their death, we should possess much fuller information concerning the climate and the products of Hispaniola.

That you may inform your apothecaries, druggists, and perfumers concerning the products of this country and its high temperature, I send you some seeds of all kinds, as well as the bark and the pith of those trees which are believed to be cinnamon trees. If you wish to taste either the seeds or the pith or the bark, be careful, Most Illustrious Prince, only to do so with caution; not that they are harmful, but they are very peppery, and if you leave them a long time in your mouth, they will sting the tongue. In case should burn your tongue a little in tasting them, take some water, and the burning sensation will be allayed. My messenger will also deliver to Your Eminence some of those black

[8] The letter of Columbus here mentioned is not known to exist.

[9] The first Spanish settlement was named Isabella, as was likewise the cape on which it stood. Long after it was abandoned and had fallen into ruin, the site was reputed to be haunted. See Las Casas, *Historia de las Indias*, vol. i., p. 72.

[10] There were certainly not as many as thirteen priests with Columbus. The text reads . . . . *divina nostro ritu sacra sunt decantata tredecim sacerdotibus ministrantibus*. The number doubtless includes all laymen who took any part, as acolytes, etc., in the ceremonies.

and white seeds out of which they make bread. If you cut bits of the wood called aloes, which he brings, you will scent the delicate perfumes it exhales.

Fare you well.

From the Court of Spain, the third day of the calends of May, 1494.

BOOK III

TO CARDINAL LUDOVICO D'ARAGON

You desire that another skilful Phaeton should drive the car of the Sun. You seek to draw a sweet potion from a dry stone. A new world, if I may so express myself, has been discovered under the auspices of the Catholic sovereigns, your uncle Ferdinand and your aunt Isabella, and you command me to describe to you this heretofore unknown world; and to that effect you sent me a letter of your uncle, the illustrious King Frederick.[1] You will both receive this precious stone, badly mounted and set in lead. But when you later observe that my beautiful Nereids of the ocean are exposed to the furious attacks of erudite friends and to the calumnies of detractors, you must frankly confess to them that you have forced me to send you this news, despite my pressing occupations and my health. You are not ignorant that I have taken these accounts from the first reports of the Admiral as rapidly as your secretary could write under my dictation. You hasten me by daily announcing your departure for Naples in company of the Queen, sister of our King and your paternal aunt, whom you have accompanied to Spain. Thus you have forced me to complete my writings. You will observe that the first two chapters are dedicated to another, for I had really begun to write them with a dedication to your unfortunate relative

[1] Frederick III., of Aragon, succeeded his nephew Frederick II., as King of Naples in 1496. Five years later, when dispossessed by Ferdinand the Catholic, he took refuge in France, where Louis XII. granted him the duchy of Anjou and a suitable pension. He died in 1504.

Ascanio Sforza, Cardinal and Vice-chancellor. When he fell into disgrace,[2] I felt my interest in writing also decline. It is owing to you and to the letters sent me by your illustrious uncle, King Frederick, that my ardour has revived. Enjoy, therefore, this narrative, which is not a thing of the imagination.

Fare you well.

From Granada, the ninth of the calends of May of the year 1500.

I have narrated in a preceding book how the Admiral Columbus, after having visited the cannibal islands, landed at Hispaniola on the fourth day of the nones of February, 1493, without having lost a single vessel. I shall now recount what he discovered while exploring that island and another neighbouring one, which he believed to be a continent.

According to Columbus, Hispaniola is the island of Ophir mentioned in the third book of Kings.[3] Its width covers five degrees of south latitude, for its north coast extends to the twenty-seventh degree and the south coast to the twenty-second;

[2] Upon the death of Innocent VIII., four members of the Sacred College were conspicuous *papabili:* Raffaele Riario and Giuliano della Rovere, nephews of Sixtus IV., and Roderigo Borgia and Ascanio Sforza. Borgia was elected and took the title of Alexander VI. He rewarded Cardinal Sforza for his timely assistance in securing his elevation, by giving him the Vice-Chancellorship he had himself occupied as Cardinal, the town of Nepi and the Borgia Palace in Rome. Dissensions between Alexander and the Sforza family soon became acute; Giovanni Sforza, Lord of Pesaro and sometime husband of Lucrezia Borgia, was expelled, and his brother, Cardinal Ascanio was included in the papal disfavour. He sought refuge in Lombardy, where he was taken prisoner by Louis XII., of France. Peter Martyr had foreseen, in a measure, the turbulent events of Alexander's pontificate; the Spanish sovereigns charged him to express to Cardinal Sforza their disapproval of his action in supporting the Borgia party, that Cardinal, though a Spaniard, being *persona non grata* to them; and in so doing he wrote to his friend the dubious augury, "God grant he may be grateful to you."

[3] Ortelius, in his *Geographia Sacra*, gives the name of Ophir to Hayti; and it was a commonly held opinion that Solomon's mines of Ophir were situated in America. Columbus shared this belief, and he later wrote of Veragua, when he discovered the coasts of Darien, that he was positive the gold mines there were those of Ophir.

its length extends 780 miles, though some of the companions of Columbus give greater dimensions. Some declare that it extends to within forty-nine degrees of Cadiz, and others to an even greater distance. The calculation concerning this has not been made with precision.

The island is shaped like a chestnut leaf. Columbus decided to found a town[4] upon an elevated hill on the northern coast, since in that vicinity there was a mountain with stone-quarries for building purposes and chalk to make lime. At the foot of this mountain a vast plain[5] extends for a distance of sixty miles in length, and of an average of twelve leagues in breadth, varying from six in the narrowest part to twenty in the broadest. This plain is fertilised by several rivers of wholesome water, of which the largest is navigable and empties into a bay situated half a stadium from the town. As the narrative proceeds you will learn how fruitful this valley is, and how fertile is its soil. The Spaniards laid out parcels of land on the river bank, which they intended to make into gardens, and where they planted all kinds of vegetables, roots, lettuces, cabbages, salads, and other things. Sixteen days after the sowing, the plants had everywhere grown; melons, pumpkins, cucumbers, and other similar products were ripe for picking thirty-six days after they were planted, and nowhere had our people tasted any of finer flavour. Throughout the whole year one might thus have fresh vegetables. Cane-roots, from the juice of which sugar is extracted (but not crystallised sugar), grew to a height of a cubit within fifteen days after planting, and the same happened to graftings of vines. Excellent grapes may be eaten from these vines the second year after planting, but on account of their exaggerated size, the bunches were not numerous. A certain peasant planted a foot of wheat about the calends of February, and wonderful to say, in the sight of everybody he brought into the town a bunch of ripe grain on the third day of the calends of April, which fell in that year on the eve of Easter. Two harvests of vegetables may be counted upon

[4] The town of Santo Domingo, standing at the mouth of the Ozama river.
[5] This valley is the actual Vega Real.

within the year. I have repeated what is told to me about the fertility of the country by all those, without exception, who have returned from there. I would notice, however, that according to some observations wheat does not grow equally well throughout the whole country.

During this time the Admiral despatched some thirty of his men in different directions to explore the district of Cipangu, which is still called Cibao. This is a mountainous region covered with rocks and occupying the centre of the island, where, the natives explained by signs, gold is obtained in abundance. The Admiral's explorers brought back marvellous reports of the riches of the country. Four large rivers rise in these mountains, into which other streams flow, thus dividing the island by an extraordinary natural arrangement into four almost equal parts. The first, which the natives call Junua, lies towards the east; the second, which borders on it and extends to the west, is called Attibinico; the third lies to the north and is called Iachi, while the fourth, Naiba, lies to the south.

But let us consider how the town was founded. After having surrounded the site with ditches and entrenchments for defence against possible attacks by the natives on the garrison he left there, during his absence, the Admiral started on the eve of the ides of March accompanied by all the gentlemen and about four hundred foot-soldiers for the southern region where the gold was found. Crossing a river, he traversed the plain and climbed the mountain beyond it. He reached another valley watered by a river even larger than the former one, and by others of less importance. Accompanied by his force he crossed this valley, which was in no place more elevated than the first one, and thus he reached the third mountain which had never been ascended. He made the ascent and came down on the other side into a valley where the province of Cibao begins. This valley is watered by rivers and streams which flow down from the hills, and gold is also found in their sands. After penetrating into the interior of the gold region a distance of some seventy-two miles from the town, Columbus resolved to establish a fortified post on an eminence commanding the river banks, from which he might study more closely the mysteries of this region. He named this place San Tomas.

While he was occupied in building this fortification he was delayed by the natives, who came to visit him in the hope of getting some bells or other trifles. Columbus gave them to understand that he was very willing to give them what they asked, if they would bring him gold. Upon hearing this promise the natives turned their backs and ran to the neighbouring river, returning soon afterwards with hands full of gold. One old man only asked a little bell in return for two grains of gold weighing an ounce. Seeing that the Spaniards admired the size of these grains, and quite amazed at their astonishment, he explained to them by signs that they were of no value; after which, taking in his hands four stones, of which the smallest was the size of a nut and the largest as big as an orange, he told them that in his country, which was half a day's journey distant, one found here and there ingots of gold quite as large. He added that his neighbours did not even take the trouble to pick them up. It is now known that the islanders set no value on gold as such; they only prize it when it has been worked by a craftsman into some form which pleases them. Who amongst us pays attention to rough marble or to unworked ebony? Certainly nobody; but if this marble is transformed by the hand of a Phidias or a Praxiteles, and if it then presents to our eyes the form of a Nereid with flowing hair, or a hamadryad with graceful body, buyers will not be wanting. Besides this old man, a number of natives brought ingots, weighing ten or twelve drachmas,[6] and they had the effrontery to say that in the region where they had found them, they sometimes discovered ingots as big as the head of a child whom they indicated.

During the days he passed at San Tomas, the Admiral sent a young nobleman named Luxan, accompanied by an escort, to explore another region. Luxan told even more extraordinary things, which he had heard from the natives, but he brought back

[6] The Greek drachma weighed one eighth of an ounce.

nothing; it is probable that he did this in obedience to the Admiral's orders. Spices, but not those we use, abound in their forests, and these they gather just as they do gold; that is to say, whenever they wish to trade with the inhabitants of the neighbouring islands for something which pleases them; for example, long plates, seats, or other articles manufactured out of a black wood which does not grow in Hispaniola. On his return journey, towards the ides of March, Luxan found wild grapes of excellent flavour, already ripe in the forest, but the islanders take no account of them. The country, although very stony (for the word Cibao means in their language *rocky*), is nevertheless covered with trees and grasses. It is even said that the growth on the mountains, which strictly speaking is only grass, grows taller than wheat within four days after it has been mown. The rains being frequent, the rivers and streams are full of water, and as gold is everywhere found mixed with the sand of the river-beds, it is conjectured that this metal is washed down from the mountains by the streams. It is certain that the natives are extremely lazy, for they shiver with cold among their mountains in winter, without ever thinking of making clothes for themselves, although cotton is found in abundance. In the valleys and lowlands they have nothing to fear from cold.

Having carefully examined the region of Cibao, Columbus returned on the calends of April, the day after Easter, to Isabella; this being the name he had given to the new city. Confiding the government of Isabella and the entire island to his brother[7] and one Pedro Margarita, an old royal courtier, Columbus made preparations for exploring the island which lies only seventy miles from Hispaniola, and which he believed to be a continent. He had not forgotten the royal instructions, which urged him to visit the new coasts, without delay, lest some other sovereign might take possession of them. For the King of Portugal made no secret of his intention also to discover unknown islands. True it is

[7] According to the judgment of Las Casas, Bartholomew Columbus was a man of superior character and well qualified to rule, had he not been eclipsed by his famous brother. *Hist. Ind.*, ii., p. 8.

that the Sovereign Pontiff, Alexander VI., had sent to the King and Queen of Spain his bull, sealed with lead, by which it was forbidden to any other sovereign to visit those unknown regions. To avoid all conflict, a straight line from north to south had been drawn, first at one hundred leagues and afterwards by common accord at three hundred leagues west of the parallel of the isles of Cape Verde. We believe these islands to be those formerly called the Hesperides. They belong to the King of Portugal. The Portuguese mariners have continued their explorations to the east of that line; following the coast of Africa on their left, they directed their course to the east, crossing the Ethiopian seas, and up to the present time none of them has yet sailed to the west of the Hesperides, or towards the south.

Leaving Hispaniola,[8] the Admiral sailed with three vessels in the direction of the land he had taken for an island on his first voyage, and had named Juana. He arrived, after a brief voyage, and named the first coast he touched Alpha and Omega, because he thought that there our East ended when the sun set in that island, and our West began when the sun rose. It is indeed proven that on the west side India begins beyond the Ganges, and ends on the east side. It is not without cause that cosmographers have left the boundaries of Ganges India undetermined.[9] There are not wanting those among them who think that the coasts of Spain do not lie very distant from the shores of India.

The natives called this country Cuba.[10] Within sight of it, the Admiral discovered at the extremity of Hispaniola a very commodious harbour formed by a bend in the island. He called this harbour, which is barely twenty leagues distant from Cuba, San Nicholas.

[8] He left Hispaniola on April 24th.

[9] This was the general opinion of cosmographers and navigators at that period; contemporary maps and globes show the Asiatic continent in the place actually occupied by Florida and Mexico. See map of Ptolemeus de Ruysch, *Universalior coquiti orbis tabula ex recentibus confecta observationibus*, Rome, 1508.

[10] Always deeming Cuba to be an extension of Asia, Columbus was anxious to complete his reconnaissance, and then to proceed to India and Cathay.

Columbus covered this distance, and desiring to skirt the south coast of Cuba, he laid his course to the west; the farther he advanced the more extensive did the coast become, but bending towards the south, he first discovered, to the left of Cuba, an island called by the natives Jamaica,[11] of which he reports that it is longer and broader than Sicily. It is composed of one sole mountain, which rises in imperceptible gradations from the coasts to the centre, sloping so gently that in mounting it, the ascent is scarcely noticeable. Both the coast country and the interior of Jamaica are extremely fertile and populous. According to the report of their neighbours, the natives of this island have a keener intelligence and are cleverer in mechanical arts, as well as more warlike than others. And indeed, each time the Admiral sought to land in any place, they assembled in armed bands, threatening him, and not hesitating to offer battle. As they were always conquered, they ended by making peace with him. Leaving Jamaica to one side, the Admiral sailed to the west for seventy days with favourable winds. He expected to arrive in the part of the world underneath us just near the Golden Chersonese, which is situated to the east of Persia. He thought, as a matter of fact, that of the twelve hours of the sun's course of which we are ignorant he would have only lost two.

It is known that the ancients have only followed the sun during the half of its course, since they only knew that part of the globe which lies between Cadiz and the Ganges, or even to the Golden Chersonese.

During this voyage, the Admiral encountered marine currents as impetuous as torrents, with great waves and undercurrents, to say nothing of the dangers presented by the immense number of neighbouring islands; but he was heedless of these perils, and was determined to advance until he had ascertained whether Cuba was an island or a continent. He continued, therefore, coasting the shores of the island, and always towards the west, to a dis-

[11] The island is about eighty-five miles from Cuba. The name Jamaica, which has survived, meant in the native tongue "land of wood and water." It was really discovered on May 13th, but was not colonised until 1509.

tance, according to his report, of two hundred and twenty-two leagues, which is equal to about one thousand three hundred miles. He gave names to seven thousand islands, and moreover beheld on his left hand more than three thousand others rising from the waves. But let us return to those matters worthy to be remembered which he encountered during this voyage.

While the Admiral was carefully examining the character of these places, coasting along the shore of Cuba, he first discovered, not far from Alpha (that is from the end of it), a harbour sufficient for many ships. Its entrance is in the form of a scythe, shut in on the two sides by promontories that break the waves; and it is large and of great depth. Following the coast of this harbour, he perceived at a short distance from the shore two huts, and several fires burning here and there. A landing was made, but no people were found; nevertheless there were wooden spits arranged about the fire, on which hung fish, altogether of about a hundred pounds' weight, and alongside lay two serpents eight feet long.[12] The Spaniards were astonished, and looked about for some one with whom to speak, but saw nobody. Indeed, the owners of the fish had fled to the mountains on seeing them approach. The Spaniards rested there to eat, and were pleased to find the fish, which had cost them nothing, much to their taste; but they did not touch the serpents. They report that these latter were in no wise different from the crocodiles of the Nile, except in point of size. According to Pliny, crocodiles as long as eighteen cubits have been found; while the largest in Cuba do not exceed eight feet. When their hunger was satisfied, they penetrated into the neighbouring woods, where they found a number of these serpents tied to the trees with cords; some were attached by their heads, others had had their teeth pulled out. While the Spaniards busied themselves in visiting the neighbourhood of the harbour, they discovered about seventy natives who had fled at their approach, and who now sought to know what these un-

12 As will be later seen, these so-called serpents are iguanas. They are still a common article of food throughout the islands, and *tierra caliente* of Mexico and Central America, and make savoury dishes.

known people wanted. Our men endeavoured to attract them by gestures and signs, and gentle words, and one of them, fascinated by the gifts which they exhibited from a distance, approached, but no nearer than a neighbouring rock. It was clear that he was afraid.

During his first voyage the Admiral had taken a native of Guanahani (an island near by Cuba), whom he had named Diego Columbus, and had brought up with his own children. Diego served him as interpreter, and as his maternal tongue was akin to the language of the islander who had approached, he spoke to him. Overcoming his fears, the islander came amongst the Spaniards, and persuaded his companions to join him as there was nothing to fear. About seventy natives then descended from their rocks and made friends, and the Admiral offered them presents.

They were fishermen, sent to fish by their cacique, who was preparing a festival for the reception of another chief. They were not at all vexed when they found that their fish had been eaten and their serpents left, for they considered these serpents the most delicate food. Common people among them eat less often of the serpents than they would with us of pheasants or peacocks. Moreover they could catch as many fish as the Spaniards had eaten, in one hour. When asked why they cooked the fish they were to carry to their cacique, they replied that they did so to preserve it from corruption. After swearing a mutual friendship they separated.

From that point of the Cuban coast which he had named Alpha, as we have said, the Admiral sailed towards the west. The middle portions of the shores of the bay were well wooded but steep and mountainous. Some of the trees were in flower, and the sweet perfumes they exhaled were wafted out across the sea,[13] while others were weighted with fruit. Beyond the bay the country was more fertile and more populous. The natives were likewise more civilised and more desirous of novelties, for, at the

[13] The fragrant odours blown out to sea from the American coasts are mentioned by several of the early explorers.

sight of the vessels, a crowd of them came down to the shore, offering our men the kind of bread they ate, and gourds full of water. They begged them to come on land.

On all these islands there is found a tree about the size of our elms, which bears a sort of gourd out of which they make drinking cups; but they never eat it, as its pulp is bitterer than gall, and its shell is as hard as a turtle's back. On the ides of May the watchers saw from the height of the lookout an incredible multitude of islands to the south-west; two of them were covered with grass and green trees, and all of them were inhabited.

On the shore of the continent there emptied a navigable river of which the water was so hot that one could not leave one's hand long in it. The next day, having seen a canoe of fishermen in the distance, and fearing that these fishermen might take to flight at sight of them, the Admiral ordered a barque to cut off their retreat; but the men waited for the Spaniards without sign of fear.

Listen now to this new method of fishing. Just as we use French dogs to chase hares across the plain, so do these fishermen catch fish by means of a fish trained for that purpose. This fish in no wise resembles any that we know. Its body is similar to that of a large eel, and upon its head it has a large pouch made of a very tough skin. They tie the fish to the side of the boat, with just the amount of cord necessary to hold it under the water; for it cannot stand contact with the air. As soon as a large fish or turtle is seen (and these latter are as large as a huge shield), they let the fish go. The moment it is freed, it attacks, with the rapidity of an arrow, the fish or turtle, on some part exposed from the shell, covering it with the pouch-like skin, and attaching itself with such tenacity that the only way to pull it off alive is by rolling a cord round a pole and raising the fish out of the water, when contact with the air causes it to drop its prey. This is done by some of the fishermen who throw themselves into the water, and hold it above the surface, until their companions, who remained in the barque, have dragged it on board. This done, the cord is loosened enough for the fisherman-fish to drop back into the water, when it is fed with pieces of the prey which has been caught.

The islanders call this fish *guaicano*, and our people call it *riverso*.[14] Four turtles which they caught in this fashion and presented to the Spaniards almost filled a native barque. They highly prize the flesh of turtles, and the Spaniards made them some presents in exchange which highly pleased them. When our sailors questioned them concerning the size of the land, they answered that it had no end towards the west. They insisted that the Admiral should land, or should send some one in his name to salute their cacique, promising moreover that if the Spaniards would go to visit the cacique, the latter would make them various presents; but the Admiral, not wishing to retard the execution of his project, refused to yield to their wishes. The islanders asked him his name, and told him the name of their cacique.

Continuing his route towards the west, the Admiral arrived several days later in the neighbourhood of a very lofty mountain, where, because of the fertility of the soil, there were many inhabitants. The natives assembled in crowds, and brought bread, cotton, rabbits, and birds on board the ships. They inquired with great curiosity of the interpreter, if this new race of men was descended from heaven. Their king, and a number of wise men who accompanied him, made known by signs that this land was not an island. Landing on another neighbouring island, which almost touched Cuba, the Spaniards were unable to discover a single inhabitant; everybody, men and women, had fled on their approach. They found there four dogs which could not bark and were of hideous aspect. The people eat them just as we do kids. Geese, ducks, and herons abound in that island. Between these islands and the continent there were such strong currents that the Admiral had great difficulty in tacking, and the water was so shallow that the keels of the ships sometimes scraped the sand.

---

[14] A sea-lamprey, also called *remora* and *echineis*. Oviedo gives details concerning the manner of catching, raising, and training the young lampreys to serve as game-fish. *Hist. delle Indie*, cap. x., in Ramusio. The account is interesting and despite obvious inaccuracies may have a basis of truth.

For a space of forty miles the water of these currents was white, and so thick that one would have sworn the sea was sprinkled with flour. Having finally regained the open, the Admiral discovered, eighty miles farther on, another very lofty mountain. He landed to replenish his supply of water and food. In the midst of the thick palm and pine groves two springs of sweet water were found. While the men were busy cutting wood and filling their barrels, one of our archers went off in the woods to hunt. He there suddenly encountered a native, so well dressed in a white tunic, that at the first glance he believed he saw before him one of the Friars of Santa Maria de la Merced, whom the Admiral had brought with him. This native was soon followed by two others, likewise coming out of the forest, and then by a troop of about thirty men, all of them clothed. Our archer turned and ran shouting, as quickly as he could, towards the ships. These people dressed in tunics shouted after him, and tried by all means of persuasion in their power to calm his fears. But he did not stop in his flight. Upon hearing this news, the Admiral, delighted finally to discover a civilised nation, at once landed a troop of armed men, ordering them to advance, if necessary, as far as forty miles into the country, until they should find those people dressed in tunics, or at least some other inhabitants.[15] The Spaniards marched through the forest and emerged on an extensive plain overgrown with brush, amidst which there was no vestige of a path. They sought to cut a pathway through the undergrowth, but wandered about so hopelessly that they hardly advanced a mile. This underbrush was indeed as high as our grain when ripe. Worn out and fatigued, they returned without having discovered a trail. The next day the Admiral sent out a new troop of twenty-five men, urging them to use the greatest diligence to discover

---

[15] None of the natives of the islands wore white tunics, nor indeed any but the most scanty covering. It has been surmised that the soldier who made this report may indistinctly and from a distance have descried a flock of tall white cranes, otherwise he was either the victim of an hallucination or an inventor of strange tales to astonish his fellows. Humboldt (*Histoire de la Géographie du nouveau Continent*) quotes an instance of the colonists of Angostora once mistaking a flock of cranes for a band of soldiers.

the inhabitants of that country. They, however, having come upon the tracks of some large animals, amongst which they thought they recognised those of lions, were terrified and retraced their steps.[16] In the course of their march, they had found a forest overgrown with wild vines, which hung suspended from the loftiest trees, and also many other spice-producing trees. They brought back to Spain heavy and juicy bunches of grapes. As for the other fruits they collected, it was impossible to bring them to Spain, because there were no means of preserving them on board the ships; hence they rotted, and when they were spoiled they threw them into the sea. The men said that they had seen flocks of cranes twice as large as ours in the forest.

Pursuing his course, the Admiral sailed towards other mountains; he observed upon the shore two huts, in which only one man was found, who, when he was brought on board the ships, shook his head and hands, indicating by signs that the country about these mountains was very populous. All along this coast the Admiral encountered numerous canoes which came to meet him, and on one side and the other friendly signals were exchanged. The man Diego, who, from the beginning of the voyage understood the language of the islanders, did not understand that of this newcomer. It was known, indeed, that the languages vary in the different provinces of Cuba. The natives gave it to be understood that a powerful sovereign, who wore clothes, lived in the interior of the country. The whole of the coast was inundated by waters, the beach being muddy and strewn with trees like in our swamps. When they landed to replenish their supply of water, they found some shells with pearls in them. Columbus nevertheless continued on his way, for he sought at that time, in obedience to the royal instructions, to explore the greatest possible extent of sea. As they proceeded on their course, lighted fires were observed on all the hilltops of the coast country, so far as to another mountain eighty miles distant. There was not a single lookout upon the rocks from which smoke did not rise.

[16] There were no lions nor large beasts of prey in the island; it has been suggested that these tracks may have been footprints of an alligator.

It was doubtful whether these fires had been lighted by the natives for domestic purposes or whether it was their custom in time of war thus to signal to warn their neighbours to provide for their safety and unite their forces to repel our attacks.

What is more probable is that they assembled to inspect our ships, as though they were something prodigious, concerning which they knew not what course to adopt. The coast-line began to recede in a southerly direction, and the sea continued to be encumbered with islands. Some of the ships, which had been scraped by the reefs, had sprung; ropes, sails, and other tackle were rotted, and provisions were spoiled by the humidity. The Admiral was, consequently, obliged to retrace his course.[17] The extreme point of this country reached by him, and which he believed to be a continent, he named Evangelista.

During the return voyage, Columbus passed among many other islands more distant from the continent, and reached a sea where he found such numbers of huge turtles that they obstructed the advance of his fleet. He likewise crossed currents of whitish water, similar to those he had already seen.[18] Fearing to sail amongst these islands he returned, and coasted along the one he believed to be a continent.

As he had never maltreated the natives, the inhabitants, both men and women, gladly brought him gifts, displaying no fear. Their presents consisted of parrots, bread, water, rabbits, and most of all, of doves much larger than ours, according to the Admiral's account. As he noticed that these birds gave forth an aromatic odour when they were eaten, he had the stomach of one of them opened, and found it filled with flowers. Evidently that is what gave such a superior taste to these doves; for it is credible that the flesh of animals assimilates the qualities of their food.

While assisting at Mass one day, Columbus beheld a man eighty

[17] Two or three days more would have sufficed to demonstrate the insular character of Cuba, and would doubtless have made Columbus the discoverer of Yucatan.

[18] The milky colour was produced by quantities of chalky sand, churned up from the bottom by the currents.

years old, who seemed respectable though he wore no clothes, coming towards him, accompanied by a number of his people. During the rest of the ceremony this man looked on full of admiration; he was all eyes and ears. Then he presented the Admiral with a basket he was carrying, which was filled with native fruits, and finally sitting beside him, made the following speech which was interpreted by Diego Columbus, who, being from a neighbouring country, understood his language:

"It is reported to us that you have visited all these countries, which were formerly unknown to you, and have inspired the inhabitants with great fear. Now I tell and warn you, since you should know this, that the soul, when it quits the body, follows one of two courses; the first is dark and dreadful, and is reserved for the enemies and the tyrants of the human race; joyous and delectable is the second, which is reserved for those who during their lives have promoted the peace and tranquillity of others. If, therefore, you are a mortal, and believe that each one will meet the fate he deserves, you will harm no one."

Thanks to his native interpreter, the Admiral understood this speech and many others of the same tenor, and was astonished to discover such sound judgment in a man who went naked. He answered: "I have knowledge of what you have said concerning the two courses and the two destinies of our souls when they leave our bodies; but I had thought until now that these mysteries were unknown to you and to your countrymen, because you live in a state of nature." He then informed the old man that he had been sent thither by the King and Queen of Spain to take possession of those countries hitherto unknown to the outside world, and that, moreover, he would make war upon the cannibals and all the natives guilty of crimes, punishing them according to their deserts. As for the innocent, he would protect and honour them because of their virtues. Therefore, neither he nor any one whose intentions were pure need be afraid; rather, if he or any other honourable man had been injured in his interests by his neighbours he had only to say so.

These words of the Admiral afforded such pleasure to the old man that he announced that, although weakened by age, he would gladly go with Columbus, and he would have done so if his wife and sons had not prevented him. What occasioned him great surprise was to learn that a man like Columbus recognised the authority of a sovereign; but his astonishment still further increased when the interpreter explained to him how powerful were the kings and how wealthy, and all about the Spanish nation, the manner of fighting, and how great were the cities and how strong the fortresses. In great dejection the man, together with his wife and sons, threw themselves at the feet of Columbus, with their eyes full of tears, repeatedly asking if the country which produced such men and in such numbers was not indeed heaven.

It is proven that amongst them the land belongs to everybody, just as does the sun or the water. They know no difference between *meum* and *tuum*, that source of all evils. It requires so little to satisfy them, that in that vast region there is always more land to cultivate than is needed. It is indeed a golden age, neither ditches, nor hedges, nor walls to enclose their domains; they live in gardens open to all, without laws and without judges; their conduct is naturally equitable, and whoever injures his neighbour is considered a criminal and an outlaw. They cultivate maize, yucca, and ages, as we have already related is the practice in Hispaniola.

On his return from Cuba to Hispaniola, the Admiral again came in sight of Jamaica, and this time he skirted its southern coast from west to east. Upon reaching the eastern extremity of this island, he beheld in the north and on his left high mountains, which he believed to be the southern coast of Hispaniola which he had not before visited. On the calends of September he reached the port he had named San Nicholas, and there repaired his ships, intending to again ravage the cannibal islands and burn the canoes of the natives. He was determined that these rapacious wolves should no longer injure the sheep, their neighbours; but his project could not be realised because of his bad health. Long watches had weakened him; borne on shore half dead by the sailors of Port Isabella, and surrounded by his two brothers and his friends, he finally recovered his former health, but he could not renew his attack on the cannibal islands, because of the disturbances which had broken out amongst the Spaniards he had left in Hispaniola. Concerning these I shall later explain. Fare you well.

BOOK IV

TO CARDINAL LUDOVICO D'ARAGON, NEPHEW OF OUR KING

When Columbus returned from the land which he believed to be the Indian continent, he learned that the Friar Boyl[1] and Pedro Margarita,[2] the nobleman who formerly enjoyed the King's friendship, as well as several others to whom he had confided the government of Hispaniola, had departed for Spain animated by evil intentions. In order that he might justify himself before the sovereigns, in case they should have been prejudiced by the reports of his enemies, and also for the purpose of recruiting colonists to replace those who had left, and to replenish the failing foodstuffs, such as wheat, wine, oil, and other provisions which form the ordinary food of Spaniards, who did not easily accustom themselves to that of the natives, he decided to betake himself to the Court, which at that time was resident at Burgos, a celebrated town of Old Castile. But I must relate briefly what he did before his departure.

The caciques of the island had always been contented with little, for they lived a peaceful and tranquil life. When they saw the Spaniards establishing themselves upon their native soil, they

---

[1] The character of Padre Boyl has been somewhat rehabilitated by Padre Fita, S. J. (*Memoires du Congr. Amer. de Madrid*, 1881), but he can hardly be deemed comparable as a missionary to the zealous, self-sacrificing friars who followed with such perfect evangelic spirit a few years later. He was at perpetual enmity with both the Admiral and his brother.

[2] Pedro de Margarita had been appointed by Columbus military commander in the island; his conduct was marked by ingratitude towards the Admiral.

were considerably troubled, and desired above all things either to expel the newcomers or to destroy them so completely that not even their memory should remain. It is a fact that the people who accompanied the Admiral in his second voyage were for the most part undisciplined, unscrupulous vagabonds, who only employed their ingenuity in gratifying their appetites. Incapable of moderation in their acts of injustice, they carried off the women of the islanders under the very eyes of their brothers and their husbands; given over to violence and thieving, they had profoundly vexed the natives. It had happened in many places that when our men were surprised by the natives, the latter strangled them, and offered them as sacrifices to their gods. Convinced that he should put down a general insurrection by punishing the murderers of the Spaniards, Columbus summoned the cacique of this valley, lying at the foot of the Ciguano Mountains, which are described in the preceding book. This cacique was called Guarionex. He had been pleased to give his sister to be the wife of that Diego Columbus who had been from his infancy brought up by the Admiral, and had served him as interpreter during his occupation of Cuba. Guarionex had hoped by these means to establish a more intimate friendship with the Admiral. He afterwards sent one of his officers to Caunaboa, cacique of the mountains of Cibao, which is the gold region. The people of this Caunaboa had besieged Hojeda and fifty soldiers in the blockhouse of San Tomas and, had they not heard of the approaching arrival of Columbus in person at the head of imposing reinforcements, they would never have raised the siege.[3] The Admiral chose Hojeda as his envoy, and while the latter was engaged in his mission, several caciques[4] sent from different parts to urge Caunaboa not to allow

[3] A cacique of the Vega, who was a vassal of Guarionex, Juatinango by name, had succeeded in killing ten Spaniards and in setting fire to a house which served as a hospital for forty others who were confined there ill. After these exploits, he besieged the blockhouse of Magdalena, which Luis de Arriaga only succeeded in defending by the greatest efforts. Herrera, *Hist. Ind.*, tom. i., lib. ii., cap. xvi.

[4] The principal caciques of Hayti at that time numbered five. They were: Caunaboa, who was the most powerful of all; Guarionex, Gauccanagari, Behechio, and Cotubanama.

the Christians to settle in the island, unless he wished to exchange independence for slavery; for if the Christians were not expelled to the last man from the island, all the natives would sooner or later become their slaves. Hojeda, on the other hand, negotiated with Caunaboa, urging him to come in person to visit the Admiral, and contract a firm alliance with him. The envoys of the caciques promised Caunaboa their unlimited support for the expulsion of the Spaniards, but Hojeda threatened to massacre him if he chose war rather than peace with the Christians. Caunaboa was very undecided. Besides, the consciousness of his crimes disturbed him, for he had cut off the heads of twenty of our men whom he had surprised. If, therefore, he desired peace on the one hand, on the other he feared the interview with the Admiral. Having carefully planned his treachery, he decided that under cover of peace he would seize the first occasion to destroy Columbus and his men. He set out, escorted by all his household and a large number of soldiers, armed after the fashion of the country, to meet the Admiral. When asked why he took such a numerous troop of men, he answered that it was not becoming for such a great king as he to quit his house and journey without an escort. In this event, however, things turned out differently from what he had expected and he fell into the net that he had himself prepared. Hardly had he left his house before he regretted his decision, but Hojeda succeeded by flatteries and promises in bringing him to Columbus, where he was at once seized and put in irons.[5] The souls of our dead might rest in peace.

After the capture of Caunaboa and all his household, the Admiral resolved to march throughout the whole island. He was informed that the natives suffered from such a severe famine that more than 50,000 men had already perished, and that people continued to die daily as do cattle in time of pest.

This calamity was the consequence of their own folly; for

[5] Hojeda tricked this cacique into allowing him to fasten handcuffs on him; after which the helpless chief was carried sixty leagues through the forests. Pizarro, in his *Varones Illustres*, relates the story, as does likewise Herrera.

when they saw that the Spaniards wished to settle in their island, they thought they might expel them by creating a scarcity of food. They, therefore, decided not only to plant no more crops, but also to destroy and tear up all the various kinds of cereals used for bread which had already been sown, and which I have mentioned in the first book. This was to be done by the people in each district, and especially in the mountainous region of Cipangu and Cibao; that was the country where gold was found in abundance, and the natives were aware that the principal attraction which kept the Spaniards in Hispaniola was gold. At that time the Admiral sent an officer with a troop of armed men to reconnoitre the southern coast of the island, and this officer reported that the regions he had visited had suffered to such an extent from the famine, that during six days he and his men had eaten nothing but the roots of herbs and small plants, or such fruits as grow on the trees. Guarionex, whose territory had suffered less than the others, distributed some provisions amongst our people.

Some days later Columbus, with the object of lessening journeys and also to provide more numerous retreats for his men in case of sudden attack by the natives, had another blockhouse built, which he called Concepcion. It is situated between Isabella and San Tomas in the territory of Cibao, upon the frontiers of the country of Guarionex. It stands upon an elevation, well watered by a number of fresh streams. Seeing this new construction daily nearing completion, and our fleet half ruined lying in the port, the natives began to despair of liberty and to ask one another dejectedly whether the Christians would ever evacuate the archipelago.

It was during these explorations in the interior of the mountainous district of Cibao that the men of Concepcion obtained an ingot of massive gold, shaped in the form of a sponge-like stone; it was as large as a man's fist, and weighed twenty ounces. It had been found by a cacique, not on a river bank but in a dry mound. I saw it with my own eyes in a shop at Medina del Campo in Old Castile, where the Court was passing the winter; and to my great admiration I handled it and tested its weight. I also saw a piece of native tin, which might have served for bells or apothecaries' mortars or other such things as are made of Corinthian brass. It was so heavy that not only could I not lift it from the ground with my two hands, but could not even move it to the right or left. It was said that this lump weighed more than three hundred pounds at eight ounces to the pound. It had been found in the courtyard of a cacique's house, where it had lain for a long time, and the old people of the country, although no tin has been found in the island within the memory of any living man, nevertheless knew where there was a mine of this metal. But nobody could ever learn this secret from them, so much were they vexed by the Spaniards' presence. Finally they decided to reveal its whereabouts, but it was entirely destroyed, and filled in with earth and rubbish. It is nevertheless easier to extract the metal than to get out iron from the mines, and it is thought that if workmen and skilled miners were sent out, it would be possible to again work that tin mine.

Not far from the blockhouse of Concepcion and in these same mountains, the Spaniards discovered a large quantity of amber, and in some caverns was distilled a greenish colour very much prized by painters. In marching through the forest there were places where all the trees were of a scarlet colour which are called by Italian merchants *verzino*, and by the Spaniards brazil wood.

At this point, Most Illustrious Prince, you may raise an objection and say to yourself: "If the Spaniards have brought several shiploads of scarlet wood and some gold, and a little cotton and some bits of amber back to Europe, why did they not load themselves with gold and all the precious products which seem to abound so plenteously in the country you describe?"

Columbus answered such questions by saying that the men he had taken with him thought more of sleeping and taking their ease than about work, and they preferred fighting and rebellion to peace and tranquillity. The greater part of these men deserted him. To establish uncontested authority over the island, it was necessary to conquer the islanders and to break their power. The Spaniards have indeed pretended that they could not endure the cruelty and hardship of the Admiral's orders, and they have formulated many accusations against him. It is in consequence of these difficulties that he has not so far thought about covering the expenses of the expeditions. I will nevertheless observe that in this same year, 1501, in which I am writing to you, the Spaniards have gathered 1200 pounds of gold in two months.

But let us return to our narrative. At the proper time I will describe to you in detail what I have only just touched upon in this digression.

The Admiral was perfectly aware of the alarm and disturbance that prevailed amongst the islanders, but he was unable to prevent the violence and rapacity of his men, whenever they came into contact with the natives. A number of the principal caciques of the frontier regions assembled to beg Columbus to forbid the Spaniards to wander about the island because, under the pretext of hunting for gold or other local products, they left nothing uninjured or undefiled. Moreover, all the natives between the ages of fourteen and seventy years bound themselves to pay him tribute in the products of the country at so much per head, promising to fulfil their engagement. Some of the conditions of this agreement were as follows: The mountaineers of Cibao were to bring to the town every three months a specified measure filled with gold. They reckon by the moon and call the months moons. The islanders who cultivated the lands which spontaneously produced spices and cotton, were pledged to pay a fixed sum per head. This pact suited both parties, and it would have been observed by both sides as had been agreed, save that the famine nullified their resolutions. The natives had hardly strength to hunt food in the forests and for a long time they contented themselves with roots, herbs, and wild fruits. Nevertheless the majority of the caciques, aided by their followers, did bring part of the established tribute. They begged as a favour of the Admiral to have pity on their misery, and to exempt them till such time as the island might recover its former prosperity. They bound themselves then to pay double what was for the moment failing.

Owing to the famine, which had affected them more cruelly than the others, very few of the mountaineers of Cibao paid tribute. These mountaineers did not differ in their customs and language from the people of the plain more than do the mountaineers of other countries differ from those who live in the capital. There exist amongst them, however, some points of resemblance, since they lead the same kind of simple, open-air life.

But let us return to Caunaboa, who, if you remember, had been taken prisoner.

This cacique, when he found himself put in irons, gnashed his teeth like an African lion and fell to thinking, night and day, upon the means to recover his liberty.[6] He begged the Admiral, since the region of Cipangu was now under his authority, to send Spanish garrisons to protect the country against the attacks of neighbours who were his ancient enemies. He said that it was reported to him that the country was ravaged, and the property of his subjects considered by his enemies as their lawful plunder. As a matter of fact it was a trap he was preparing. He hoped that his brother and other relatives in Cibao would, either by force or by trickery, capture as many Spaniards as would be required to pay his ransom. Divining this plot, Columbus sent Hojeda, but with an escort of soldiers sufficient to overcome all resistance of the inhabitants of Cibao. Hardly had the Spaniards entered that region when the brother of Caunaboa assembled about 5000 men, equipped in their fashion, that is to say, naked, armed with arrows without iron points, clubs, and spears. He succeeded in surrounding the Spaniards, and held them besieged in a small house. This chief showed himself under the circumstances to be a veritable soldier. When he had approached within a distance of

[6] Las Casas (*Hist. de las Indias*, tom. i., p. 102) relates that Caunaboa never forgave Columbus for his treatment of him, while he had, on the contrary, great respect for Hojeda, the latter's clever ruse, deftly executed, being precisely the kind of trickery he was able to appreciate and admire.

one stadium, he divided his men into five groups, stationing them in a circle, and assigning to each one his post, while he himself marched directly against the Spaniards. When all his arrangements were completed, he ordered his soldiers to advance, shouting all together, so as to engage in a hand-to-hand combat. He hoped that, by thus surrounding the Spaniards, none of them would escape. But our men, persuaded that it was better to attack than to await their assault, fell upon the most numerous band they saw in the open country. The ground was adapted for cavalry manœuvres and the horsemen, opening their charge, rode down the enemy, who were easily put to flight. Those who awaited the encounter were massacred; the others, overcome with fright, fled, abandoning their huts, and seeking refuge in the mountains and upon inaccessible rocks. They begged for mercy, promising and swearing to observe all the conditions imposed upon them, if they were only permitted to live with their families. The brother of the cacique was finally captured, and each of his men was sent to his own home. After this victory that region was pacified.

The mountain valley where the cacique lived is called Magona. It is traversed by auriferous rivers, is generously productive and marvellously fertile. In the month of June of this same year occurred a frightful tempest; whirlwinds reaching to the skies uprooted the largest trees that were swept within their vortex. When this typhoon reached the port of Isabella, only three ships were riding at anchor; their cables were broken, and after three or four shocks—though there was no tempest or tide at the time—they sank. It is said that in that year the sea penetrated more deeply than usual into the earth, and that it rose more than a cubit. The natives whispered that the Spaniards were the cause of this disturbance of the elements and these catastrophes. These tempests, which the Greeks called typhoons, are called by the natives *huracanes.*[7] According to their accounts hurricanes are

---

[7] The word *hurricane* is from *Hurakan*, the name of the god or culture hero who, in the mythology of Yucatan, corresponded to Quetzalcoatl of the Mexicans. Being the god of the winds, storms were ascribed to his fury, and

sufficiently frequent in the island, but they never attain such violence and fury. None of the islanders living, nor any of their ancestors remembers that such an atmospheric disturbance, capable of uprooting the greatest trees, had ever swept the island; nor, on the other hand, had the sea ever been so turbulent, or the tidewater so ravaged. Wherever plains border the sea, flowery meadows are found nearby.

Let us now return to Caunaboa. When it was sought to take them to the sovereigns of Spain, both he and his brother died of grief on the voyage. The destruction of his ships detained the Admiral at Hispaniola; but, as he had at his disposal the necessary artisans, he ordered two caravels to be built immediately.

While these orders were being carried out, he despatched his brother, Bartholomew Columbus,—Adelantado, the Spaniards call him, of the island,—with a number of miners and a troop of soldiers, to the gold mines, which had been discovered by the assistance of the natives sixty leagues from Isabella in the direction of Cipangu. As some very ancient pits were found there, the Admiral believed that he had rediscovered in those mines the ancient treasures which, it is stated in the Old Testament, King Solomon of Jerusalem had found in the Persian Gulf. Whether this be true or false is not for me to decide. These mines cover an area of six miles. The miners, in sifting some dry earth gathered at different places, declared that they had found such a great quantity of gold hidden in that earth that a miner could easily collect three drachmas in a day's work. After they had explored that region, the Adelantado and the miners wrote to Columbus acquainting him with their discovery. The ships being then ready, Columbus immediately and with great delight embarked to return to Spain; that is to say, the fifth day of the ides of March in the year 1495.[8] He confided the government of the province with full powers to his brother, the Adelantado, Bartholomew Columbus.

---

the typhoons and tempests which broke out at times with destructive violence over the seas and countries were called by his name.

[8] Columbus sailed on March 10, 1496.

BOOK V

TO CARDINAL LUDOVICO D'ARAGON, NEPHEW OF OUR KING

Acting upon the parting counsel of his brother, the Adelantado, Bartholomew Columbus, constructed a blockhouse at the mines, which he called El Dorado,[1] because the labourers discovered gold in the earth with which they were building its walls. It required three months to manufacture the necessary tools for washing and sifting the gold, but famine obliged him to abandon this enterprise before it was terminated. At a place sixty miles farther on, where he and the greater part of his soldiers went, he succeeded in procuring from the islanders a small quantity of the bread they make, to such a bad state were affairs at that time reduced. Unable to prolong his stay, he left ten men at El Dorado, furnishing them with a small part of the bread that remained. He moreover left with them an excellent hunting dog for chasing the game, which I have above said resembles our rabbits, and which are called *utias;* after which he left to return to Concepcion. It was at that time that the tribute from the cacique Guarionex and one of his neighbours called Manicavex was due. The Adelantado remained there the whole month of June, and obtained from the caciques, not only the sum total of the tribute, but also provisions necessary to support himself and the 400 men of his escort.

About the calends of July three caravels arrived, bringing provisions—wheat, oil, wine, and salted pork and beef. In obedi-

---

[1] The name first given to the place was San Cristobal.

84

ence to the orders from Spain, they were distributed amongst all the Europeans, but as some of the provisions had rotted, or were spoiled by the damp, people complained. Fresh instructions from the sovereigns and from the Admiral were sent to Bartholomew Columbus by these ships. After frequent interviews with the sovereigns, Columbus directed his brother to transfer his residence to the southern coast of the island, nearer to the mines. He was likewise ordered to send back to Spain, in chains, the caciques who had been convicted of assassinating the Christians, and also those of their subjects who had shared their crimes. Three hundred islanders were thus transported to Spain.[2]

After having carefully explored the coast, the Adelantado transferred his residence and built a lofty blockhouse near a safe harbour, naming the fort Santo Domingo, because he had arrived at that place on a Sunday. There flows into that harbour a river, whose wholesome waters abound in excellent fish, and whose banks are delightfully wooded. This river has some unusual natural features. Wherever its waters flow, the most useful and agreeable products flourish, such as palms and fruits of all kinds. The trees sometimes droop their branches, weighted with flowers and fruit over the heads of the Spaniards, who declare that the soil of Santo Domingo is as fertile, or even perhaps more so, than at Hispaniola. At Isabella there only remained the invalids and some engineers to complete the construction of two caravels which had been begun, all the other colonists coming south to Santo Domingo. When the blockhouse was finished, he placed there a garrison of twenty men, and prepared to lead the remainder of his people on a tour of exploration through the western parts of the island, of which not even the name was known. Thirty leagues distant from Santo Domingo, that is to say, at the ninetieth mile, they came upon the river Naiba, which flows south from the mountains of Cibao and divides the island into two equal parts. The Adelantado crossed this river, and sent two captains, each with an escort of twenty-five soldiers, to explore the territory of the caciques who possessed forests of red

[2] This transport marks the beginning of the slave trade in America.

trees. These men, marching to the left, came upon forests, in which they cut down magnificent trees of great value, heretofore respected. The captains piled the red-coloured wood in the huts of the natives, wishing thus to protect it until they could load it on the ships. During this time the Adelantado, who had marched to the right, had encountered at a place not far from the river Naiba a powerful cacique, named Beuchios Anacauchoa, who was at that time engaged in an expedition to conquer the people along the river, as well as some other caciques of the island. This powerful chieftain lives at the western extremity of the island, called Xaragua. This rugged and mountainous country is thirty leagues distant from the river Naiba, but all the caciques whose territory lies in between are subject to him.[3] All that country from the Naiba to the western extremity produces no gold. Anacauchoa, observing that our men put down their arms and made him amicable signs, adopted a responsive air, either from fear or from courtesy, and asked them what they wanted of him. The Adelantado replied: "We wish you to pay the same tribute to my brother, who is in command here in the name of the Spanish sovereigns, as do the other caciques." To which he answered: "How can you ask tribute from me, since none of the numerous provinces under my authority produce gold?" He had learned that strangers in search of gold had landed on the island, and he did not suspect that our men would ask for anything else. "We do not pretend," continued the Adelantado, "to exact tribute from anybody which cannot be easily paid, or of a kind not obtainable; but we know that this country produces an abundance of cotton, hemp, and other similar things, and we ask you to pay tribute of those products." The cacique's face expressed joy on hearing these words, and with a satisfied air he agreed to give what he was asked, and in whatever quantities they desired; for he sent away his men, and after despatching messengers in advance, he himself acted as guide for the Adelantado, conducting him to his residence, which, as we have already said,

[3] Xaragua includes the entire western coast from Cape Tiburon to the island of Beata on the south.

was situated about thirty leagues distant. The march led through the countries of subject caciques; and upon some of them a tribute of hemp was imposed, for this hemp is quite as good as our flax for weaving ships' sails; upon others, of bread, and upon others, of cotton, according to the products of each region.

When they finally arrived at the chieftain's residence in Xaragua, the natives came out to meet them, and, as is their custom, offered a triumphal reception to their king, Beuchios Anacauchoa, and to our men. Please note amongst other usages these two, which are remarkable amongst naked and uncultivated people. When the company approached, some thirty women, all wives of the cacique, marched out to meet them, dancing, singing, and shouting; they were naked, save for a loin-girdle, which, though it consisted but of a cotton belt, which dropped over their hips, satisfied these women devoid of any sense of shame. As for the young girls, they covered no part of their bodies, but wore their hair loose upon their shoulders and a narrow ribbon tied around the forehead. Their face, breast, and hands, and the entire body was quite naked, and of a somewhat brunette tint. All were beautiful, so that one might think he beheld those splendid naiads or nymphs of the fountains, so much celebrated by the ancients. Holding branches of palms in their hands, they danced to an accompaniment of songs, and bending the knee, they offered them to the Adelantado. Entering the chieftain's house, the Spaniards refreshed themselves at a banquet prepared with all the magnificence of native usage. When night came, each, according to his rank, was escorted by servants of the cacique to houses where those hanging beds I have already described were assigned to them, and there they rested.

Next day they were conducted to a building which served as a theatre, where they witnessed dances and listened to songs, after which two numerous troops of armed men suddenly appeared upon a large open space, the king having thought to please and interest the Spaniards by having them exercised, just as in Spain Trojan games (that is to say, tourneys) are celebrated. The two armies advanced and engaged in as animated a combat as though

they were fighting to defend their property, their homes, their
children or their lives. With such vigour did they contest, in the
presence of their chieftain, that within the short space of an hour
four soldiers were killed and a number were wounded; and it was
only at the instance of the Spaniards that the cacique gave the
signal for them to lay down their arms and cease fighting. After
having advised the cacique to henceforth plant more cotton along
the river banks, in order that he might more easily pay the
tribute imposed on each household, the Adelantado left on the
third day for Isabella to visit the invalids, and to see the ships in
construction. About three hundred of his men had fallen victims
to divers maladies, and he was therefore much concerned and
hardly knew what course to adopt, for everything was lacking,
not only for caring for the sick, but also for the necessities of
life; since no ship had arrived from Spain to put an end to his
uncertainty, he ordered the invalids to be distributed in the
several blockhouses built in different provinces. These citadels,
existing in a straight line from Isabella to Santo Domingo, that is
to say, from north to south, were as follows: thirty-six miles
from Isabella stood Esperanza; twenty-four miles beyond Esperanza came Santa Caterina; twenty miles beyond Santa Caterina,
Santiago. Twenty miles beyond Santiago had been constructed a
fortification stronger than any of the others; for it stood at the
foot of the mountains of Cibao, in a broad and fertile plain which
was well peopled. This was called La Concepcion. Between La
Concepcion and Santo Domingo, the Adelantado built an even
stronger fortress, which stood in the territory of a chieftain, who
was obeyed by several thousands of subjects. As the natives called
the village where their cacique lived, *Bonana*, the Adelantado
wished the fortress to have the same name.

Having distributed the invalids amongst these fortresses or in
the houses of the natives in the neighbourhood, the Adelantado
left for Santo Domingo, collecting tribute from the caciques he
encountered on his way. He had been at Santo Domingo but a
few days when the report was brought that two of the caciques
in the neighbourhood of La Concepcion were driven to despera-

tion by the Spaniards' rule, and were planning a revolt. Upon the
reception of this news he set out for that region by rapid
marches.

He learned upon his arrival that Guarionex had been chosen by
the other caciques as their commander-in-chief. Although he had
already tested and had reason to fear our arms and our tactics, he
had allowed himself to be partly won over. The caciques had
planned a rising of about 15,000 men, armed in their fashion, for a
fixed day, thus making a new appeal to the fortunes of battle.
After consultation with the commander at La Concepcion and
the soldiers he had with him, the Adelantado determined to take
the caciques in their villages, while they were off their guard and
before they had assembled their soldiers. Captains were thus sent
against the caciques, and surprising them in their sleep, before
their scattered subjects could collect, invaded their houses which
were unprotected either by ditches, walls, or entrenchments;
they attacked and seized them, binding them with cords, and
bringing them, as they had been ordered, to the Adelantado. The
latter had dealt with Guarionex himself, as he was the most
formidable enemy, and had seized him at the appointed hour.
Fourteen caciques were thus brought prisoners to La Concepcion, and shortly afterwards two of those who had corrupted
Guarionex and the others, and who had favoured the revolt were
condemned to death. Guarionex and the rest were released, for
the Adelantado feared that the natives, affected by the death of
the caciques, might abandon their fields, which would have occasioned a grievous damage to our people, because of the crops.
About six thousand of their subjects had come to solicit their
freedom. These people had laid down their arms, making the air
ring and the earth shake with their clamour. The Adelantado
spoke to Guarionex and the other caciques, and by means of
promises, presents, and threats, charged them to take good care
for the future to engage in no further revolt. Guarionex made a
speech to the people, in which he praised our power, our
clemency to the guilty, and our generosity to those who remained faithful; he exhorted them to calm their spirits and for the

future neither to think nor to plan any hostilities against the
Christians, but rather to be obedient, humble, and serviceable to
them, unless they wished worse things to overtake them. When
he had finished his speech, his people took him on their shoulders
in a hammock, and in this wise they carried him to the village
where he lived, and within a few days the entire country was
pacified.

Nevertheless the Spaniards were disturbed and depressed, for
they found themselves abandoned in a strange country. Fifteen
months had elapsed since the departure of the Admiral. The
clothes and the food to which they were accustomed were
wanting, and so they marched with sad faces and eyes bent on the
ground.[4] The Adelantado strove as best he might to offer conso-
lation. At this juncture, Beuchios Anacauchoa, for such was the
name of the king of the western province of Xaragua of which
we have before spoken, sent to the Adelantado notifying him that
the cotton and other tribute he and his subjects were to pay,
were ready. Bartholomew Columbus marched thither, therefore,
and was received with great honours, by the cacique and by his
sister. This woman, formerly the wife of Caunaboa, King of
Cibao, was held in as great esteem throughout the kingdom as her
brother. It seems she was gracious, clever, and prudent.[5] Having
learned a lesson from the example of her husband, she had persuaded her brother to submit to the Christians, to soothe and to
please them. This woman was called Anacaona.

Thirty-two caciques were assembled in the house of Anacauchoa, where they had brought their tribute. In addition to
what had been agreed upon, they sought to win favour by adding

---

[4] The story of the disorders, privations, and unrest, as told by Las Casas,
Columbus, and others, makes cheerless reading; the misfortunes of the
colonists were due to their inveterate idleness, their tyranny, which had
alienated the good-will of the natives, and to the disillusionment that had
dispersed their hope of speedily and easily won riches.

[5] Herrera (iii., 6) speaks of her as *la insigne Anacaona . . . mujer pru-
dente y entendida . . .* etc. She composed with unusual talent the *arreytos*
or folk-ballads the natives were fond of singing. Las Casas describes her
dreadful death in his *Brevissima Relacion*.

numerous presents, which consisted of two kinds of bread, roots, grains, utias, that is to say, rabbits, which are numerous in the island, fish, which they had preserved by cooking them, and those same serpents, resembling crocodiles, which they esteem a most delicate food. We have described them above, and the natives call them iguanas. They are special to Hispaniola.[6] Up to that time none of the Spaniards had ventured to eat them because of their odour, which was not only repugnant but nauseating, but the Adelantado, won by the amiability of the cacique's sister, consented to taste a morsel of iguana; and hardly had his palate savoured this succulent flesh than he began to eat it by the mouthful. Henceforth the Spaniards were no longer satisfied to barely taste it, but became epicures in regard to it, and talked of nothing else than the exquisite flavour of these serpents, which they found to be superior to that of peacocks, pheasants, or partridges. If, however, they are cooked as we do peacocks and pheasants, which are first larded and then roasted, the serpent's flesh loses its good flavour. First they gut them, then wash and clean them with care, and roll them into a circle, so that they look like the coils of a sleeping snake; after which they put them in a pot, just large enough to hold them, pouring over them a little water flavoured with the pepper found in the island. The pot is covered and a fire of odorous wood which gives very little light is kindled underneath it. A juice as delicious as nectar runs drop by drop from the insides. It is reported that there are few dishes more appetising than iguana eggs cooked over a slow fire. When they are fresh and served hot they are delicious, but if they are preserved for a few days they still further improve. But this is enough about cooking recipes. Let us pass on to other subjects.

The tribute of cotton sent by the caciques filled the Adelantado's hut, and, in addition, he accepted their promise to furnish him all the bread he needed. While waiting for the bread to be made in the different districts, and brought to the house of Beuchios Anacauchoa, King of Xaragua, he sent to Isabella direct-

[6] Iguanas are found in all the *tierras calientes* of the continent.

ing that one of the caravels he had ordered to be built be brought to him promising the colonists that he would send it back to them loaded with bread. The delighted sailors made the tour of the island with alacrity, and landed on the coast of Xaragua. As soon as that brilliant, prudent, and sensible woman called Anacaona, sister of Beuchios Anacauchoa, heard that our ship had reached the coast of her country, she persuaded her brother to accompany her to visit it. The distance from the royal residence to the coast was only six miles. They halted for the night at a village about halfway, where the queen kept her treasure; this treasure did not consist of gold, silver, or pearls, but of utensils necessary to the different requirements of life, such as seats, platters, basins, cauldrons, and plates made of black wood, brilliantly polished; they display great art in the manufacture of all these articles. That distinguished savant, your doctor, Joannes Baptista Elysius, thinks that this black wood is ebony. It is to the manufacture of these articles that the islanders devote the best of their native ingenuity. In the island of Ganabara which, if you have a map, you will see lies at the western extremity of Hispaniola and which is subject to Anacauchoa, it is the women who are thus employed; the various pieces are decorated with representations of phantoms which they pretend to see in the night-time, and serpents and men and everything that they see about them. What would they not be able to manufacture, Most Illustrious Prince, if they knew the use of iron and steel? They begin by softening the inner part of pieces of wood in the fire, after which they dig them out and work them with shells from the rivers.

Anacaona presented to the Adelantado fourteen seats and sixty earthen vessels for the kitchen, besides four rolls of woven cotton of immense weight. When they all reached the shore where the other royal town is situated, the Adelantado ordered out a barque fully equipped. The king also commanded two canoes to be launched, the first for the use of himself and his attendants, the second for his sister and her followers, but Anacaona was unwilling to embark on any other than the boat which carried the Adelantado. As they approached the ship, a cannon was fired at a given signal. The sound echoed over the sea like thunder, and the air was filled with smoke. The terrified islanders trembled, believing that this detonation had shattered the terrestrial globe; but when they turned towards the Adelantado their emotion subsided. Upon approaching closer to the ship the sound of flutes, fifes, and drums was heard, charming their senses by sweet music, and awakening their astonishment and admiration. When they had been over the whole ship, from stern to prow, and had carefully visited the forecastle, the tiller, and the hold, the brother and sister looked at one another in silence; their astonishment being so profound that they had nothing to say. While they were engaged in visiting the ship, the Adelantado ordered the anchor to be raised, the sails set, and to put out on the high sea. Their astonishment was redoubled when they observed that, without oars or the employment of any human force, such a great boat flew over the surface of the water. It was blowing a land wind, which was favourable to this manœuvre, and what astonished them most was to see that the ship which was advanced by the help of this wind likewise turned about, first to the right and then to the left, according to the captain's will.

At the conclusion of these manœuvres the ship was loaded with bread, roots, and other gifts, and the Adelantado after offering them some presents took leave of Beuchios Anacauchoa and his sister, their followers and servants of both sexes. The impression left upon the latter by this visit was stupefying. The Spaniards marched overland and returned to Isabella. On arriving there, it was learned that a certain Ximenes Roldan, formerly chief of the miners and camp-followers, whom the Admiral had made his equerry and raised to the grade of chief justice, was ill-disposed towards the Adelantado. It was simultaneously ascertained that the Cacique Guarionex, unable longer to put up with the rapacity of Roldan and the other Spaniards at Isabella, had been driven by despair to quit the country with his family and a large number of his subjects, taking refuge in the mountains which border the northern coast only ten leagues to the west of Isabella. Both these mountains and their inhabitants bear the same name, *Ciguaia*. The

chief of all the caciques inhabiting the mountain region is called
Maiobanexios, who lived at a place called Capronus. These mountains are rugged, lofty, inaccessible, and rise from the sea in a
semicircle. Between the two extremities of the chain, there lies a
beautiful plain, watered by numerous rivers which rise in these
mountains. The natives are ferocious and warlike, and it is
thought they are of the same race as the cannibals, for when they
descend from their mountains to fight with their neighbours in
the plain, they eat all whom they kill. It was with the cacique of
these mountains that Guarionex took refuge, bringing him gifts,
consisting of things which the mountaineers lack. He told him
that the Spaniards had spared him neither ill-treatment nor
humiliation nor violence, while neither humility nor pride had
been of the least use in his dealings with them. He came, therefore, to him as a suppliant, hoping to be protected against the
injustice of these criminals. Maiobanexios promised him help and
succour to the extent of his power.

Hastening back to La Concepcion the Adelantado summoned
Ximenes Roldan, who, accompanied by his adherents, was prowl-
ing amongst the villages of the island, to appear before him.
Greatly irritated, the Adelantado asked him what his intentions
were. To which Roldan impudently answered: "Your brother,
the Admiral is dead, and we fully understand that our sovereigns
have little care for us. Were we to obey you, we should die of
hunger, and we are forced to hunt for provisions in the island.
Moreover, the Admiral confided to me, as well as to you, the
government of the island; hence, we are determined to obey you
no longer." He added other equally misplaced observations. Before the Adelantado could capture him, Roldan, followed by
about seventy men, escaped to Xaragua in the western part of the
island, where, as the Adelantado reported to his brother, they
gave themselves over to violence, thievery, and massacre.

While these disturbances were in progress, the Spanish sovereigns fully granted the Admiral eight vessels, which Columbus
promptly ordered to sail from the town of Cadiz, a city consecrated to Hercules. These ships were freighted with provisions

for the Adelantado. By chance they approached the western coast of the island, where Ximenes Roldan and his accomplices were. Roldan won over the crews by promising them fresh young girls instead of manual labour, pleasures instead of exertion, plenty in place of famine, and repose instead of weariness and watching.

During this time Guarionex, who had assembled a troop of allies, made frequent descents upon the plain, killing all the Christians he surprised, ravaging the fields, driving off the workmen, and destroying villages.

Although Roldan and his followers were not ignorant that the Admiral might arrive from one day to another, they had no fears, since they had won over to their side the crews of the ships that had been sent on ahead. In the midst of such miseries did the unfortunate Adelantado await from day to day the arrival of his brother. The Admiral sailed from Spain with the remainder of the squadron but instead of sailing directly to Hispaniola, he first laid his course to the south.[7] What he accomplished during this new voyage, what seas and countries he visited, what unknown lands he discovered, I shall narrate, and I shall also explain at length the sequel of these disorders in the following books. Fare you well.

[7] This was the third voyage of Columbus.

BOOK VI

TO THE SAME
CARDINAL LUDOVICO D'ARAGON

On the third day of the calends of June, 1498,[1] Columbus sailed from the port of San Lucar de Barrameda, which is situated at the mouth of the Guadalquivir not far from Cadiz. His fleet consisted of eight heavily freighted ships. He avoided his usual route by way of the Canaries, because of certain French pirates who were lying in wait for him. Seven hundred and twenty miles north of the Fortunate Isles he sighted Madeira, which lies four degrees to the south of Seville; for at Seville, according to the mariners' report, the north star rises to the 36th degree, whereas at Madeira it is in the 32d. Madeira was, therefore, his first stop, and from thence he despatched five or six ships loaded with provisions directly to Hispaniola, only keeping for himself one ship with decks and two merchant caravels. He laid his course due south and reached the equinoctial line, which he purposed to follow directly to the west, making new discoveries and leaving Hispaniola to the north on his starboard side. The thirteen islands of the Hesperides lie in the track of this voyage. They belong to the Portuguese, and all, save one, are inhabited. They are called the Cape Verde islands, and are distant only a day's sail from the western part of Ethiopia. To one of these islands the Portuguese

---

[1] The date was May 30, 1498, and the number of ships under his command was six, instead of eight. Much delay had occurred in fitting out the fleet for the voyage, owing to the poor management of the royal functionaries, especially the Bishop of Burgos, whose enmity towards Columbus was from thenceforward relentless.

have given the name of Bona Vista;[2] and each year numerous lepers are cured of their malady by eating the turtles of this island.

The climate being very bad, the Admiral quickly left the archipelago behind, and sailed 480 miles towards the west-south-west. He reports that the dead calms and the fierce heat of the June sun caused such sufferings that his ships almost took fire. The hoops of his water barrels burst, and the water leaked out. His men found this heat intolerable. The pole star was then at an elevation of five degrees. Of the eight days during which they endured these sufferings only the first was clear; the others being cloudy and rainy, but not on that account less oppressive. More than once, indeed, did he repent having taken this course. After eight days of these miseries a favourable wind rose from the south-west, by which the Admiral profited to sail directly west, and under this parallel he observed new stars in the heavens, and experienced a more agreeable temperature. In fact, all his men agree in saying that after three days' sailing in that direction, the air was much cooler. The Admiral affirms that, while he was in the region of dead calms and torrid heat, the ship always mounted the back of the sea, just as when climbing a high mountain one seems to advance towards the sky, and yet, nevertheless, he had seen no land on the horizon. Finally, on the eve of the calends of July, a watcher announced with a joyful cry, from the crow's nest, that he saw three lofty mountains.[3] He exhorted his companions to keep up their courage. The men were, indeed, much depressed, not merely because they had been scorched by the sun, but because the water-supply was short. The barrels had been sprung by the extreme heat, and lost the water through the cracks. Full of rejoicing they advanced, but as they were about to

[2] Properly *Boavista*. A leper colony had been established here by the Portuguese.

[3] Alonzo Perez Nirando, a sailor from Huelva, made the joyous announcement, and the sailors sang the *Salve Regina* in thanksgiving. Columbus named the island *Trinidad*, having already decided to dedicate the first sighted land to the Holy Trinity. The three mountain peaks close together seemed to render the name all the more appropriate.

touch land they perceived that this was impossible, because the sea was dotted with reefs, although in the neighbourhood they descried a harbour which seemed a spacious one. From their ships the Spaniards could see that the country was inhabited and well cultivated; for they saw well-ordered gardens and shady orchards, while the sweet odours, exhaled by plants and trees bathed in the morning dew, reached their nostrils.

Twenty miles from that place, the Admiral found a sufficiently large port to shelter his ships, though no river flowed into it. Sailing farther on he finally discovered a satisfactory harbour for repairing his vessels and also replenishing his supply of water and wood. He called this land Punta del Arenal.[4] There was no sign of any habitation in the neighbourhood of the harbour, but there were many tracks of animals similar to goats, and in fact the body of one of those animals, closely resembling a goat, was found. On the morrow, a canoe was seen in the distance carrying eighty men, all of whom were young, good-looking, and of lofty stature. Besides their bows and arrows they were armed with shields, which is not the custom among the other islanders. They wore their hair long, parted in the middle, and plastered down quite in the Spanish fashion. Save for their loin-cloths of various coloured cottons, they were entirely naked.

The Admiral's opinion was that this country was nearer to the sky than any other land situated in the same parallel and that it was above the thick vapours which rose from the valleys and

---

[4] The narrative at this point is somewhat sketchy, but the author, doubtless, faithfully recounted the events as they were reported to him. The ships approached the island from the east, and then coasted its shore for five leagues beyond the cape named by Columbus *La Galera*, because of its imagined resemblance to a galley under sail. The next day he continued his course westwards, and named another headland *Punta de la Playa*; this was a Wednesday, August the first; and as the fleet passed between La Galera and La Playa, the South American continent was first discovered, some twenty-five leagues distant. Fernando Columbus affirms that his father, thinking it was another island, called it *Isla Santa;* but in reality Columbus named the continent *Tierra de Gracia*. Punta del Arenal forms the southwestern extremity of the island and is separated by a channel, according to Columbus, two leagues broad.

swamps, just as the high peaks of lofty mountains are distant from the deep valleys. Although Columbus declared that during this voyage he had followed without deviation the parallel of Ethiopia, there are the greatest possible physical differences between the natives of Ethiopia and those of the islands; for the Ethiopians are black and have curly, woolly hair, while these natives are on the contrary white, and have long, straight, blond hair. What the causes of these differences may be, I do not know. They are due rather to the conditions of the earth than to those of the sky; for we know perfectly well that snow falls and lies on the mountains of the torrid zone, while in northern countries far distant from that zone the inhabitants are overcome by great heat.

In order to attract the natives they had met, the Admiral made them some presents of mirrors, cups of bright polished brass, bells, and other similar trifles, but the more he called to them, the more they drew off. Nevertheless, they looked intently and with sincere admiration at our men, their instruments and their ships, but without laying down their oars. Seeing that he could not attract them by his presents, the Admiral ordered his trumpets and flutes to be played, on the largest ship, and the men to dance and sing a chorus. He hoped that the sweetness of the songs and the strange sounds might win them over, but the young men imagined that the Spaniards were singing preparatory to engaging in battle, so in the twinkling of an eye they dropped their oars and seized their bows and arrows, protecting their arms with their shields, and, while waiting to understand the meaning of the sounds, stood ready to let fly a volley against our men. The Spaniards sought to draw near little by little, in such wise as to surround them; but the natives retreated from the Admiral's vessel and, confident in their ability as oarsmen, they approached so near to one of the smaller ships that from the poop a cloak was given to the pilot of the canoe, and a cap to another chief. They made signs to the captain of the ship to come to land, in order that they might the more easily come to an understanding; but when they saw that the captain drew near to the Admiral's vessel to ask permission to land, they feared some trap, and quickly jumped into their canoe and sped away with the rapidity of the wind.

The Admiral relates that to the west of that island and not far distant he came upon a strong current flowing from east to west.[5] It ran with such force that he compared its violence to that of a vast cataract flowing from a mountain height. He declared that he had never been exposed to such serious danger since he began, as a boy, to sail the seas. Advancing as best he could amongst these raging waves, he discovered a strait some eight miles long, which resembled the entrance of a large harbour. The current flowed towards that strait, which he called Boca de la Sierpe, naming an island beside it, Margarita. From this strait there flowed another current of fresh water, thus coming into conflict with the salt waters and causing such waves that there seemed to rage between the two currents a terrible combat. In spite of these difficulties, the Admiral succeeded in penetrating into the gulf, where he found the waters drinkable and agreeable.

Another very singular thing the Admiral has told me, and which is confirmed by his companions (all worthy of credence and whom I carefully questioned concerning the details of the voyage), is that he sailed twenty-six leagues, that is to say, one hundred and forty-eight miles, in fresh water; and the farther he advanced to the west, the fresher the water became.[6] Finally, he sighted a very lofty mountain, of which the eastern part was inhabited only by a multitude of monkeys with very long tails. All this side of the mountain is very steep, which explains why no people live there. A man, sent to reconnoitre the country, reported however that it was all cultivated and that the fields were sown, though nowhere were there people or huts. Our own peasants often go some distance from their homes to sow their fields. On the western side of the mountain was a large plain. The Spaniards were well satisfied to drop anchor in such a great

---

[5] Columbus was then near the mouth of the Orinoco River.

[6] The fresh waters of the estuary are in fact driven a considerable distance out to sea.

river.[7] As soon as the natives knew of the landing of an unknown race on their coasts, they collected about the Spaniards anxious to examine them, and displaying not the slightest fear. It was learned by signs that that country was called Paria, that it was very extensive, and that its population was most numerous in its western part. The Admiral invited four natives to come on board and continued his course to the west.

Judging by the agreeable temperature, the attractiveness of the country, and the number of people they daily saw during their voyage, the Spaniards concluded that the country is a very important one, and in this opinion they were not wrong, as we shall demonstrate at the proper time. One morning at the break of dawn the Spaniards landed, being attracted by the charm of the country and the sweet odours wafted to them from the forests. They discovered at that point a larger number of people than they had thus far seen, and as they were approaching the shore, messengers came in the name of the caciques of that country, inviting them to land and to have no fears. When Columbus refused, the natives urged by curiosity, flocked about the ships in their barques. Most of them wore about their necks and arms, collars and bracelets of gold and ornaments of Indian pearls, which seemed just as common amongst them as glass jewelry amongst our women. When questioned as to whence came the pearls, they answered by pointing with their fingers to a neighbouring coast; by grimaces and gestures they seemed to indicate that if the Spaniards would stop with them they would give them basketfuls of pearls. The provisions which the Admiral destined for the colony at Hispaniola were beginning to spoil, so he resolved to defer this commercial operation till a more convenient

---

[7] This was the first landing of the Spaniards on the American continent, but Columbus, being ill, did not go on shore. Pedro de Torreros took possession in the Admiral's name (Navarrete, tom. iii., p. 569). Fernando Columbus states that his father suffered from inflamed eyes, and that from about this time he was forced to rely for information upon his sailors and pilots (*Storia*, cap. lxv.–lxxiii.). He seemed nevertheless to divine the immensity of the newly discovered land, for he wrote to the sovereigns *y creo esta tierra que agora mandaron discrubir vuestras altezzas sea grandissima.*

opportunity. Nevertheless he despatched two boats loaded with soldiers, to barter with the people on land for some strings of pearls and, at the same time, to discover whatever they could about the place and its people. The natives received these men with enthusiasm and pleasure, and great numbers surrounded them, as though they were inspecting something marvellous. The first who came forward were two distinguished persons, for they were followed by the rest of the crowd. The first of these men was aged and the second younger, so that it was supposed they were the father and his son and future successor. After exchanging salutations the Spaniards were conducted to a round house near a large square. Numerous seats of very black wood decorated with astonishing skill were brought, and when the principal Spaniards and natives were seated, some attendants served food and others, drink. These people eat only fruits, of which they have a great variety, and very different from ours. The beverages they offered were white and red wine, not made from grapes but from various kinds of crushed fruits, which were not at all disagreeable.

This repast concluded, in company with the elder chief, the younger one conducted the Spaniards to his own house, men and women crowding about in great numbers, but always in separate groups from one another.

The natives of both sexes have bodies as white as ours, save those perhaps who pass their time in the sun. They were amiable, hospitable, and wore no clothes, save waist-cloths of various coloured cotton stuffs. All of them wore either collars or bracelets of gold or pearls, and some wore both, just as our peasants wear glass jewelry. When they were asked whence the gold came, they indicated with the finger that it was from a mountainous country, appearing at the same time to dissuade our men from going there, for they made them understand by gestures and signs that the inhabitants of that country were cannibals. It was not, however, entirely clear whether they meant cannibals or savage beasts. They were much vexed to perceive that the Spaniards did not understand them, and that they possessed no means of making themselves intelligible to one another. At three o'clock in the afternoon the men who had been sent on shore returned, bringing several strings of pearls, and the Admiral, who could not prolong his stay, because of his cargo of provisions, raised anchor and sailed. He intends, however, after putting the affairs of Hispaniola in order, shortly to return. It was another than he who profited by this important discovery.

The shallowness of the sea and the numerous currents, which at each change of the tide dashed against and injured the lesser vessels, much retarded the Admiral's progress, and to avoid the perils of the shallows he always sent one of the lighter caravels ahead; this vessel being of short draught took repeated soundings and the other larger ones followed. At that time two provinces of the vast region of Paria, Cumaná and Manacapana, were reached, and along their shores the Admiral coasted for two hundred miles. Sixty leagues farther on begins another country called Curiana. As the Admiral had already covered such a distance, he thought the land lying ahead of him was an island, and that if he continued his course to the west he would be unable to get back to the north and reach Hispaniola. It was then that he came upon the mouth of a river whose depth was thirty cubits, with an unheard-of width which he described as twenty-eight leagues. A little farther on, always in a westerly direction though somewhat to the south, since he followed the line of the coast, the Admiral sailed into a sea of grass of which the seeds resemble those of the lentil. The density of this growth retarded the advance of the ships.

The Admiral declares that in the whole of that region the day constantly equals the night. The north star is elevated as in Paria to five degrees above the horizon, and all the coasts of that newly discovered country are on the same parallel. He likewise reports details concerning the differences he observed in the heavens, which are so contradictory to astronomical theories that I wish to make some comments. It is proven, Most Illustrious Prince, that the polar star, which our sailors call Tramontane, is not the point of the arctic pole upon which the axis of the heavens turns. To realise this easily, it is only necessary to look through a small hole at the pole star itself, when the stars are rising. If one then looks through the same aperture at the same star when dawn is paling the stars, it will be seen that it has changed its place; but how can it be in this newly discovered country that the star rises at the beginning of twilight in the month of June to a height of only five degrees above the horizon, and when the stars are disappearing before the sunrise, it should be found by the same observer to be in the fifteenth degree? I do not at all understand it, and I must confess the reasons the Admiral gives by no means satisfy me. Indeed, according to his conjectures, the terrestrial globe is not an absolute sphere, but had at the time of its creation a sort of elevation rising on its convex side, so that instead of resembling a ball or an apple, it was more like a pear, and Paria would be precisely that elevated part, nearest to the sky. He has also persisted in affirming that the earthly paradise[8] is situated on the summit of those three mountains, which the watcher from the height of the crow's nest observed in the distance, as I have recounted. As for the impetuous current of fresh water which rushed against the tide of the sea at the beginning of that strait, he maintains that it is formed of waters which fall in cascades from the heights of these mountains. But we have had enough of these things which to me seem fabulous. Let us return to our narrative.

Seeing his course across that vast gulf had, contrary to his expectation, been arrested, and fearing to find no exit towards the north through which he might reach Hispaniola, the Admiral retraced his course and sailing north of that country he bent towards the east in the direction of Hispaniola.

Those navigators who later explored this region more carefully believe that it is the Indian continent, and not Cuba, as the Admiral thought; and there are not wanting mariners who pre-

---

[8] Speaking of the earthly paradise, Columbus describes it as *adonde ne puede llegar nadie, sabro par voluntad divina.* Vespucci it was who thought it would be found in the New World: *se nel mondo e alcun paradiso terrestre.*

tend that they have sailed all round Cuba. Whether they are right or whether they seek to gratify their jealousy of the author of a great discovery, I am not bound to decide.[9] Time will decide, and Time is the only truthful judge. The Admiral likewise discusses the question whether or not Paria is a continent; he himself thinks it is. Paria lies to the south of Hispaniola, a distance of 882 leagues, according to Columbus. Upon the third day of the calends of September of the year 1498, he reached Hispaniola, most anxious to see again his soldiers and his brother whom he had left there. But, as commonly happens in human affairs, fortune, however favourable, mingles with circumstances, sweet and pleasant, some grain of bitterness. In this case it was internecine discord which marred his happiness.

[9] Rivalry and perhaps jealousy existed among the navigators, each bent on eclipsing the achievements of his fellows, and the former feeling was a spur to enterprise. Yañez Pinzon, Amerigo Vespucci, Juan Diaz de Solis all explored the American coasts, discovering Yucatan, Florida, Texas, and Honduras.

BOOK VII

TO THE SAME
CARDINAL LUDOVICO D'ARAGON

Upon his arrival at Hispaniola, the Admiral found an even greater state of disorder than he had feared, for Roldan had taken advantage of his absence to refuse obedience to his brother, Bartholomew Columbus. Resolved not to submit to him who had formerly been his master and had raised him in dignity, he had stirred up the multitude in his own favour and had also vilified the Adelantado and had written heinous accusations to the King against the brothers. The Admiral likewise sent envoys to inform the sovereigns of the revolt, begging them at the same time to send soldiers to put down the insurrection and punish the guilty, according to their crimes. Roldan and his accomplices preferred grave charges against the Admiral and the Adelantado, who, according to them, were impious, unjust men, enemies to the Spaniards, whose blood they had profusely shed. They were accused of torturing, strangling, decapitating and, in divers other ways, killing people on the most trifling pretexts. They were envious, proud, and intolerable tyrants; therefore, people avoided them as they would fly from wild beasts, or from the enemies of the Crown. It had in fact been discovered that the sole thought of the brothers was to usurp the government of the island. This had been proven by different circumstances, but chiefly by the fact that they allowed none but their own partisans to work the gold-mines.

In soliciting reinforcements from the sovereigns, sufficient to deal with the rebels according to their merits, the Admiral explained that those men who dared thus to accuse him were guilty of misdemeanours and crimes; for they were debauchees, profligates, thieves, seducers, ravishers, vagabonds. They respected nothing and were perjurers and liars, already condemned by the tribunals, or fearful, owing to their numerous crimes, to appear before them. They had formed a faction amongst themselves, given over to violence and rapine; lazy, gluttonous, caring only to sleep and to carouse. They spared nobody; and having been brought to the island of Hispaniola originally to do the work of miners or of camp servants, they now never moved a step from their houses on foot, but insisted on being carried about the island upon the shoulders of the unfortunate natives, as though they were dignitaries of the State. Not to lose practice in the shedding of blood, and to exercise the strength of their arms, they invented a game in which they drew their swords, and amused themselves in cutting off the heads of innocent victims with one sole blow. Whoever succeeded in more quickly landing the head of an unfortunate islander on the ground with one stroke, was proclaimed the bravest, and as such was honoured. Such were the mutual accusations bandied about between the Admiral and the partisans of Roldan, not to mention many other imputations.

Meanwhile the Admiral, desiring to put a stop to the dangerous attacks of the Ciguana tribe which had revolted under the leadership of Guarionex, sent his brother the Adelantado with ninety foot-soldiers and some horsemen against them. It may be truthfully added that about three thousand of the islanders who had suffered from the invasions of the Ciguana tribe, who were their sworn enemies, joined forces with the Spaniards. The Adelantado led his troops to the bank of a great river which waters the plain between the sea and the two extremes of the mountain chain of Ciguana, of which we have already spoken. He surprised two of the enemy's spies who were concealed in the underbrush, one of whom sprang into the sea, and, swimming across the river at its mouth, succeeded in escaping to his own people. From the one who was captured, it was learned that six thousand natives of Ciguana were hidden in the forest beyond the river and were

prepared to attack the Spaniards when they crossed over. The
Adelantado therefore marched along the river bank seeking a
ford. This he soon found in the plain, and was preparing to cross
the river when the Ciguana warriors rushed out from the forest
in compact battalions, yelling in a most horrible manner. Their
appearance is fearsome and repulsive, and they march into battle
daubed with paint, as did the Thracians and Agathyrses. These
natives indeed paint themselves from the forehead to the knees,
with black and scarlet colours which they extract from certain
fruits similar to pears, and which they carefully cultivate in their
gardens. Their hair is tormented into a thousand strange forms,
for it is long and black, and what nature refuses they supply by
art. They look like goblins emerged from the infernal caverns.
Advancing towards our men who were trying to cross the river,
they contested their passage with flights of arrows and by throwing pointed sticks; and such was the multitude of projectiles that
they half darkened the light of the sun, and had not the Spaniards
received the blows on their shields the engagement would have
ended badly for them.

A number of men were wounded in this first encounter, but the
Adelantado succeeded in crossing the river and the enemy fled,
the Spaniards pursuing them, though they killed few, as the
islanders are good runners. As soon as they gained the protection
of the woods, they used their bows to repulse their pursuers, for
they are accustomed to woods, and run naked amongst underbrush, shrubs, and trees, like wild boars, heedless of obstacles.
The Spaniards, on the contrary, were hindered amongst this
undergrowth by their shields, their clothes, their long lances, and
their ignorance of the surroundings. After a night passed use-
lessly in the woods the Adelantado, realising the next morning
that they could catch nobody, followed the counsel of those
islanders who are the immemorial enemies of the Ciguana tribe,
and under their guidance marched towards the mountains where
the King Maiobanexius lived at a place called Capronus. Twelve
miles' march brought them to the village of another cacique,

which had been abandoned by its terrified inhabitants, and there he established his camp. Two natives were captured, from whom it was learned that King Maiobanexius and ten caciques with eight thousand soldiers were assembled at Capronus. During two days there were a few light skirmishes between the parties, the Adelantado not wishing to do more than reconnoitre the country. Scouts were sent out the following night under the guidance of some islanders who knew the land. The people of Ciguana caught sight of our men from the heights of their mountains, and prepared to give battle, uttering war-cries as is their custom. But they did not venture to quit their woods, because they thought the Adelantado had his entire army with him. Twice on the following day, when the Adelantado marched on with his men, the natives tested the fortune of war; hurling themselves against the Spaniards with fury, they wounded many before they could protect themselves with their shields, but the latter, getting the better of them, pursued them, cutting some in pieces, and taking a large number prisoners. Those who escaped took refuge in the forests, from which they were careful not to emerge.

The Adelantado selected one of the prisoners, and sending with him one of his allies, he despatched them both to Maiobanexius with the following message: "The Adelantado has not undertaken to make war upon you and your people, O Maiobanexius, for he desires your friendship; but he formally demands that Guarionex, who has taken refuge with you and has drawn you into this conflict to the great damage of your people, shall be delivered to him to be punished as he merits. He counsels you, therefore, to give up this cacique; if you consent, the Admiral will count you among his friends and protect and respect your territory. If you refuse you will be made to repent, for your entire country will be devastated with fire and sword, and all you possess will be destroyed." Maiobanexius, upon hearing this message, replied: "Everybody knows that Guarionex is a hero, adorned with all the virtues, and therefore I have esteemed it right to assist and protect him. As for you, you are violent and

perfidious men, and seek to shed the blood of innocent people: I
will neither enter into relations with you, nor form any alliance
with so false a people."

When this answer was brought to the Adelantado, he burnt the
village where he had established his camp and several others in
the neighbourhood. He again sent envoys to Maiobanexius, to ask
him to name one of his trusty advisers to treat for peace. Maiobanexius consented to send one of the most devoted of his
counsellors, accompanied by two other chiefs. The Adelantado
earnestly conjured them not to jeopardise the territory of Maiobanexius solely in the interests of Guarionex. He advised Maiobanexius, if he did not wish to be ruined himself and to be treated
as an enemy, to give him up. When his envoys returned, Maiobanexius called together his people and explained the conditions.
The people cried that Guarionex must be surrendered, cursing
and execrating the day he had come amongst them to disturb
their tranquillity. The cacique reminded them, however, that
Guarionex was a hero, and had rendered him services when he
fled to him for protection, for he had brought him royal presents.
Moreover, he had taught both the cacique himself and his wife to
sing and dance, a thing not to be held in mediocre consideration.
Maiobanexius was determined never to surrender the prince who
had appealed to his protection, and whom he had promised to
defend. He was prepared to risk the gravest perils with him
rather than to merit the reproach of having betrayed his guest.
Despite the complaints of the people, the cacique dissolved the
assembly, and calling Guarionex to him, he pledged himself for
the second time to protect him and to share his fortunes as long as
he lived.

Maiobanexius resolved to give no further information to the
Adelantado: on the contrary he ordered his first messenger to
station himself with some faithful soldiers at a place on the road
where the Adelantado's envoys usually passed, and to kill any
Spaniards who appeared, without further discussion. The Adelantado had just sent his messengers, and both these men, one of

whom was a prisoner from Ciguana and the other from amongst the native allies, were decapitated. The Adelantado, escorted by only ten foot-soldiers and four horsemen, followed his envoys and discovered their bodies lying in the road, which so incensed him that he determined to no longer spare Maiobanexius. He invaded the cacique's village of Capronus with his army. The caciques fled in every direction, abandoning their chief, who withdrew with his entire family into places of concealment in the mountain districts. Some others of the Ciguana people sought to capture Guarionex, since he was the occasion of the catastrophe; but he succeeded in escaping and concealed himself almost alone amidst the rocks and desert mountains. The soldiers of the Adelantado were exhausted by this long war, which dragged on for three months; the watches, the fatigues, and the scarcity of food. In response to their request they were authorised to return to Concepcion, where they owned handsome plantations of the native sort; and thither many withdrew. Only thirty companions remained with the Adelantado, all of whom were severely tried by these three months of fighting, during which they had eaten nothing but cazabi, that is to say, bread made of roots, and even they were not always ripe. They also procured some utias, or rabbits, by hunting with their dogs, while their only drink had been water, which was sometimes exquisitely fresh, but just as often muddy and marshy. Moreover the character of the war obliged them to pass most of the time in the open air and per-petual movement.

With his little troop the Adelantado determined to scour the mountains to seek out the secret retreats where Maiobanexius and Guarionex had concealed themselves. Some Spaniards, who had been driven by hunger to hunt utias for want of something better, met two servants of Maiobanexius, whom the cacique had sent into the villages of his territory, and who were carrying back native bread. They forced these men to betray the hiding-place of their chief, and under their leadership, twelve soldiers who had stained their bodies like the people of Ciguana succeeded by trickery in capturing Maiobanexius, his wife, and his son, all of whom they brought to the Admiral at Concepcion. A few days later hunger compelled Guarionex to emerge from the cavern where he was concealed, and the islanders, out of fear of the Admiral, betrayed him to the hunters. As soon as he learned his whereabouts, the Admiral sent a body of foot-soldiers to take him, just at the moment when he was about to quit the plain, and return to the mountains. These men caught him and brought him back, after which that region was pacified, and tranquillity restored.

A relative of Maiobanexius who was married to a cacique whose territory had not yet been invaded, shared the former's misfortunes. Everybody agreed in saying that she was the most beautiful of the women nature had created in the island of Hispaniola. Her husband loved her dearly, as she merited, and when she was captured by the Spaniards he almost lost his reason, and wandered distractedly in desert places, doubtful what course to pursue. Finally he presented himself before the Admiral, promising that he and his people would submit without conditions, if he would only restore him his wife. His prayer was granted and at the same time several others of the principal captives were likewise freed. This same cacique then assembled five thousand natives who instead of weapons carried agricultural implements, and went himself to labour and plant the crops in one of the largest valleys in his territories. The Admiral thanked him by means of presents, and the cacique came back rejoicing. This news spread throughout Ciguana, and the other caciques began to hope that they too might be treated with clemency, so they came in person to promise they would in future obey the orders given them. They asked that their chief and his family might be spared, and in response to their petition, the wife and child were delivered to them, but Maiobanexius was held a prisoner.

While the Admiral was thus engaged in administering the affairs of Hispaniola, he was ignorant of the intrigues his adver-

saries were carrying on against him at the Spanish Court.[1]
Wearied by these continuous quarrels, and above all annoyed at
receiving but a small quantity of gold and valuable products
because of these dissensions and revolts, the sovereigns appointed
another Governor,[2] who, after a careful enquiry, should punish
the guilty and send them back to Spain. I do not precisely know
what has come to light against either the Admiral or his brother
the Adelantado, or their enemies; but this is certain, that the
Admiral and his brother were seized, put in irons, deprived of all
their property, and brought to Spain; and of this, Most Illustrious
Prince, you are not ignorant. It is true that the sovereigns, when
they learned that the Columbus brothers had arrived at Cadiz
loaded with irons, promptly sent their secretaries to order their
release and that their children should be allowed to visit them;
nor did they conceal their disapproval of this rough treatment.[3]
It is claimed that the new Governor has sent to the sovereigns
some letters in the handwriting of the Admiral, but in cipher, in
which the latter summoned his brother the Adelantado, who was
at that time absent with his soldiers, to hasten back and repel
force with force, in case the Governor sought to use violence.
The Adelantado preceded his soldiers, and the Governor seized
him and his brother before their partisans could rejoin them.
What will be the outcome, time will show, for time is the
supreme arbiter of events. Fare you well.

[1] One of the most inveterate of his enemies was Juan de Fonseca, afterwards Bishop of Burgos, who was unfortunately in a position to do
Columbus serious harm.

[2] Francisco de Bobadilla, commander of Calatrava.

[3] The sovereigns made what amends they could for the abusive execution
of their orders by over-zealous agents; they sent Columbus a present of two
thousand ducats—not an insignificant sum at the time—and wrote him a
letter, full of affectionate expressions of confidence; he was admitted to
audience on December 17th.

FROM
A HISTORY OF ANCIENT MEXICO
By FRAY BERNARDINO DE SAHAGÚN

TRANSLATED BY
FANNY R. BANDELIER
FROM THE SPANISH VERSION
OF
CARLOS MARIA DE BUSTAMENTE

BOOK I

THE GODS WHICH ANCIENT MEXICANS ADORED

PROLOGUE

All writers endeavor to give to their writings the best authority possible; some do so by means of trustworthy witnesses; others consult other authors who wrote on the same subject before them and whose information is considered as trustworthy; while still others rely on the holy scriptures. I have not had all these fundamentals to prove what I have written in these twelve books, nor do I find other sources to vouch for my assertions; all I can do is to put down here an account of the efforts I made to find out the truth of all there is contained in these books. As I have stated in other prologues of the present work, I was ordered by my Superior to write, in the Mexican language, what to me would seem useful for the culture, support, and teaching of Christianity among these natives of New Spain, and which would at the same time be of assistance to the workers and ministers of the Christian Faith. Upon receiving this order, I at once made out in Spanish a memorandum of all the matters I intended to touch, which was what is contained in the twelve books, in the glossary, and the songs.

This (work) was started in the village of Tepeopulco, in the

From *A History of Ancient Mexico* by Fray Bernardino de Sahagún, Translated by Fanny R. Bandelier from the Spanish of Carlos Maria de Bustamente, Fisk University Press, 1932, Volume I, pp. 21–71. (Footnotes partially deleted.)

province of Culhuacán or Tezcoco, and was accomplished in the following manner: In said village I had all the prominent men assemble with the chieftain of the place, whose name was Don Diego de Mendoza, an old man of great dignity and intelligence, well versed in local matters, in warfare and politics, and even in idolatries. Having gathered them all, I told them what I intended to do and begged them to find me intelligent and experienced men with whom I might talk, and who would be able to answer me to whatsoever I should ask them. They replied that they would discuss the matter proposed by me, that the following day they would give me their answer, and with that they took leave. The next day the chief came with the principals and, after having made a very solemn speech as in those times they used to make, they assigned to me about ten of the most prominent old men, and told me that with them I could commune and they would answer whatever I might ask them. There were also present as many as four Spanish-speaking Indians whom I had taught myself a few years previous at the College of Santa Cruz de Tlaltelolco. With these principals and the grammarians, who were also prominent men in the township, I talked for many days in almost two years (of my residence there), according to the notes I took at the time. All matters we talked about were given me by them by means of paintings, which was the mode of writing they had in ancient times. The grammarians then explained these paintings in their own language, writing this explanation underneath the pictures. Even now I have the originals of this work. At that time I also dictated the "postilla" (postilla—copy or transcript) and the songs; all this was written by the grammarians—the Indians who had been taught reading and writing, Spanish and Latin, at the college of Tlaltelolco; they wrote it for me right there at Tepeopulco. When I went to attend the Chapter meetings at Mexico at the time Father Francisco de Torál, who had entrusted me with the work, completed his hebdomade, they removed me with all my writings from Tepeopulco, and I went to live at Santiago de Tlaltelolco (again). There I once more assembled all the principal (prominent) men and told them the motive of my writings and demanded to assign to me some able leaders with whose help I might discuss and examine what I had noted down at Tepeopulco. The governor and his aides thereupon pointed out as many as 18 leaders (principals) from among them all who were the best versed in their language and in matters of their ancient culture. With these men and five or six collegians all of whom were trilingual, I worked for a year and a little over, confined in the college. We corrected what we had worked out, and added all the material I had brought from Tepeopulco, and then all of it was copied in very poor writing, because it was all written in a great hurry. Of all the students the one who did most of the work in this scrutiny or investigation was Martin Jacobita, who at that time was principal of the college. He was a citizen of Tlaltelolco, from the city district or ward of Santa Ana.

After having accomplished (finished) all the above mentioned work at Tlaltelolco, I went to live at the convent of San Francisco of Mexico (city), taking with me all my writings (notes) and there for three years I corrected and recorrected them by myself alone; I amended them and then divided them into books, twelve in all, and each book was moreover arranged in chapters and paragraphs. After this was done and while Fray Miguel Navarro was Provincial and Fray Diego de Mendoza, General of the Order of St. Francis in Mexico, they helped me to get the entire work copied in a legible hand, all of the twelve books; also the "postilla" (here it probably means book of annotations or commentaries on the Bible), and the (book of) songs. Also an "Art of the Mexican Language" with a vocabulary appendix was prepared, which the Mexicans corrected, and to which they added a great deal. It was then copied again. Thus, the first advisory council that criticized my work was composed of the men of Tepeopulco, the second of those of Tlaltelolco, and the third by those of Mexico (city), and in all this research work several students of the college who knew Spanish and Latin helped. The principal assistant and the most learned one was Antonio Valeriano, citizen of Aztcapuzalco; another one, little less learned, was Alonso Vegerano of Cuauhtitlan; still another was Martin Jacobita, whom I have already mentioned. There was, moreover, Pedro de San Buenaventura, also of Cuauhtitlan; all these were well versed in three languages: Latin, Spanish and Indian, i.e., Aztec or Mexican. The copyists who copied all the above mentioned books in clear handwriting were Diego Degrado of the city ward of San Martin, Mateo Severino of Xuchimilco, near Ullac. As soon as all this was copied, through the kindness of the two Fathers above mentioned, who spent a good many tomines (pennies) to pay the copyists, the author requested the Father Commissary, Fray Francisco de Rivera, to appoint three or four monks to give their opinion on these manuscripts at the Meeting of the Provincial Chapter, which was soon to take place. These friars came (read the work), and made their report to the "definitorio" of the Chapter. They told the "definitorio" that it was a work of great value and should receive all the help possible to finish it. However, some of the *definidores* were of the opinion that it was against the (professed) poverty of the Order to spend money for the copy of these writings, and therefore they ordered the author to dismiss his copyists and that he do himself whatever he wanted to with them, copy them in his own handwriting as best he might. But since he was then over seventy years old and his hand trembled, he could not do anything with them, nor was he able to obtain dispensation (on account of that) nor revocation of the order, and thus his work remained absolutely dormant for over five years. Then at the Meeting of the next General Chapter Father Fray Miguel Navarro was appointed *custos custodum* and as Provincial Father Fray Alonso de Escalona. Meanwhile the author had prepared a summary of all the books, their respective chapters and prologues, giving a short outline of the contents. This summary was taken to Spain by Fray Miguel Navarro and his companion, Fray Geronimo de Mendieta, and so all that had been written up to that time (in abstract) about the things concerning this land remained in Spain. In the meantime the Father Provincial took all the books of the said author and distributed them among all of the convents of the province so that they were, of course, perused by many of the Franciscan monks, who considered them as very valuable and important. After a few years, when Fray Miguel Navarro came back from the Meeting of the General Chapter, where he was appointed as Commissary of the Franciscan Order in New Spain, he ordered the books to be returned to the author upon the latter's petition. After all of them had been gathered once more, within the course of a year, more or less, they were again put into the hands of their author. In all this time nothing had been done on them, nor was there anybody to offer assistance for the translation of what remained into Spanish, until the Commissary General, Fray Rodrigo de Sequera, arrived from Spain. He looked them over and was very much pleased with them, and at once ordered the author to translate what remained into Spanish, facilitating everything necessary for a new and complete copy. In this copy, the Mexican text was arranged in one column and Spanish in the other, and in this shape the work was sent to Spain, because the President of the Council of the Indies, Exmo. Señor Don Juan de Ovando, wished to purchase it, after having had information about it from the summary (abstract) which Father Navarro had taken to Spain as stated above.

All the above stated is to the effect to say that this work was examined and approved by many in the course of many years, and that great suffering and misfortune was endured to get it into the shape it is at present.

CHAPTER I

The god Vitzilopuchtli was another Hercules, exceedingly robust, of great strength and very bellicose, a great destroyer of towns and killer of people. In warfare he was like live-fire, greatly feared by his enemies. His emblem was the head of a very ferocious dragon which emitted fire from its mouth. This god was at the same time a sorcerer of the black arts and a wizard who could change himself into the shapes of diverse birds and beasts. While he lived, the magicians esteemed him very highly on account of his strength and prowess in war; after his death they venerated him as a god, offering him slaves whom they sacrificed in his presence. They endeavored to have these very well cared for and very well dressed and adorned with the well-known ear ornaments and neckpieces used in these times. All this they did in order to pay him the utmost honor.

Another god very similar to him was worshipped around Tlaxcala. He was called Camaxtle.

The god Paynal was a sort of sub-captain of the first mentioned, who commanded as captain general when war was declared against some province or other. Paynal, as his representative, served when it became necessary to make a sudden attack against the enemy. On such occasions, Paynal, which means the speedy one, had to go personally to summon men so that they might go forthwith to fight the enemy. After his death they honored him with a feast at which one of the "sátrapas," priests, took the image of Paynal, richly bedecked with ornaments like a god's, and carried him thus in a very long procession, all running at top speed, the one who carried the image as well as all the rest of the accompaniment. By so doing they demonstrated the haste which was often necessary to resist enemies who attack before one realizes that they are there, lying in ambush.

Tezcatlipoca was considered and held as the true and invisible god who walked all over the heavens and the earth and hell. They were afraid that whenever he trod on earth he caused wars, enmities and discords, all of which meant a great deal of trouble and anxieties. They said that he himself incited the people against one another, causing them to have wars, and for this reason they called him Necocyautl, which means sower of discord on both sides. They called him the only being who ruled the world, and the only one who could grant prosperity and wealth as he was also the only one who could take these away at will.

Tlaloctlamacazqui was the god of rain. They said he gave them the rains to irrigate the earth, and that these rains caused all the herbs, trees, fruits and grains to grow. It was he who also sent hail and lightning and storms on the water and all dangers of rivers and the sea. The name Tlaloctlamacazqui means that he is the god who resides in the terrestrial paradise and gives to man whatever he needs for his physical body. The celebrations held in his honor are cited in Book II among the feasts held in honor of the gods.

Quetzalcoatl, although a man, was held as a god who, they said, swept the road clear for the gods of the water. This they supposed to be a fact because always before the rainy season begins there are heavy winds and dust clouds, and this is the reason why Quetzalcoatl was called the god of the winds who swept the roads for the gods of rain so they might come on with their rain.

The sacrifices and ceremonies with which this god was honored can be found in Book II. The insignia and ornaments with which they adorned Quetzalcoatl are the following: on the head he wore a mitre with a tuft of plumes which are called quetzalli; the mitre was spotted to resemble a tiger-skin; his face and body were painted black. He wore a shirt in the form of an embroidered surplice which reached only as far as the waist; he wore turquoise ear-rings in mosaic; a gold necklace, from which hung some beautiful little sea-shells. As a device he carried on his shoulder a feather arrangement to represent flames of fire. Furthermore, he wore leggings from the knee down of tiger-skin, from which also pended little sea-shells. His feet were clad in sandals dyed black and dipped in margagita.[1] In his left hand he held a shield on which was a painting with five angles, which is called the wind-rose. In the right hand he held a sceptre in the shape of a bishop's crooked shepherd's staff, i.e.: the top of it formed a crook like a bishop's staff, richly adorned with precious stones, but it was not quite as long as a staff. The hilt looked more like the hilt of a sword. Quetzalcoatl was the high priest of the temple.

The first one of the principal goddesses adored by the Mexicans was called Civacoatl, and they say of her that she granted adverse things, such as poverty, mental depression, and sorrows. It is their belief that she frequently appeared, dressed as a lady of rank who visits a palace (frequents royalty); they also said of her that at night she called aloud or howled in the air. Civacoatl means woman of the snake; they also call her Tonantzin, which is "our mother." According to these two items it would seem that they knew what happened between our mother Eve and the snake, who deceived her. The clothes in which she appeared were white, and her hair was done up in such a way that it formed two little horns crossed on her forehead. They also say that she carried a cradle on her back like a woman who carries her child; that she mingled with the other women in the tianquiztli (market) and, suddenly disappearing, she left the cradle behind. When the other women noticed the cradle forgotten there by someone they would look into it to see what was there, and would find a piece of flint like a lance point, which was used by them to kill those

---

[1] This is probably margajita, or marcasita—marcasite, that is, white pyrite, which the Ancient Mexicans used either pulverized or in small prisms.

they sacrificed to the gods, and they at once knew that it was Civacoatl who had left the cradle in their midst.

The goddess Chicomecoatl was the goddess of food, food that is eaten as well as beverages; and they depicted her as wearing a crown on her head; in her right hand she held a goblet; in the left a shield, on which a large flower was painted, her cuoytl ycipilli (tunic) and her sandals were vermilion in color. She must have been the first woman who made bread and other sweetmeats and stews.

Now follows a goddess whom they called the mother of the gods, heart of the earth (Centeotl or Civeles) and our grandmother. She was the goddess of medicine and medicinal herbs. She was venerated by physicians and surgeons, by those who bled people, and also by midwives and those who gave herbs for abortion; by soothsayers who tell the good or bad fortune children are going to have, according to the date, time or signs of their birth. She was likewise venerated by those who predict the future with grains of corn, the ones who do it by looking into the water in a bowl, as well as those who tell fortunes by means of small strings which they tied together and called the mecatle-pouhque and all such who extracted tiny worms from mouth and eyes, and small pebbles from other parts of the body, calling this procedure tetlaquilique. She was also adored by those people who had baths or "temazcalis" in their homes, all of whom placed the image of this goddess in their baths, and they called her Temaz-calteci, which means the grandmother of the baths. All these people mentioned above made each year a feast to this goddess, and for this purpose they were wont to buy a woman whom they adorned with ornaments such as behooved this goddess, such as they are represented on pictures they have of her; and every day while her feast lasted they held dances for this woman, entertaining and feasting her greatly to prevent her getting sad or crying on account of her approaching death. They fed her delicately and urged and tempted her with all manner of food, entreating her to eat as if she were a great lady. They played war games before her in those days, and planned many different shows in distinctive devices amid great shouting and rejoicing. They presented prizes to the soldiers who fought before her in order to give her pleasure and amuse her. When the hour of her death had come and after having killed her and two others who had to accompany her in death, they flayed her and a man or Sátrapa (priest) dressed himself up in her skin, walking through the whole town and boasting a great deal in this garb. This goddess had her mouth and chin down to the throat dyed with ulli, which is a black gum, and another round mark like a plaster of the same dye on the cheek. On the head she wore a sort of cap or turban made of twisted and knotted cloth, the ends of the knot falling over her back. In the knot itself there was a tuft of feathers with plumes sticking out like flames; these hung over toward the back of the head. She wore a vipilli, which had at its lower end a wide and indented band which, ending in edges and points, looked like a saw. Her skirts were white. She wore sandals on her feet. In her left hand she held a shield with a round gold clasp in the center. In the right hand she held a broom, which is the implement for sweeping.

Another goddess was called Tzaputlatena, because it is said she was born in the town of Tzaputla. She was also sometimes called the mother of Tzaputla, because she was the first one who invented the resin known by the name of vxitl, which is an oil obtained skilfully from pine resin, and which cures many diseases. In the first place, it is very efficient against a sort of pustules or itch (mange) which begins on the head and is called quaxococuixtli; it is also good against another similar outbreak of pustules on the head called chaquachiciuztli; likewise is this oil used for head-itch, for hoarseness, against fissures (cracks) in the skin of the feet and cracked lips and the ringworm on face or hands, as well as against eczema and many other complaints. As this woman must have been the first one who found this oil, she was placed among the goddesses and all these who make or sell that oil, vxitl, celebrate a feast-day in her honor, offering her sacrifices.

The Civapipilti were all the women who died in giving birth to their first child, and thus became canonized as goddesses, according to Book VI, Chapter 28, where the ceremonies celebrated upon their death and their canonization, are described at length. We shall here simply state that it is said that these goddesses are said to always travel together through the air and to appear whenever they choose to those on earth, inflicting boys and girls with sickness such as palsy (paralysis) and entering into human bodies. In order to injure children, they were said to wait on crossroads, and that for this reason parents would forbid their children to leave the house on certain days of the year when these goddesses were supposed to come down to earth. Whenever anyone became ill with paralysis or another sudden disease, or when he became possessed by some demon, they said these goddesses had done it, and for that reason (in order to appease them) they celebrated a feast in their honor, offering in the temple dedicated to them, or on crossroads, bread fashioned into diverse figures; some of these looked like butterflies, others like lightning as it descends from heaven and is called Tlavitequiliztli, or else like large tamales called Xucuichtlamatzxoalli, or toasted corn, izquitl. Images of these goddesses have a whitish face as if it had been painted with some very white paint like titzatl, also the arms and legs; their ears were of gold, the hair was dressed like that of ladies of quality with their little curls or horns. Their vipil (sleeveless blouse) was painted with black waves; their skirts were of various colors, and they wore white sandals.

Chalchiuhtliycue was the goddess of water; she is depicted as a woman, for they say that she was the sister of the gods of rain they call Tlaloques. They honored her because they said that she had power over the sea and the rivers, and could drown those who navigated on the waters, causing tempests and whirlwinds that would flood the boats and barges and other vessels happening to be on the water. They made a feast to this goddess in which they call her Etzalqualiztli, which feast is described in Book II, Chapter 7, with all the ceremonies and sacrifices in her honor. Her devotees were all those who derived their livelihood and gain from the water, like men who sell goods from their canoe, and all such that sell things in big earthen jars on the market-place. They represented this goddess with a yellow face, a necklace of precious stones from which hung a gold medal, around the neck. On the head she had a crown made of paper, painted pale blue with tufts of green feathers and certain balls or pellets, some of which hung down toward the back and others toward the front of the crown, all of them light blue. Her ear-rings were made of turquoise mosaic, and she was dressed in a vipil and skirt of pale blue with fringes, from which pended small sea-shells. In the left hand she held a shield with a wide, round leaf on it, which grows in the water and is called atlacuccona; in the right hand she held a cup with a cross on it, which was made just like the cross on the tabernacle in which the holy sacrament is carried by only one man (when the tabernacle is small), this cup and cross represented the sceptre of the goddess. She wore white sandals. This goddess and two others, one Chicumecoatl, goddess of food, and Vixtocivatl, the goddess of the salt, were greatly venerated by lords and kings because these three supported and fed the common people so they might live and multiply. There is more about this goddess in the above-mentioned chapter of Book II.

Now we come to Tlaculteutl, the goddess of carnal matters, who had three different names. First, Tlaculteutl, which means goddess of carnality. The second name was Ixcuina; they called her thus because they said there were four sisters; the first born or oldest was Tiacapan; the second was the youngest and they called her Teicu, the third was the middle one, called Tlaco; the fourth was the youngest of all Xucotzin. All these four sisters were the goddesses of carnality; in these names all women are included who are fit for the carnal act. The third name of the goddess is Tlaclqüani, which means eater of filthy things. This signifies that, according to their sayings, all such carnal men and women confessed their sins to these goddesses, no matter how uncouth and filthy they might have been, and they were forgiven. It is also said that this goddess or these goddesses had the power to produce lust; that they could provoke carnal intercourse and favored illicit love affairs, and that after such sins had been committed, they also held the power of pardoning and cleansing them of the sin, forgiving them if they confessed them to their Sátrapas (priests), who were the soothsayers who kept the books of divination and of the fate of the newly born, of witchcraft and prognostication as well as of ancient traditions, which were transmitted from mouth to mouth from the ancients down to them.

When a penitent was ready for confession, he would at once go in search of one of these priests or divines to whom they were wont to confess, saying to him: "Sir, I want to go to god almighty who is the protector of all (this god almighty is called Yoallichccatlostees-tezcatlipoca) for I wanted to speak in secret of my sins." Hearing this, the Sátrapa would answer: "Be very welcome, my son, for what you say you wish to do is for your salvation and advantage." After saying this he would at once consult his book of divination which was called Tonalamatl, in order to find out by this book what day would be the most opportune for such a deed. As soon as he had found the propitious day, he would say: "Come on such and such a day, for on that day the sign is favorable to do this successfully." When the appointed day had come for the penitent to return he would buy a new mat (petate), white incense which they call copalli, and wood for the fire, over which the copalli was to be burned. If the penitent was a prominent man or invested with some official dignity, the priest would go to his house to confess him (or by chance the penitent man even being a prominent person might choose to go to the house of the priest). Upon arrival (wherever it might be), the place where the new mat was to be spread was very well swept and the confessor seated himself on the mat; the fire was lighted and he, the Sátrapa, threw the incense into it, and addressed himself to the fire, saying to it: "I wish to inform you, oh lord, who are the father and the mother of all the gods and who are the most ancient god, that there has come today one of your vassals, this your servant, who comes here weeping in deep sorrow; he comes with great suffering; by all this it is clear that he has erred, that he stumbled and met with and found some of the obscenity of sin even with serious crime worthy of death, and he is very sad about it and downcast. Our very merciful lord who are our protector and supporter, accept the penitence and listen to the anguish of your servant and vassal." This prayer finished, the priest then turned to the penitent and spoke to him as follows: "Son, you have come into the presence of god, the helper and supporter of all; you came to tell him your inward shame and rottenness, to disclose unto him the secrets of your heart; be careful not to lead a riotous life nor to throw yourself headlong into it, nor get lost by lying in the presence of our lord. Rid yourself and throw out all your shame and disgrace in the presence of our lord, whose name is Yoallichectla, that is to say, Tezcatlipoca. It is a fact that you are before him (in his presence), although you are not worthy to see him; and even if he doesn't speak to you, because he is invisible and not palpable, mind how you come before him, with what kind of a heart; do not fear to declare your secrets in his presence, tell him your life, tell your (good) deeds in the same way you confessed your excesses and offenses, pour out your evil deeds in his presence, tell them all sorrowfully to our lord god, who is the protector of all, and who holds his arms open and is ready to embrace you and to carry you. See to it that you do not omit anything out of shame or cowardice!" When the penitent had heard all this, he took the oath to tell the truth,—in their own way of taking an oath, which is touching the earth with the hand and licking off whatever had stuck to it. He then threw copal into the fire, which was another way of taking an oath. Then he seated himself opposite the priest and, considering him (in this instance), as god's representative, he began his confession, saying: "Oh, lord, who accepts and helps everyone, listen to my baseness and rottenness. In your presence I disclose myself. I throw out all my shameful acts as many as I have committed, for, to be sure, none of the wickedness I am guilty of is hidden from you, because all things are apparent and clear to you." After this he at once began to tell his sins in the order he had committed them, with entire calm and distinctness,

like a person who recites a poem or legend, very slowly and well
enunciated, or like one who goes on a very straight road without
deviating to one side or the other. After having thus confessed
everything he had done, the priest spoke to him and said, "My
son, you have spoken before our lord god, telling him of all your
wicked acts; now also in his name I shall tell you what you are
obliged to do. When the goddesses called Civapipilti come down
to earth, or when the feast to the goddesses of carnality whose
name is Yxtuiname, is celebrated, you are to fast for four days,
punishing your stomach and your mouth, and on the very day of
the feast of Yxtuiname, in the morning or at daybreak, you are to
make the proper penitence as suits your sins, and that is to pass
through your tongue from one side to the other some twigs of
what they call teucalcacatl or tlacotl, and if you should wish to
do more than that, pass them through the ears, one or the other.
This you do as penitence and atonement for your sins; it is not to
be as a merit, but as a penitence for your evil deeds. You are to
pierce first your tongue in the middle with a maguey thorn and
through that same hole you will pass the twigs, passing each one
in front of your face and, as you pull them out of the tongue,
throw them behind you toward your back. If you should wish
to unite (tie) all of them, you may attach one to the other, be
there four hundred or eight hundred, in short, just as many as
you wish to pass through your tongue; doing this, all the wickedness and filth you committed will be forgiven you." If the
penitent has not committed neither very many nor serious sins,
the priest to whom he confesses tells him, "My son, you are to
fast; tire your stomach by hunger and your mouth by thirst,
eating only once a day at noon and repeating this for four days,"
or he might tell some penitent to go and offer papers at the
accustomed places and make images and to cover these images—
as many and fashioned as his devotion would command,—with
these papers and go through the devotional ceremony of singing
and dancing, as is customary in their presence. Or he might say:
"You offended god by getting drunk, so you must appease the
god of wine, called Totochti, and when you go to comply with

your penance you are to go at night, naked with only a paper in front and one at the back to cover your privy parts; when you are ready to return after your prayers are offered, you are to throw the papers that had covered your front and back at the feet of the gods that are there."

Once his confession made and after having received the penance he was to make, the penitent would go home and try never again to incur in the same sins he had just confessed, because it was said that if these same sins were repeated then there was no more absolution.

Confessions of great sins, such as adultery, were only made by old men, and this for the simple reason to escape worldly punishment meted out for such sins; to escape from being condemned to death, which was either having their head crushed or ground to powder between two stones. It must be said that the priests who heard confessions were utterly discreet, never disclosing what they had learned in confession; this was because they considered that it was not they personally who had heard these confessions, but their god, who was the only one before whom sin was revealed, hence it was not supposed that any human heard them, nor had they been told to human ears, only to god (in his representative). It is well known that even after Christianity had been implanted, they (those Indians) insisted on confessing the most serious and nefarious sins, such as homicide, adultery, etc., and that by carrying out the penitence (penance) imposed in expiation as in times past, the courts of justice also would pardon them. Even now, if one of them kills or commits adultery, he will come to our homes or monasteries and without saying a word about their evil deeds, simply say that he wants to do penance. They will work in the orchard, they will sweep the house, or do anything else they are ordered; after a few days they will go to confession, and after that will tell about their crimes, and give the reason why they came to do penance. After confession they ask a statement signed by the confessor with the intention to show it to those in power, be it the governor or the mayors, and thus let them know that they have done penance and have gone to confession, therefore justice has no case against them. Hardly any of the friars (monks) nor of the civil authorities understand this, mainly because they do not know anything about that ancient custom mentioned above, but rather think that the Indians ask for the certificate to show compliance with religious duties (to show that they have confessed that year). We are well aware of this condition on account of the great experience we acquired among them. It is said that the old men confessed their great (serious) sins of the flesh from which fact we may deduce that they probably had greatly sinned in their youth but did not confess until they were old, but that they could continue sinning while young, for it was their belief that once confessed they could not sin again. From the above we may safely deduce that those Indians of New Spain considered it their obligation to go to confession at least once in their lifetime, and that they did this even long before they had any knowledge of the Christian faith.

Now we come to the minor gods. The first one of these is Xiuhtecutli, who has two other names, one being Yxcocauhqui, meaning yellow face; the other is Cuecaltzin, which means flame of fire. He was also called Viveteutl, which is ancient god; he was considered by all as a father according to the effects he caused, because he burns and the flame lights and burns. All these are effects which cause fear, but he has other attributes which call for love and reverence, such as the heat that warms those who are cold, it cooks the food to eat, frying, baking, boiling and toasting it. It (the fire or heat from it) produces the salt (by evaporation of the brine), and the thick honey, coal and lime. It heats the baths for bathing, it makes the oil called Uxitl. With fire we can heat the lye and water to wash soiled and old clothes, so that they will become almost new. The feast to this god was celebrated each year at the end of the month called 13 calli[2] and they dressed his image with all the vestments, ornaments and plumes of the principal lord; in Mocthecuzuma's time they dressed this god to resemble him, and even in times of other rulers of the past they were wont to dress him like one of these and place him upon his

2 That is the feast called Hucy Micailhuitl, or feast of the great deceased.

altar or throne. In his presence they decapitated many quails, sprinkling their blood in front of him, offering him copal (incense) as to a god; also a sort of cakes called quilltamalli made of wild amaranth seed, which they also ate themselves in his honor; in all districts of the town, in every house they offered them, however, first to the fire before eating them, and if they were not first offered, they would not touch them. The priests designated to the service of this god and who were called Ybebeyoban, which means "his old men" danced before him all day, singing as they danced in their own way, playing on conch-shells like horns, beating drums and teponaztli, which are drums made of wood, and in their hands they held rattles to accompany their singing. These rattles are like the toy or baby rattles with which children are quieted when they cry, and also like those used in the fields. On that day they (the Mexican people in general) did not cook bread in comal (the flat earthenware pan in which maize cakes are cooked in Mexico), and they took care that no one should do it anywhere; nor could they cook anything else in comal, to avoid that anyone should touch the fire, since it was the first day of the year on which this kind of tamales were eaten and offered (to the god). On the occasion of this same feast the fathers and mothers of children caught snakes, some caught frogs, or a kind of fish which is called joviles (today juiles) or small water-lizards called axélotl, or birds or any other tiny animal, and these they threw into the home fire, and when they were well toasted the children would eat them, saying, "Our father the fire eats toasted things." That night the old men and women drank uctli, which is wine of the land; before they tasted it themselves, however, they sprinkled some in the four directions (parts) of the house, saying that by so doing they gave the fire a taste of it, humoring it thus as a god in the form of an offering or sacrifice. Every four years a very solemn feast was offered to this god by the lord of the land with all his principal citizens (chieftains), and he arranged a dance in front of the house or temple of that god. At this feast celebrated every four years, not only old men and women, but everybody, youths and maidens, boys and girls, drank wine, or pulque, for which reason this feast was called "pillavano," which means a feast at which children drink wine or pulque. The parents of children this day selected godfathers and godmothers for their children, giving them some presents. These godparents had to carry their godchildren on their backs to the temple of the god of the fire, whom they also called Yxcocauhqui; there, in the temple, in front of the god, they perforated the children's ears in the presence of the godparents, who were called Ymavivanyntlavan. After this ceremony all, parents, godparents, and the children, ate together. The image of this god represents a naked man whose chin was dyed black with a resin called ulli, and a bib of red stone in the parting of the chin. On the head he had a crown of paper painted in different colors and with diverse designs; on top of the crown were several green feather tufts imitating flames, on each side hung a few feather balls, looking like pendants over the ears. In the perforations of the ears he wore ear-rings of turquoise mosaic. He carried on his shoulder (or back) a plumage made to look like a dragon's head, fashioned of yellow feathers and small sea-shells; jingles were attached around the ankles; in his left hand he carried a shield with five green stones which are called chalchivites, placed in the form of a cross over a gold plate covering almost the entire shield; in his right hand he held a sort of sceptre consisting of a round gold plate with a hole through the center and at the top of this sceptre as crown or termination there were two globes, one larger than the other, with a point on the smaller one. They call this sceptre Tlachicloni, which means look-out or observatory, because he (the god) hid his face behind it, looking out through the opening in the center of the gold-plate.

Another divinity was called Macuilxochitl, and was also considered as a god, like the god of the fire. He was especially the god of those who dwelt in the houses of lords or in the palaces of the chiefs. The feast celebrated in his honor was the one called Xochilhuitl, which was a movable feast and is described in Book IV under divinatory art. All those who celebrated this feast, men or women, fasted for four days previous, and if during this fast any man had intercourse with a woman or vice versa, they said he or she soiled their fast, and this offended the god terribly, so he gave them dreadful diseases of the privy parts if they did misbehave, such as piles, furuncles, venereal diseases, bubo, etc., and it was understood that all such ailments were punishments meted out by this god for reasons above given, and they made him promises and vows to relieve them and relent his resentment, lifting the scourge off them. When the day of the feast Xochilhuitl, or feast of the flowers, was due, and after they all had fasted during four preceding days on which they did not eat any chillioaxi and only ate once a day at noon and at midnight they drank a sort of pap or gruel called Tlaquilolatulli, which means colored or tinted gruel with a flower placed in the center on top of it; this sort of fast was called the fast of the flowers. Even those who did not leave off eating chilli and other such tasty things only ate them once a day, at noon. Others fasted, eating unleavened bread (panes acimos),—that is, that the corn of which they make this kind of bread is not mixed with lime before grinding it, thus producing a kind of fermentation, but ground it dry and made their bread with this flour, cooking it in comal (earthenware pan); they did not eat chilli nor anything else with it and also only ate once a day, at noon.

On the fifth day, which was the day of the feast, everyone dressed in the same clothes as the god, as if they were his image or someone who meant the same as the god, and, attired in that way, they held dances and chants accompanied by drums and jingles (rattles—toponaztli). At noon of the same day they cut the heads off of many quails, spilling the blood in front of the god and his image; some bled their own ears in front of him; still others pierced their tongues with maguey thorns, passing a number of straws (twigs) through the opening, bleeding freely; they made many other votive offerings in the temple. One of the ceremonies was to make five tamales of corn, neither very thick nor very round, which they called pan de ayuno (unleavened bread). These loaves were large and had an arrow stuck in the center. These they called xuchimitl, offering of the people. Such individuals as felt like doing so offered five such tamales of small size on a wooden plate, with some chilmolli in a cup; again others offered two cakes called tzoalli, instead of ulli, black gum, which many offered on wooden plates. One of these two cakes was . . . . . ,[3] the other vermilion. In general people offered many diverse things, toasted corn, toasted corn mixed with honey and flour made of the seeds of wild amaranthus; bread adorned with a certain figure in the shape of lightning as it crosses the skies and which they call Xonecuilli; or bread shaped like butterflies; unleavened bread called yotlaxcalli; cakes of seeds of the wild amaranthus, cakes shaped like shields of that same seed; also shaped like arrows or swords; even dolls they made out of that same dough.

For this same feast, all the chieftains and Calpixques (stewards or rent-gatherers) of the district of Mexico which bordered on the surrounding war-districts, brought the captives they had either made themselves or bought and delivered them to the stewards of Mexico (city) for these latter to keep until the time came to sacrifice them before the idols. If one of these slaves or captives ran away in the meantime the Calpixque in whose care they had been given was obliged to buy another one to replace the one who had fled.

The image of this god looked like a naked man whose skin had been stripped off or dyed with vermilion; his mouth and chin were painted white, black and light blue; the face a bright red; he had a crown dyed a light green, with feather tufts of the same color; a few tassels hung from the crown towards the back; he carried a device or plumage on the shoulders (back) that looked like a flag or banner stuck on a hill; at the top of this banner were green feather tufts. His body was clothed in a bright red mantle which hung to his thigh; this mantle had a fringe, from which hung little sea-shells. His feet were clad in sandals very elaborately made. In his left hand he had a shield, which was white and had four stones in the center, two and two together; lastly also a sceptre, which was shaped like a heart with green feather

[3] There is evidently a word left out in Bustamente's copy.

tufts on top, while from the bottom of it hung other tufts of green and yellow feathers.

Omecatl, which means two canes, is the god of invitations (treats) who, they say, has power (rules) over invitations (festivities) and guests. When, for instance, some prominent men, chieftains or lords, invited all their relatives to give them to eat, present them with blankets and flowers, that they might dance, whirl about and sing in their homes, the one who gave this festivity went to get the image of that god to take it to his house. Some of the priests in the service of this god in his temple would carry the image to the host's house. They said that if they did not do this honor to the god as they should, he would get angry and appear to the host in his dreams to scold and blame him, saying: "You bad man, why did you not honor me as is due me? Do you know that now I shall leave you, I shall forsake you, and you will pay me fully the affront you committed." If he was very angry he showed his anger by mixing animal or human hair with the food and drink in order to sadden the guests and dishonor their host, and when the latter went to communion on the god's feast day, he often would become ill, or when he ate or drank, would choke on the food or beverage, or when he walked, would stumble and often fall. When they celebrated the feast of this god, which took place at night, they communed with their body, that is, by fasting, and for this communion the chiefs and stewards and all those who had charge of the districts, made the figure of a big, thick bone, round like an elbow, and called it the bone of the god. Before communion they ate and drank pulque. At dawn, after having been eating and drinking, they pricked the stomach of the one who represented the image of this god with pins or something of the kind until hurting him. After that they distributed the figure of this dough, which they called Tzoalli, dividing it into three parts and each one ate as much as he could. All those who communed here, had it said and understood that the coming year on the feast of this god they were to contribute toward it providing everything necessary to be spent for it.

The image of this deity was that of a man seated on a bunch of cypress; his face was spotted black and white with a paper crown tightly adjusted around the forehead, with a long and wide scarf, which was tied at the back of the head, laced by something that looked like tassels. Around the crown were wound a few beads of chalchivites (Mexican emeralds). His mantle was like a net; a wide fringe with flowers strewn in it, these latter woven into the same fringe; he had a shield standing close by, from which hung wide tassels at the bottom. In his right hand he held a sceptre which had a round, perforated medallion on it, like a bull's eye (skylight or spy-hole). This sceptre was resting on the edge of a round table, and above it had a pyramidal capital. This sceptre was called tlachialia, which means observatory (watch-tower or lookout), because he covered his face with the medallion and looked through the spy-hole.

To Yxtlilton, which means the little Negro, by another name also called Tlaltetecuin, they made a tabernacle of painted boards where his image stood. In his oratory or temple were a good many glazed earthenware tubs and water jars with water, all of which were covered with boards or comales; the water they contained was called tlilalt, meaning "black water". When a child was ill they took it to the temple of god Yxtlilton and, uncovering one of these jars, they gave the sick child some of that water to drink, and it cured it, and if anyone wished to show his devotion to this god by celebrating a feast, he would take his image to his home. This image was neither a statue nor a painting, but simply one of his priests who dressed himself in the insignia, and when they came to take him from the temple they burnt incense or copal in front of him until he reached the house where the celebration was to take place. This consisted of dances and songs, customary among them. Their way of dancing and whirling about is different from ours, and they called these dances macevalistli. For this many got together and paired off in twos and threes, in a large circle, according to their number. They carried flowers in their hands and with their finery they wore plumes. They all made the same motion with body, feet and hands at one time, which was worth seeing, for being very artistic. Their motions were executed to the beating of drums and rattles. They all sang together in chorus, with very sonorous voices, the praise of the god whose feast they celebrated. They have the same custom today, only dedicated to another personality. They govern their motions in posture and dress according to what they sing; they dispose of a great many different movements as well as a great variety of tunes for their singing, but it is all very graceful and even highly mystical. Idolatry is not uprooted as yet.

As soon as the image reached the house of the man who was offering the god this celebration, they ate and drank first, then commenced the dancing and singing with the god whom they so honored. After he had danced with the others a long while, he entered into the house and went to the storeroom where they kept the pulque or wine which they were wont to drink, in many jars all of them covered with boards or comales (earthenware pans), all roughly plastered onto the jugs. These jars had been thus covered for four days, and the god now opened one or many of them, and this opening ceremony was called tlaiacaxapotla, which means "this wine is new." As soon as the jars had thus been opened, the god and these with him drank of that wine, going out into the courtyard of the home where the ceremonies took place. They now went to where the jars of the black water were kept, dedicated to this god, and which had also been sealed for four days. The priest who represented the god opened them and if, after they had thus been opened, there appeared in any of them a bit of dirt, such as a little straw, a human or animal hair or a bit of charcoal, they at once pronounced the host of this festivity a bad man, an adulterer, a thief, or a man given to the carnal sins. They forthwith faced him with the accusation that he was an addict of one of these vices or that he was a sower of discord or corrupting vice, making these accusations in presence of everyone. When the priest who played the part of the god left that house (such a house) they gave him rugs or shawls which they called ixquen, which means opening of the face (of the eyes), because the host of such a festivity felt ashamed if any impurity was found in that black water. The manner of dress of this god will be explained at the end of this book.

The god called Opuchtli was counted among the deities whose collective name was Tlaloques, which means inhabitants of the earthly paradise, although they knew that he was a mere man. They attributed to him the invention of fishing nets as well as of an implement to kill fish and which they call minacachalli, which is like a "fisga"[4] although it has only three points in triangle like a trident with which they injure the fish; they also kill birds with it. Opuchtli also invented the lazoes to kill birds and the oars to row.

When the fishermen and people of the water front who derive their livelihood from that element and who adore him as their god celebrated his feast, they offered him food and wine of the kind they call uctli, by another name, pulque. They also offered him green corn-stalks, flowers, smoke canes which they call yietl, white incense called copalli, an odoriferous herb the name of which is yiauhtli, which they strew in front of him in the same way they spread mats of rattan, rush-rugs, for processions to pass. During this festivity they also used timbrels placed in hollow sticks and which sounded almost like rattles; furthermore, they throw in front of the image toasted corn called mumuchtli, a sort of corn which when toasted opens up and shows the white marrow (popcorn), forming a very white flower. They said this represented hail, which is attributed to the water gods. The old priests, in whose care this god was given, and the old women, sang the songs of praise to him. His image represents a naked man painted entirely black with a grayish face more or less the color of quail-feathers. He wore a paper crown of different colors, fashioned like a rose, one row of petals overlapping the other, and on top there was a green feather tuft which came out of a yellow tassel; large and long tassels hung down towards the back from this crown. He wore a green stole crossed (in front) like the one worn by priests when celebrating mass. Around the waist he wore green paper bands which hung down as far as the knees; his

[4] Fisga—harpoon.

feet were clad in white sandals; in his left hand he held a shield painted red, and in the center of the red field there was a white flower with four leaves which formed a cross, and from these leaves projected again four points which also were leaves (petals) of the same flower. His right hand held a sceptre in the shape of a chalice with something like a socket with arrows (quiver?).

Xipetotec, meaning flayed, was the god honored by all those who lived on the seashore. He was originary of Zapotlan, a town in the state of Xalisco. To this god they attributed the following diseases: small-pox, tumours that form anywhere on the body, itch, also diseases of the eyes such as the soreness of eyes resulting from excessive drinking, and all other eye complaints. Anyone suffering from the above-mentioned diseases made a promise to this god to dress in a (human) skin when his feast was to be celebrated, which feast was called Tlacaxipealiztli, that is, "flaying of men." In the course of this festivity they executed a dance which looks very much like the Spanish "Juege de cañas" namely, a skirmish on horseback, in Spain, with spear-throwing, these spears being made of a light reed (caña). Two bands would be stationed opposite each other, the first one was the band of the image of Totec or the god himself, all his followers dressed in skins of men they had just killed and flayed, all of them still fresh and bleeding. The other band consisted of the daring and courageous soldiers and other martial and fighting men, to whom death meant nothing, and who now, fearless and bold, of their own free-will, stepped forth to fight their opponents in sham battle, pursuing each other close to the enemy line running in full flight back to their own place. After the ammunition was exhausted on both sides the party of the god Totec, dressed in human skins, went through the whole town, entering every house to beg alms, anything, for the love of their god. In the houses they entered the people would make them sit on little bundles of branches of the tzapote tree, throwing about their necks strings of ears of corn and chains of flowers which reached down to their armpits; they adorned them with garlands and gave them pulque to drink, which is their wine.

If a woman fell ill with any of the above mentioned diseases she would present her votive offering on the feast of that god in the way she had promised. The image of this deity represents a naked man with one half of his body painted yellow, the other half tawny; his face is ornamented on both sides by a narrow band which reaches from the forehead down to the chin. On the head he wears a little cap of diverse colors, with tassels that hang down towards the back. He is clothed in the skin of a man; the hair is parted into two braids, the ears are of gold. He wears a short green skirt as far as the knees, with small sea-shells around the bottom. His feet are clad in sandals; he has a yellow shield with a red coping all around. He holds his sceptre with both hands, and it is of the shape of the heart of a poppy with a little quiver stuck straight into it.

It is supposed that Yiacatecutli, god of merchants, was the one who started trading among those people, and that for this reason the guild of the merchants adopted him as their god and honored him in different ways, one being to offer him paper with which they covered his statues wherever they found them. They also venerated the cane (stick) with which they walked, which was a solid cane called utatl (also otate). They have still another kind of cane or walking stick made of a solid light black cane without a knot, and which looks like reed such as is used in Spain.[5] All merchants used that kind of cane on the road. When they reached the place where they were to spend the night, they would gather all their canes and tie them into one bundle, which they then stuck at the head of the sleeping place or camp. They would sprinkle blood in front of this bundle, which blood they obtained by bleeding their own ears, tongue, arms or legs. Then they offered incense by building a fire and burning copal in front of this bundle of sticks, which they considered as the image of the god Yiacatecutli, and by this means they asked him to protect them from all danger. These merchants traveled over the whole land, bartering, trading, buying in some place and selling in another what they had purchased. They also travel through

[5] The well known Malacca cane.

towns, along the seashore, and in the interior. There isn't a place they do not pry into and visit, here buying, there selling; it is neither too hot for them in this place nor too cold in that one. They don't shun a road because it is too rough nor too difficult to search for whatever is there, either pretty or valuable or advantageous to buy and sell again. These traders suffer great hardships and are exceedingly daring; they go anywhere, even if it should be an enemy's domain and they are very sly in their deals with strangers, in learning their languages, as well as in their tactics, attaining through kindness what they want, thus gaining their confidence. They find out where the feathers (plumes) and the precious stones can be had, or the gold; there they purchase them and take them to where they are worth a great deal. They also know where to go to find exquisite and valuable skins of beasts, and where to resell them at high prices. Likewise do they deal in precious cups of many different kinds and material adorned with diverse painted figures, and which are used in all the different districts; some of these cups have covers made of tortoise shells and spoons of the same to stir the cocoa; there are cups with covers painted in different colors and figures, made to resemble a leaf of the "vinarbol"[6] and with various kinds of beautiful sticks with which they stirred their cocoa. If they are forced to enter an enemy's realm, they first learn the language of these people; they adopt their mode of dress so they might not be taken for strangers, but for people of that same country. It often happened that the enemy recognized them, capturing and killing them. If one or two or more were able to escape, they were wont to notify the chief or principal lord of the province, as, for instance, Mocthecuzuma or any of his predecessors, bringing him as an offering some of the treasures of those countries, making a present of these things in remuneration of their sufferings, and in order to be honored by their people and considered courageous. They would give him an amber bib, which is a large, transparent, yellow stone which hangs from the lower lip as a sign that he was brave and noble, too; this bib was highly valued.

[6] Probably a name for the grape-vine.

Whenever these traders or merchants left for such a voyage to foreign lands they took leave of their relatives amid great ceremonies, in accordance with ancient rites. They remained absent many years, and when they returned they brought back great riches (many treasures). In order to display what they had and to give an account of the countries they had visited and the things they had seen, soon upon their return they would invite all the traders (merchants), especially the principal ones, as well as the chieftains of the town, and arranged a great festivity for them. These festivities they called "washing of feet." The guests did great honor to the cane (walking-stick) with which the traveler had gone and come back; considered it the image of Yiacatecutli, god of the merchants, who had favored them to travel the roads and brought them back safely. In order to do due honor to the cane they placed it in one of the temples they had in the different quarters of the town, and which they call calpulli, which means church of the district or parish. In the calpulli to which this particular trader belonged, he put the cane in an honored place, and when the dinner was served to his guests, he first placed food, flowers, and acayietl (small tube containing incense of odoriferous herbs which was burned in front of the stick); and even afterwards, after the invitation was over, each time the trader was about to eat he first placed food and all the other things in front of the stick (cane), which he now kept in his own home, in the private oratory thereof. All these traders, after returning from one of their voyages, as they now were wealthy, would buy male and female slaves, whom they offered to their god on his feast, this generally being Yiacatecutli, who had five brothers and one sister, all being held as deities, and according to the size of their devotion, they would sacrifice slaves to each one of them separately on his personal feast, or to all together, or to the sister alone. One of the brothers was called Chiconquiavitl, the other Xomocuil, the next Nacxitl, another Cochimetl, the fifth Yacapitzaoac; the sister's name was Chalmecacioatl. To each one of these or to one or the other they offered one or more slaves, sacrificing (killing) them in front of these gods, dressed in the insignia of the respective one as if he were his image. There was a regular fair in a town (village) called Azcapotzalco, at two leagues from Mexico where slaves, men and women, were sold. There those who wanted any went to select among a great number of them, for they were very careful that the slave, male or female, should be without blemish of body and free of disease of any kind. After having purchased these slaves, men or women, they treated them very well; they bathed them in hot water, gave them well to eat and drink and in abundance, so that these slaves grew fat, for they were to be eaten and offered to their god. They also feasted them, making them dance and sing at times on the flat roofs of their houses or on the public square; there they sang all the songs they knew until they became tired of singing. They did in no way fear or mind the sort of death awaiting them.

These slaves were killed at the feast called panquetzalistli, and all the time before that feast they were treated to everything, as we have said.

If among these slaves there was a man who appeared to have fair judgment, was quick and intelligent in serving and perhaps could sing well, or if there was a woman among them who was willing and able to prepare food and drink, could embroider or weave, the chiefs or prominent people would buy them for their own service in their homes, and thus these escaped from being sacrificed.

The image of this god represents an Indian who travels with his cane; the face was spotted black and white; in his hair he wore two tassels of the fine feathers (plumes) called quetzalli; these plumes were tied in the center of the head where the hair was gathered like a sheaf at the top (of head). His ears were of gold; he wore a blue mantle, and over the blue was thrown a black net so that the blue shone through the meshes of the net. The mantle had a fringe all around with flowers woven into it. Around the ankles he wore yellow leather straps from which hung diminutive sea-shells. His feet were clad in sandals gracefully made and very elaborate. His shield was yellow with a light blue spot in the center quite plain, without any ornamentation; in his right hand he held a cane such as traders (travelers) carry on the road.

Napatecutli is the god of those who make cypress (rush) mats, and he belongs to the class they call Tlalocs. The say that he is the one who invented the art of making mats, and it is for this reason that the makers of mats are called "petates," and also those who weave seats for stools, icpales and hurdles, are tolqüextli. They said that through the grace of this god cypress, reed and rush were planted and grew, thus enabling them to work at their trade. At the same time they believed this god to produce rain. They celebrated his feast wherever the above-mentioned things were made, and revered and worshipped him, demanding of him to give them what he was wont to give, namely, water, reeds, or rush for their work, etc. For this feast they bought a slave to sacrifice in front of him, dressing him in the ornaments of this god as if he, the slave, were his image. On the day this slave was to die and after he had been dressed as we just said, they placed a glass with water in his hand, and gave him a branch of willow, and with this he had to sprinkle them all like one who sprinkles holy water. If for devotion anyone wanted to make a feast in honor of this god, he would first go to his (the god's) priests and report; then they all would dress one of their number with the god's vestments to represent his image, and he then would sprinkle water with the willow branch wherever he passed. When they reached the house where the festivity was to be held, they put him in his place (of honor) and performed the reglamentary (usual) ceremonies in his presence, entreating him to grant favors to that house. He who had offered the festivity gave food and drink to the god, those who had accompanied him, and to all he had invited. He did this in gratitude for the prosperity and wealth he was already enjoying, believing that the god had given these to him. They performed dances, sang songs, as is their custom, in honor of Napatecutli, and to have him see how grateful his devotee was, he would spend everything he had, saying: "I do not mind to remain without a thing so long as I have served my god with this celebration. Should he choose to grant me more or leave me without anything, let him do as he pleases." After saying this he would cover the priest, who had come in representation of Napatecutli, with a white blanket, and then this latter would return to the temple with his companions. After they had left, the host and his relatives sat down to eat.

The men who make petates (mats) and whatever else of rush or reed took great care to provide and arrange, sweep and clean and strew cypress in the temple of their god. They were also mindful to put mats on the floor, stools, icpales, for seats, so that everything would be nice and clean and well furnished, and not even a little straw nor anything else could be seen in the temple.

The image of Napatecutli represented a man dyed all black but for a few white specks among the black in the face. He wore a crown of paper painted black and white, and a few tassels hanging from the crown onto his back; from these tassels came a plume or tuft of three green plumes which rose towards the back of the head. Around the waist he wore a sort of short skirt to the knees painted black and white, and on it were small sea-shells. He had white sandals. In his left hand he held a shield fashioned like a water-lily, which is an aquatic plant, wide and resembling a large plate. In the right hand he held a flowering stalk or cane, the flowers being made of paper. He also wore a wide band like a stole from the right shoulder across the chest crossing under the left arm, black flowers painted on white.

All prominent mountain peaks, especially such around which rain-clouds will gather, they imagined to be gods, therefore they made of each an image according to their idea. They also thought that certain diseases which are due to the cold or inclement weather came from the mountains, and that these mountains had the power to cure them. Therefore, all those who became ill of such diseases made a vow to offer a feast and offering to such and such a mountain closest to which they happened to live, or to which they were most devoted. Similar promises were made by anyone who was in imminent danger of drowning in a river or in the sea. The various diseases for which they made promises to the Tlalocs were the gout (rheumatism) in hands or feet or any other part of the body; also contraction of tendons in any part of the body; for appearance of blotches (stains or spots) on the body (so-called liverspots, et al.), or contraction of any member, limbs or arms, or for paralysis. All those afflicted by any one of these ailments made a solemn vow to make the images of the following Tlalocs: the god or Tlaloc of the air, goddess of the water, god of rain, as well as the image of the volcano called Popocatepetl and the one of the Sierra Nevada, and of a mountain called Poiauhtecatl, or of any other mountain or hill they wanted to worship. They could make a vow to one or more, and the image or images were made of a dough called tzoalli in human shape: it was not permitted, however, to the worshipper himself to fashion them; he had to go to the different priests of these deities who were experienced in this sort of work, and whose duty it was, besides, to do it. The Sátrapa in making the image would give it teeth of pumpkin seeds, and for eyes black beans, which are as large as (lima) beans, though of a different shape, and which they call ayecotli. As for their dress and ornaments, they fashioned them according to the image of the Tlaloc they represented. Thus they make the god of the wind look like Quetzalcoatl, the one of water like the goddess of the water, rain like the god of rain, and all the mountains according to the paintings they make of them. To these figures they offered the paper they make, consisting of a sheet (of it), onto which they dripped a great many drops of the gum called ulli, which they melted first. This paper they would hang around the neck of the image so that the latter was covered from the chest down, and at the lower end they snatched off the paper. Similar papers dripped all over with ulli they would hang on strings, one alongside the other, in front of the images, and the wind would shake them, for these strings of paper were tied at each end to canes stuck in the ground, the strings or "mecatl" being tied to the upper end. To these images wine—uctli, or pulcre,[7] which is the wine of the country, was offered in cups which were made in the following way: there are some pumpkins, smooth, round and mottled between green and white, or

---

[7] Pulque, but it is very frequently spelled as above.

else spotted, which they call tzilacayutli, of the size of a large melon. These they cut in halves and emptied the seeds so that they now looked like cups, and these they used for the uctli, or wine, they placed in front of the images. To them these gourd cups represented those made of precious stones, called chalchivitl. All this was done by the priests, who knew how to do them, and who were appointed specially for these sacrifices. The rest of the people never made them, even if it were for their own home. After these images were made for the devotional ceremony, the ones who had ordered them invited the priests for the fifth day after their confection, when the celebration was to take place. When that day had come they spent that night (the eve) in wake, singing and dancing in honor of the images and of the gods they represented. During that night they offered tamales, which are a sort of cake made of corn, at four different times, to all those who danced and sang, namely, the priests who had made the images and those invited to partake of the feast. Four times a meal was served to all of them, and as many times they played their musical instruments, the whistling was done by placing the little finger in the mouth; they played on shells and flutes of the kind they used. This was done by jugglers who played that sort of music (at feasts), and to whom they also gave food. At daybreak the Sátrapas decapitated all the images they had made of dough, twisting their heads, and they took all that dough and carried it to the house where they, the priests, all lived together, and which is called calmecac, while the hosts, whose vows had caused the images to be made, immediately returned home and joined their guests. They remained together all that day and in the evening toward night all the old men and women drank pulcre (pulque) or uctli, because they all had permission to drink it, and after they all were half or entirely drunk, they went home; some were crying, others made fierce threats like the braves and were dancing and showing off; still others were quarreling with each other. The hosts of such a festivity invited and provided also for the innkeepers, who made (brewed) the pulque, entreating them to make good wine, and the latter did their best to have it as good as possible. In order to attain this, that is, to brew good pulque, they abstained for four days of all intercourse with women, because it was their belief that if in those days they should hold any intercourse with women, the wine (pulque) would turn sour and would spoil. They also re-frained during that period from drinking either pulque or the honey (aqua miel) of which they brewed it, not even a finger would they dip in it to taste it until on the fourth day, when it would be officially tasted in the ceremony mentioned above. They held the superstition that if anyone drank of that wine, even if it were ever so little, before the official ceremony of the opening of the jugs as mentioned before, his mouth would twist to one side as a punishment of his sin. They also said that if anyone suffered from a shriveled hand or foot, or if the face, mouth or lips would begin to tremble (from palsy) or that he became possessed by some evil spirit, all this happened to him because these Tlalocs were angry with him.

The day after the feast, in the morning, the host gathered all his relatives, his friends and those of his parish (city precinct), and everybody of his own household, to finish eating the food left over and to drink the rest of the pulque, and this they called apealo, which means adding to what had been eaten and drunk before; nothing at all would be left for the next day. It was said that if those afflicted with gout or any other disease of those above mentioned, also those who escaped any calamity on river or sea, arranged and celebrated such a festivity, they fulfilled their vows. Once this feast was over, all the papers and ornaments which had adorned the images of the Tlalocs, all the vessels that had been used for the guests, were carried to a gutter (sewer) in the lagoon of Mexico, called pantitlan, and there they threw it all into the water.

Even in the past, the wine or pulcre (pulque) of the country was considered as pernicious (bad) on account of the bad effects it caused. Some of those intoxicated by its use would throw themselves from a rock or other height, others would hang themselves, still others would throw themselves into the water, where they would drown, or they would kill one another when drunk. All these calamities were blamed on the god of the wine and on the wine itself, and not on the drunkard who abused it. Furthermore, it was their belief that if anyone spake ill of that beverage or even murmured against it, some disaster (catastrophe) would befall him. The same was said if a drunken man was murmuring against it, insulting it, even if he was simply saying or doing a thousand villainies (in that condition), he was to be punished for it, because, as they said, it wasn't really he who committed or did these things, but the god or, better still, the demon who was in him, and who was Tezcatzoncatl, god of the wine (pulque), or one of the others. Tezcatzoncatl was a relative or brother of the other deities of wine, who were called: Yzyuitecalt, Yiauhteatl, Acolóa, Tlilhóa, Pantecatl, Tultecatl, Papaztac, Tlatecaivoa, Umetuchtli, Tepuztecalt, Chimapalnecatl, and Colhoatzincatl. By the above statement we can clearly see that whatever they did while drunk they did not consider as sin, no matter how serious a misdeed it might be. We might even adduce with good reason that they deliberately became intoxicated in order to commit what they had in mind, and which would not be held against them as sin or crime in that condition, hence he who did it escaped blameless. Even now that they have become Christians, they try to excuse their deeds by saying that they were drunk when they did it. They evidently think that the erroneous conception held by them previous to their Christianization is valid today. Of course, they are very much mistaken, and it is necessary to impress them of their error in confession as well as on other occasions.

BOOK II

FEASTS AND SACRIFICES
WITH WHICH THE NATIVES
HONOURED THEIR GODS
IN THE TIMES OF THEIR PAGANISM

CHAPTER I

The first month of the year was called among the Mexicans Atlacahualco, and elsewhere Quavitleloa. This month began on the second day of the month of February, when we celebrate the Purification of our Lady (the Virgin). On this first day of the month they celebrated a festival in honor (according to some) of the gods Tlaloc, whom they considered as the gods of rain. But, according to others, it was in honor of their sister Chalchiutlicue, the goddess of the water; still others pretended it was in honor of the great priest or god of the winds, Quetzalcoatl, so we may safely say that this feast was probably held in honor of all of them. This month, like all the others, which in all are eighteen, counted twenty days.

CALENDAR

ATLACAHUALCO OR QUAVITLELOA

In this month they killed many children; they sacrificed them in many places on the top of mountains, tearing out their hearts in honor of the gods of rain, so that they might grant them abundant rain.

They adorned the children thus to be sacrificed with many ornaments and carried them on their shoulders in litters. These were adorned with plumes and flowers and they played musical instruments, sang and danced in front of them.

If the children who were to be killed cried a great deal and shed many tears they were glad of it, for they took it as a prognostication of a great deal of rain for that year.

They also killed a great many prisoners in that month in honor of the same gods of water. First they stabbed them with knives, fighting with them as they were tied on to a stone which looked like a millstone, from which they routed them by means of knife-thrusts. They then took them to the temple called Yopico, where their hearts were torn out.

When these slaves were to be killed, their owners, who had captured them, danced, magnificently dressed (with plumes on the head) ahead of them, demonstrating their courage. This happened on all the days of this month. A good many ceremonies which took place at this festival are described at length on fol. 15 of their history.

The second month was called Tlacaxipeoaliztli. On the first day of this month they celebrated a festival in honor of the god Totec, who is also called Xippe, when they killed and flayed a number of slaves and captives.

Tlacaxipeoaliztli

The captives were killed by scalping them, taking the scalp off the top of the head, which was kept by their owners as a relic. The ceremony was performed in the calpul in front of the fire.

When the masters of these captives took their slaves to the temple where they were to be killed, they dragged them by the hair. As they pulled them up the steps of the Cú, some of these captives would faint, so their owners had to drag them by the hair as far as the block where they were to die.

As soon as they had dragged them to the block, which was a stone three spans (3 palmos—24 inches) high, more or less, by almost two in width, they threw them down on their back, five men holding them, two by the feet, two by the arms, and one by the head. Then at once the priest, who was to kill him, would come and strike him a blow on the chest with both hands, holding a flint knife shaped like the iron of an anchor, cutting a hole. Into this hole he would thrust one hand and tear out the heart, which he then offered to the sun; later he put it into a bowl or jar.

After thus having torn their hearts out, and after pouring their blood into a jicara (bowl made of a gourd), which was given to the master of the dead slave, the body was thrown down the temple steps. From there it was taken by certain old men called Quaquaquilti, and carried to their calpul (or chapel), cut in to pieces, and distributed [by] them to be eaten.

Before cutting them up they would flay the bodies of the captives; others would dress in their skins and fight sham battles with other men.

After the above, they would kill other captives, fighting again with them while they were tied around the waist with a rope which ran through the hole in the center of a stone like a millstone. The rope was so long that the men could walk around the stone on all sides. He was given his weapons to fight with; four men, armed with sword and shield, would now come to fight with him until they slew him.

The third month was called Tozoztontli. On the first day of this month they celebrated the festival of the god called Tlaloc, who is the god of rain. At this feast they killed many children on the tops of hills, offering them in sacrifice to this god and his companions, so that they might give them water (rain).

Tozoztontli

On this festival they offered the first flowers that had come out that year at the Cú, called Yopico, and before they were thus offered, no one dared smell of a flower.

The officials (priests or guardians) of the flowers called Sochimanque made the festival to their goddess Coatlycue, or by another name Coatlantona.

In this month also those who were dressed in the skins of the dead they had flayed the previous month went to place them in a cave of the Cú called Topico. They went in procession with many ceremonies, and they smelled bad like dead dogs. After having left the skins there, they went to wash themselves with great ceremony. Some sick persons would make promises to be present at this procession in order to become cured, and they say that some did.

The owners of captives, with their entire household, did penance for twenty days, during which time they neither bathed nor did they wash themselves until (this should be "while") they wore the skins of the dead captives. In the above mentioned cave it is said they did penance for their dead captives.

After this penance was over they bathed and washed themselves, then invited all their relatives and friends, offering them meals, and they performed many ceremonies with the bones of the dead captives.

For all of those twenty days until the beginning of the following month, they rehearsed songs in the houses called cuicatlacalli; they did not dance, but remained seated, singing the praise of their gods. They performed a great many more ceremonies, all of which are described at length in the history of the gods, fol. 27.

The fourth month was called Veytocoztli (according to Clavijero Huytozoztli). On the first day of this month they celebrated the feast in honor of the god Cinteutl, who was regarded as the god of corn (maize). To honor him they fasted four days previous to the festival.

VEYTOCOZTLI

For this festival they put branches of reed-mace by the doors of their houses and sprinkled them with blood from their ears or from the shin-bone. (This might also mean the blackheads which draw blood when dug out.) The nobles and also the wealthy adorned their whole houses besides the reed-mace with branches or wreaths which are called acxoatl, and likewise they placed wreaths around the gods each one had in his house, and put flowers before them.

After this they went into the cornfields and brought back some cornstalks (which were still small), arranged them with flowers, and then went to put them in front of their gods in the oratory they call Calpulli. They also put food before them.

After having done this in the different city districts (wards) they went to the Cú (temple) of the goddess whom they called Chicomecoatl and there, in front of her, they represented sham battles, and all the girls carried ears of corn of the previous year on their backs and walked in procession up to the goddess to present them to her; then they took them back home with them as blessed objects. From this corn they gathered the seed for the following year's sowing. They also used such ears of corn as "hearts" of the corn bins, because they had been blessed. Of the dough called azoalli they made the image of this goddess in the court-yard of her Cú, and in front of this they placed as offerings all the different kinds of corn, of beans and of chian, the leaves of which are eaten as vegetables and the seeds are used for flavoring, like sesame, because they believed her to be the creator and giver of these things, which are the food-staples of these people.

According to reports of some people, they collected the children they sacrificed in the first month, buying them from their mothers and then killed them at all subsequent festivals until the rainy season came in full force. Thus they killed a few in the first month called Quavitleoa, others in the second called Tlacaxipeoaliztli, others in the third, Tozoztontli, and again some in the fourth, Veytocoztli. As a matter of fact, therefore, they crucified[1] children at all the festivals until the rainy season set in. They celebrated a great many other ceremonies at this feast.

The fifth month was Toxcatl, and on its first day they celebrated a big feast in honor of the god Titlacaoa, known by one other name as Tezcatlipoca, and whom they held to be the god of gods. In his honor they killed on the day of his festival a

---

[1] This no doubt should be "sacrificed" and not crucified.

chosen young man without a blemish on his body and who had
been kept in all the delights of life for a whole year, being instructed to play musical instruments, to sing and speak (recite).

Toxcatl

This was the principal festival of all. It was like Easter, and came
very close to the Christian Easter, perhaps a few days later. The
youth, educated as told above, was very well grown and chosen from
among many. He wore his hair long, as far down as his waist.

When they killed the youth whom they had maintained for a
whole year for this purpose, they at once chose another one who,
before being sacrificed one year hence, went through the whole
town very well dressed, with flowers in his hand, and accompanied by certain personalities (probably prominent people). He
would bow graciously to all whom he met, and they all knew he
was the image of Tezcatlipoca and prostrated themselves before
him, worshipping him wherever they met him. Twenty days
previous to the festival they gave this youth (who was to die)
four maidens, well prepared and educated for this purpose.
During these twenty days he had carnal intercourse with these
maidens. His clothes were changed when they first brought them
to him; they cut his hair as for a captain, and gave him some other
luxuries of dress.

Five days before he was to die they gave festivities for him,
banquets held in cool and gay places, and many chieftains and
prominent people accompanied him. On the day of the festival
when he was to die they took him to a Cú or oratory, which they
called Tlacuchcalco. Before reaching it, at a place called Tlapi-
tuoaian, the women (maidens) stepped aside and left him. As he
got to the place where he was to be killed, he mounted the steps
(staircase) by himself and on each one of these he broke one of
the flutes which he had played during the year. Once at the top
they threw him down onto the block and tore his heart out, then
brought his body down on their hands (arms); down at the foot
they cut the head from the trunk and impaled it on a pole called

Tzonpantli. Many other ceremonies were celebrated during this festival, all of which are described at length on fol. 53 of the Ms.

The sixth month was called Etzalcualiztli, and on its first day the festival to the gods of rain took place, and in order to honor them, the priests of their sanctuaries fasted for four days before the festival, that is to say, the four days of the previous month.

ETZALCUALIZTLI

To celebrate this festival, the Sátrapas (priests) of the idols first when to Citlaltepec for cypress, which grew very tall and very beautiful in a lagoon called Temilco, and from there they brought them to Mexico to adorn the Cús. All along the way nobody else showed himself; travelers on that road would hide for fear of those priests; if they happened to meet anyone they took everything he possessed from him, leaving him naked and should he attempt to defend himself, they so ill-treated him that they left him for dead, even if he was a man who carried the taxes for Mocthecuzuma, which they took from him. For all this they were never punished, because, being the priests (ministers) of the idols, they had complete liberty to do not alone thus, but even worse without fear of punishment. The temple priests celebrated a great many other ceremonies in the four days the festival lasted, all of which are fully described in the account of this celebration.

On the feast of Etzalcualitztli everybody made a sort of delicacy in the way of cooking which is called etzalli (delicate dish to taste) and everybody ate at home and gave to those who came in. A great many crazy things they would do on that day.

It was at this festival that all ministers (priests) of the gods who had committed some fault or other in their service were terribly punished in the waters of the lagoon, so much so that they left them almost dead on the bank near the water's edge; their parents or relatives took care of them, carrying them home more dead than alive.

During this month they killed a great many captives and slaves, dressed in the finery of these Tlalocs in whose honor they killed them, in their respective oratories, the Cús. The hearts of those they killed they threw into the whirlpool or sewer in the lagoon of Mexico, which then was clearly visible.

Many other ceremonies were celebrated.

The seventh month they called Tecuilhiutontli, and its first day was dedicated to the goddess of the salt, whose name was Vixtocioatl; they said that she was the oldest sister of the Tlalocs, and in her honor they killed (sacrificed) a woman dressed in the ornaments of the goddess.

TECUILHIUTONTLI

On the eve of that festival all the women, old and young, as well as young girls, danced and sang. They were holding on to short cords which they held in their hands, one holding one end and her neighbor the other. These cords were called xochimecatl; they all wore garlands of ascension flowers called iztahyatl, and were led by some old men who also led the singing. In their midst went the woman representing the image of the goddess in her finery and ornaments, and who was going to be sacrificed.

On the eve of the festival the women spent the night with the one that was to be sacrificed, singing and dancing all night. In the morning all the priests dressed in festive garb and performed a very solemn dance, and all those present carried in their hands the flowers called cempoalxochitl. Thus dancing, they led many captives to the Cú (temple) of Tlaloc, and with them the woman who was to be killed, representing the image of the goddess Vixtocioatl. In the Cú they first killed the captives and then the woman.

Many other ceremonies took place at this festival; there also was much drunkenness, all of which is described at length on fol. 76 (Sahagún Ms.).

Veytecuilhiutl was the eighth month, on the first day of which they celebrated a festival in honor of the goddess called Xilonem (goddess of the Xilotes). At this feast they fed the poor, men and women, the old of both sexes, boys and girls, to honor the goddess. On the tenth day of the month they killed a woman arrayed in the finery of the image they painted of Xilonem.

VEYTECUILHIUTL

They fed men and women, young and old, for eight continuous days previous to the feast. Very early in the morning they gave them to drink a sort of (thin) mush they call chiempinolli. Everyone drank as much as he liked. At noon they placed them all in their order in rows, seated, and then fed them (with) tamales.

The one who distributed these tamales would put into the hand of each one as many as he could hold in one hand, and if anyone misbehaved by taking twice they ill-treated him and took away those he had already taken, leaving him without any. This the lords (wealthy) did to console the poor, because at that time of the year there was generally a shortage of provisions (food staples). During all of these eight days there was general dancing, the men whirling around with the women, all of them attired in their very richest clothes and jewels; the women wore their hair loose, and thus, with it hanging down onto their shoulders, loose, they danced and sang with the men. They began this dance at sunset, dancing continuously until nine o'clock; they carried many torches of candlewood and there were furthermore many fires burning, lighted in the court itself where they were dancing. In this dance they crossed hands or else were in each other's arms, the arm of one around the shoulders of his partner, both, men and women alike. On the day before they killed the woman who was to be sacrificed to honor the goddess Xilonem, the women who attended her in her Cú (temple) and who were called Cioatlamacazque, danced in the court of the Cú, singing the songs in praise of the goddess; they surrounded the victim, who was dressed in the ornaments (insignia) of this goddess. Thus singing and dancing, they spent the night until daybreak of the day when she was to be sacrificed. At early dawn the nobles and the warriors held a dance in the same court, and the woman (victim) danced with them, together with many other women attired like her. The men danced in a group alone, in front, the women following after them. In that manner, dancing, they finally reached the Cú. They lifted her up the steps and once up there they cut her head off, then tore out her heart, offering it to the sun. Many other ceremonies took place at that festival.

The ninth month they called Tlaxochimaco, the first day of which was dedicated to the god of war, Vitzilopuchtli, offering him at that festival the first flowers of the year.

TLAXOCHIMACO

On the eve of that festival all were busy killing chickens and dogs to use their meat in making tamales and other things to eat. Then, very early on the day of the feast the priests serving the idols adorned the statue of Vitzilopuchtli with a great many flowers, and after that they adorned the statues or images of all the other gods with garlands, wreaths, and necklaces of flowers; then they did the same with the statues in the Calpules and Telpuchcales and in the houses of the Calpixques and of the principals (chieftains) and macehuales; in fact, everybody adorned the statues they had in their houses with flowers.

Once all the statues were thus adorned, they would begin to eat all those viands they had prepared on the previous night, and a little while after eating they commenced a special sort of dance, at which the noble men and women danced together, either holding hands or with their arms around each other's necks. They did not dance in their usual way, nor did they whirl and twist their bodies as in their ordinary dances, but went step by step to the sound of those who played the instruments and sang, and who were all standing a short ways apart from the dancers, near a round altar called mumuztli.

This singing lasted until night, not only in the courts of the Cús, but everywhere in all the houses of chiefs and macehuales they were playing music and singing with great shouts until night. The old men and women drank uctli, but no young man or maiden, and if any one did, they would be punished severely.

Many other ceremonies were held which are fully described in their proper place.

Xocohuetzi was the tenth month, and on its first day they celebrated the festival of the god of fire called Xiutecutli, or Ihcocauhui. At this celebration they threw many slaves, their feet and hands tied, alive into the fire, and before they were entirely dead, they pulled them out in order to tear out their hearts in front of the image of the god.

Xocohuetzi

During the festival to Tlaxochimaco they went into the woods to cut a tree of 25 fathoms (6 feet) in height and brought it—hauling or dragging it behind them to the court of the Cú of this god; there they pruned it completely and then raised it up and left it standing thus until the eve of the festival of Xocohuetzi, when they again felled it, being very careful that it should not get bruised, using many implements to prevent that. On the eve of the festival, very early in the morning, a number of carpenters would come with their implements, and they peeled it, making it very smooth. After having peeled it, they adorned it with many kinds of paper, then tied ropes and strings to it, raising it with big shouts and great noise, and moored it very well.

As soon as the pole or tree was raised and trimmed with all its ornaments, those who owned slaves whom they were to throw alive into the fire, dressed themselves in their rich vestments and plumes, painted their bodies yellow, which is the livery of the fire, and, taking their slaves with them, performed their dances during that entire day until nightfall.

After having watched over the captives (slaves) throughout the night in the Cú, and having performed many ceremonies with them, they powdered their faces with a powder called yiauchtli to make them lose consciousness and so would not feel their death so much. They now tied their feet and hands and thus tied, carried them on their backs, walking with this load as if they

were dancing, around a big fire and a large heap of live coal.
While they marched this way they thrust them into the live coal,
now one, then another one, and they let each one they had
thrown into the fire burn quite awhile, but while he was still alive
and nauseated and only partly overcome, they pulled him out
with any sort of a pothook or grapple and threw him onto the
slaughter-block (or sacrificial stone), and opening his breast, tore
out the heart. In this manner all these poor captives died. The
tree (or pole) was tied with many ropes at (or near) the top, like
the rigging of a ship that is hanging downward from the top
(sail?). At the top (of the pole) was fastened, standing up, the
image of that god Xiutecutli made of the dough which they call
tzoalli. After the sacrifice above mentioned, all the young men
attacked (one another) with great impetus. A great many other
events took place during this festival, as is described at length
elsewhere.

The eleventh month they call Ochpaniztli; on its first day they
celebrated a festival in honor of this goddess; they danced in
silence and also in silence they killed a woman dressed in the
manner of the image of this goddess.

Ochpaniztli

Five days previous to the beginning of this month, they stopped all
festivities and rejoicing of the past month. The first eight days of
Ochpaniztli they danced without singing and without playing the
teponaztli. After these eight days the woman representing the image
of Teteuinna appeared dressed in the ornaments of that image. With
her came a great number of women, especially the women healers
(doctors) and the midwives. They separated into two groups, fighting
one another by pelting each other with pellets of pachtli, also tuna-
leaves, and pellets made of reed-mace leaves and also flowers called
cempoatl-xuchitl. This rejoicing lasted four days.

After these and other similar ceremonies were over, they tried
to prevent the woman who was destined to die from knowing it,

in order to prevent her from crying or getting sad, for this they considered a bad omen. As soon as the night on which she was to die had come, they dressed her very richly, giving her to under-stand that she was being taken where a great lord (or chief) was to sleep with her. Amid great silence they took her to the Cú where she was to die. Arrived at the top a man lifted her on his back, her back to his, and they quickly cut her head off, then flayed her, and a strong youth dressed himself in her skin.

At once they took this youth who had put on the skin of the sacrificed woman with great solemnity and in company also of many captives to the Cú of Vitzilopuchtli. There, in front of this god, this youth tore the heart from four captives himself; the rest of them he left for the Sátrapas (priests) to kill.

In this month the chieftain of all the warriors passed muster of all the young men who had not gone to war yet. There were many other ceremonies celebrated at this festival, which can be read elsewhere in this history.

The twelfth month was called Teotleco, which means arrival of the gods. They celebrated this festival in honor of all the gods because they said these had gone to other parts. On the last day of the month they made a great feast because their gods had returned.

TEOTLECO

On the fifteenth day of this month the young men and boys en-wreathed all the altars and oratories of the gods as well as those within houses and the ones on roads and cross-roads, and for this work they were given corn as reward. Some gave them a chiquivitl full of corn, others a few ears.

On the eighteenth day Tlamatzincatl, the god who had re-mained a bachelor, also called Titlacaban, arrived. They said that on account of his being a bachelor and strong, he walked faster and therefore arrived first. They at once offered a meal in his Cú, and that night they all ate and drank and rejoiced, especially the old people; men and women drank wine (pulque) on the occasion of the god's arrival, saying that by so doing they washed his feet.

On the last day of this month they celebrated the big festival, for on that day, they pretended the gods were all returning. On the eve (of that day), at night, they placed on a straw mat (petate) a very compact little heap of stacked corn in the shape of a bone. On this heap the gods imprinted the sole of one foot as a sign that they had returned. All night the head-priest kept watch; he would come and go many times during his vigil to see whether the imprint was there.

As soon as he saw the sign of the foot, he would shout: "Our lord has arrived," and at once all the priests of the Cú (temple) would blow cornets (horns), shells, and trumpets, and all other instruments they had then. As soon as the people heard this music, they came to offer food at all the oratories and temples, and again they would rejoice, "washing the gods' feet," as mentioned above.

On the following day the old gods were arriving after all the others for they said that, as they were old, they could not walk quite so fast. For this day they gathered many of their captives to burn them alive. When the fire was so well started that there were heaps of live coal, certain young men, disguised as monsters and thus dancing around it, would throw those unfortunate captives (creatures) into the fire, as stated before. There were a good many other ceremonies to celebrate this day, all of which are fully described elsewhere.

The thirteenth month was Tepeilhuitl, in the course of which they honored all the prominent peaks all over this New Spain, around the summits of which clouds were wont to gather. The images they made of them were human in shape, fashioned of the dough they call tzoalli, and before these images they sacrificed, honoring in them the mountains they represented.

Tepeilhuitl

In honor of the mountains they made snakes of wood or roots of trees, fashioning the head like a snake's. They also cut thick pieces of wood about a wrist's length, calling them ecatolonti; these, as well as the wooden snakes, they covered with the dough tzoal and shaped them like mountains, making the top in the shape of a human head. Similar figures were made in memory of all those who had drowned or died (otherwise), only so they were not burnt but buried.

After having placed the above-mentioned images on their respective altars, amid great ceremonials they offered to them tamales and other food; furthermore, they sang songs in their praise and drank wine (pulque) in their honor.

When the festival in honor of the mountains commenced they killed four women and one man. The first one of these women was called Tepoxoch, the second one Matlalhue, the third Xochtecatl, and the fourth Mayabel. The man was called Milnaoatl. They dressed these women and the man in many papers covered with ulli (gum) and carried them in litters borne on the shoulders of richly dressed women to the place where they were going to kill them.

As soon as they were killed they would tear the hearts out and then let them slide slowly down the steps, and once down at the foot they cut their heads off and took the bodies to the house called Calpul, where they distributed the pieces of flesh for eating. The heads were impaled. The papers with which they had adorned the images of the mountains, after having broken these to pieces to eat them, they hung up in the Calpul. They celebrated a good many more ceremonies on that occasion, all of which are described at length in the corresponding chapters.

The fourteenth month is Quecholli; in this month the god called Miscoatl was feasted. This also was the month in which they made arrows and darts for their wars; they killed many slaves in honor of this god.

QUECHOLLI

When they made the arrows and darts during five days, they would also bleed themselves from the ears. The blood they thus squeezed out they smeared on their own temples, saying they did penance in order to hunt deer. They took the blankets away from all those who in that time failed to bleed themselves, as a punishment. No man slept with his wife during that time, nor did the old men and women drink pulque, because they did penance.

When the four (five?) days on which they made arrows and darts had passed they also made some very small arrows, tying them into fours, with every four torches, and thus, having made small bundles of four torches and four arrows each, they offered them on the graves of the dead, at the same time placing two tamales with each such bundle. This was left on the grave for a whole day. At night they then burned them. At this same festival they performed many other ceremonies in honor of the dead.

On the tenth day of that month all the Mexicans and Tlatelulcanos went to the mountain chain they call Cacatepec and which they say is their mother. That day they built xacales (huts) of straw and lodges, and built fires, but did nothing else.

At daybreak the following day they all ate breakfast and then went to the open country (fields), where they formed a great wing (made a wing-like move) and so closed in on a great many animals, deer, rabbits, and other game, closing the circle little by little until they had them all driven into close quarters and now each could attack and kill what he wanted.

After this hunt was over they killed captives and slaves in a Cú called Tlamatzinco, tying them hands and feet, and thus carrying them up the steps of the Cú (as if one carried a deer tied feet and hands to kill it), and then killed them amid great ceremonies. The man and the woman who represented the images of the god Mexcoatl[2] and his wife were also killed, but in another Cú called

---

[2] This is spelled both ways, Miscoatl and Mexcoatl and evidently both are accepted.

Miscoateupatl. There were many other ceremonies, at this festival, all of which are described, etc.

Panquetzaliztli they called the fifteenth month, and during this month they celebrated the festival of the god of war, Vitzilopuchtli. Previous to this festival the priests of the idols fasted for forty days and did other heavy (severe) penance, such as to go naked at midnight into the woods to gather bunches of flowers.

PANQUETZALIZTLI

On the second day of this month they began their dances and to sing the songs of Vitzilopuchtli in the court of his Cú (temple). Men and women danced together. They began these songs in the afternoon and finished about 10 o'clock. These songs and dances lasted for twenty days.

On the ninth day of the month they prepared, amid great ceremonies, all those they were going to kill, painting them in many colors and adorning them with a great many papers, and then danced with them. For this dance there were couples of men and women singing and dancing together.

On the sixteenth day of this month the owners of slaves began to fast and on the nineteenth they began a certain kind of dance in which all held hands, men and women, and in this manner danced winding and twisting about the court of the said Cú; certain old men played and sang while the others danced.

After those who were to die during this festival had gone through a number of ceremonies, Vitzilopuchtli descended from the Cú (temple), that is he, the god, was represented by a man, dressed in the ornaments and insignias of the god Paynal, and he killed four of those slaves (prepared for death) in the ball game which took place in the court called Teutlachtli; he then left and made the circuit of the entire city, running, and in a determined place in each quarter, he killed one slave. After that two parties began to fight sham battles, at which some of the fighters died.

Finally, after performing a number of ceremonies, they killed captives in the temple of Vitzilopuchtli, as well as many slaves. As soon as one had been killed, they played musical instruments; when the music ceased they killed another one, played again, and so forth till all of these poor victims had been put to death. Then they started to sing and dance, to eat and drink, and thus the festival ended.

The sixteenth month was called Atemoztli. In this month they celebrated festivals for the gods of rain, because for the greater part of this month thunderstorms came up and the rains began to show. The priests of the Tlalocs commenced to do penance and offer sacrifices to make the rains start.

ATEMOZTLI

When it started to thunder the priests at the service of the Tlalocs with great activity offered copal (incense) and other perfumes to the gods, and when they had tied their statues, they would say that then the gods are bound to come to give water to the people. They made promises to shape the images of the mountains, which they call tepictli, because those are dedicated to the gods of water. On the sixteenth day all the people prepared offerings to Tlaloc, and for four days they did penance, the men abstaining from intercourse with women, and these latter with men.

When the festival was due, on the last day of the month, they cut strips of paper which they tied or wound around long slender poles from the bottom upwards, and stuck these poles in the courtyards of their houses; they made the images of the mountains of tzoal (dough) with teeth of pumpkin seeds, eyes of a sort of bean called ayecotli, then offered them their offerings (gifts) of food, worshipping them.

After keeping vigil, playing musical instruments and singing, they cut their breasts (of the idols) with a tzotzopaztli, which is an implement used by the women for weaving, almost like a cutlass, and took out their hearts,[3] cut off their heads, and then distributed the body among themselves and ate it; the ornaments

---

[3] I.e., the innermost part of the dough-image where the heart would be.

with which they had bedecked them they burned in the courts of their houses.

After this was done, they gathered all the ashes, all the apparatus (the poles, etc.) with which they had worshipped, to the oratories called ayauhcalco, and then started to eat and drink and rejoice, and thus ended the festivity. Other ceremonies celebrated on this occasion may be found in the corresponding place of their history.

Tititl was the seventeenth month. In this month they celebrated the feast of a goddess called Tlamatecutli,[4] and by another name Tona, and still another Coscamiauh. In her honor they killed a woman. After having torn out her heart they cut her head off and held a (special) dance with it. The leader (in that dance) carried the head by its hair in his right hand, making the dance steps.

Tititl

The woman they killed at this festival was dressed in all the ornaments and clothes of the goddess whose image she represented, and whom they called Ylamatecutli, by another name Tona, which means "our mother." Donned in all this finery, she had to dance alone to the music some old men played, and while she danced she sighed and cried, remembering that she was to die. After midday the priests, dressed in the ornaments of all the gods, went ahead of her, making her go up to the Cú (temple) where she was to die. They threw her on the stone block (sacrificial stone) and tore out her heart and cut her head off, which at once one of the priests dressed like a god, took by the hair and danced with it at the head of all the rest. And he who thus carried the head in his right hand led the dance, making the dance steps with it in his hand.

On the same day they killed this woman the priests of the idols executed certain skirmishes and rejoicing, running after one another up and down the steps of the temple, performing certain ceremonies at the same time.

[4] Tlamatecutli, also Ylamatecutli and Yllamatecutli.

On the following day all the people made bags like pouches with cords of an arm's length attached to them. They inflated these bags and filled them with something soft like wool, then took them, hidden under their blanket (manta) and, once on the street and meeting a woman, hit her with this bag in fun; this game was so popular that the boys, too, made their bags and with them then mauled the girls till they made them cry.

As may be seen in the historical part of this work, there were a good many other ceremonies performed on this festival.

The eighteenth month was called Yzcalli, and it was the month dedicated to festivals to the god of fire called Xiuhtecutli Opecauhqui. In his honor they made an image which seemed to throw out flames of fire by itself. Every four years at this same festival they killed captives and slaves in honor of this god, and also perforated the ears of all the children born within these four years, and gave them godfathers and godmothers.

Yzcalli

On the tenth day of this month, at midnight, they went to obtain new fire in front of the image of Xiuhtecutli, very neatly adorned. Once the fires were all lighted, there came in the morning young men and boys with diverse animals they had hunted in the past few days, some from the water, others from land, and offered them to the old men whose duty it was to guard this god. These latter threw all the animals into the fire to roast them, and to the young men and boys they gave each a tamale made of wild amaranth, which they called vauhquiltamalli, which all the people offered on that day, and which they all ate in honor of the festival. They ate them very hot; and they drank and rejoiced.

During the usual celebration of this feast every year they did not kill anyone; they made human sacrifices only on the bissextile years, that is, every four years captives and slaves were sacrificed. The image of Xiuhtecutli was adorned with a great many precious and curious ornaments. Upon the death of these (victims) they performed many and very solemn ceremonies, far more so than at any other festival of the year, as it is explained in their history.

After having killed these slaves and captives and the image of Yzcocauhqui, who is the god of fire, all the chiefs and lords and illustrious personages and even the emperor himself were richly dressed and adorned with precious ornaments, and they held a dance of great solemnity and gravity, which they called netecuitotiliztli, which means "dance of the lords." This dance was only held every four years at this feast. Very early on this same day even before dawn, they started perforating the ears of the boys and girls, and they put a helmet on their heads made of parrotfeathers glued on with ocutzotl, which is pine-resin.

The five remaining days of the year, which are the four last days of January and the first of February, they called Nemontemi, which means "idle" (useless) days, and they considered them as unfortunate (unlucky). It is supposed that they perforated the ears of children every four years on account of these five days of nemontemi, which tally with our bissextile day in leap year.

They said that all who were born in these five days, which they considered unlucky, had to suffer many misfortunes in everything and were (always) poor and miserable; they called them neme; if they were men they were called Nemoquich, if women Nencioatl. They did no work in those days because they were considered unlucky, and they especially refrained from quarreling, because they said that anyone who quarreled in those days acquired the habit; it was also thought bad luck to stumble in those days.

The above mentioned feasts were permanent, that is, they always occurred in the respective month, with a difference of a day or two. The others were mutable, and were celebrated in the course of the twenty signs which completed their circuit of 260 days, and for this reason these feasts would occur one year in one month, another year in another, and if they came together they would somehow shift them around.

ABOUT THE MUTABLE (MOVABLE) FEASTS

1. The first movable feast was celebrated in honor of the sun, when it was in the sign of Ceocelutl, in the fourth house called Naolin. During this feast they offered to the image of the sun quail; they burned incense, and in the center of the house they killed captives in front of the image and in its honor. On that same day they all, big and small, drew blood from their ears, to honor the sun, offering that blood as a sacrifice.

2. Under this same sign, all the painters made their festival in the seventh house, and the washwomen fasted forty days, the painters another twenty in order to attain good luck to paint well or to do good weaving on their blankets or other work in hand. For this purpose they offered quail and incense; the men performed certain ceremonies for the god Chicomexochitl, and the women for the goddess Xochiquetzatl.

3. Under the third sign, Cemacatl, they celebrated a festival in the first house, in honor of the goddesses called Cisapitliti, because they said that then these goddesses would come down to earth. They dressed their images with papers and offered gifts.

4. Under the sign called Cemecatl they celebrated a great festival in the second house called Ometochtli, in honor of Yzquitecatl, who is the second god of wine, and not only for him but for all the gods of the wine, who were many. They adorned his statue very well in his Cú, offering him all sorts of food, and they sang and played before him. They placed a very large jar of pulque in the court of his Cú (temple), and the innkeepers (also meant for those who brew it) kept on filling it to overflow; all those who wished to went there to drink. The innkeepers had their (own) cups for drinking, and they continued filling the jar so that it was always full. This was especially done by those who had cut the maguey plant anew. The first honey-water (agua miel) which they obtained they carried to the temple of this god as offering of first-fruits.

5. Under the sign called Cexóchitl, the chieftains and lords prepared a great festival in the first house, where they danced and

sang in honor of that sign. There were other sorts of rejoicing, and they wore on that occasion the choicest plumes for the dance. During this festival the lord (king or chief) granted favors to the warriors, the singers, and the employees of the palace.

6. Under the sign called Ceacatl the lords and chieftains offered a big feast, in the first house, to Quetzalcoatl, god of the winds. This celebration was prepared in the house called Calmecac, which is where the priests of the idols lived and where boys were educated. In this house, which was like a monastery, was placed the image of Quetzalcoatl, which they adorned with beautiful ornaments for that festival, offering perfumes and food before it. They said that the sign Ceacatl was Quetzalcoatl's sign.

7. Under the sign of Cemiqueztli the chieftains and lords offered a great festival in the first house to Tezcatlipoca, who was the great god and they said that the above was his sign. As they all had their private oratories in their houses, where they also kept the image of this god among many others, on this day they adorned the image and offered to it perfumes and flowers and food, and they sacrificed quail in front of it, tearing their heads off. This was not only done by the chieftains and prominent people, but by everybody who knew about this feast. It was also celebrated in the calpules as well as in the Cús (temples). They all prayed, asking favors of this god, for he was their omnipotent lord.

8. Under the sign of Cequiavitl they celebrated the festival in honor of the goddesses they call Cioapipilli, in the first house. These goddesses were said to be the women who died giving birth to their first child. They became goddesses, they said, and lived in the house of the sun, and that at the time the sign above mentioned came around they descended to earth, and inflicted diverse diseases on all those they found away from their homes. Oratories in honor of these goddesses were erected in all such city wards that had two streets and called them Cioateucalli or Cioateupan. Here they kept the images of these goddesses, which they adorned for their festival with papers which they called amateteuitl. On the feast of these goddesses and in their honor

they killed those condemned to death for some crime or other, and who were kept in their prisons.

9. Under the sign called Cequiavitl they killed, in the fourth house, Nauhecatl, which was the house of very bad luck, all criminals (evil doers) who were in prison, and the chieftain also ordered slaves to be killed for the sake of superstition. All the merchants and traders made exhibits of the jewels in which they were dealing, displaying them so that everyone might see them and after this, that same night, they ate and drank. They would take flowers and tubes of perfume, seat themselves in their places, and then begin in turn to brag about their earnings and about the far away places they had reached (in their travel), and at the same time look down upon others who were (timid) and did not have as much as they, nor had traveled to such remote countries. This all gave rise to much fun among them, and lasted the greater part of the night.

10. Under the sign they called Cemallinalli they prepared a great festival in the second house called Umecoatl, because they said that this sign belonged to Tezcatlipoca. For this festival they made the image of Omacatl and anyone who was a devotee of this image carried it to his house, that the latter might be blessed and his property be increased, and if such blessings came to him, he kept the image, and was loath to let it go back (to the temple). To the contrary, if he wished the image to be put back where it belonged, he waited till this same sign came around again, and then carried the image back whence he had taken it.

11. Under the sign called Cetecpatl they took out of the first house all the ornaments of Vitzilopuchtli; they cleaned and dusted them and put them in the sun for, they said, this was his sign and the one of Camaxtle; this was the way the Hacatecos celebrated. Here (in Mexico) they cooked a great many different dishes, deliciously prepared as they are eaten by the chieftains, and they placed them all in front of his image. After they had remained there a little while, the officers (priests) of Vitzilopuchtli took them and, distributing them among themselves, they ate them; they also burned incense in front of the image and

offered it quail, which they beheaded before it, so that the blood might be spilled before the god. The chieftain or lord offered also all the beautiful flowers which are worn by the lords and chiefs, to the image.

12. They said that under the sign of Ceocumatli the goddesses called Cioapipilli descended to earth and injured the (small) children, boys and girls, afflicting them with palsy, so that if a child fell ill at that time (of the year) they immediately blamed it on the Cioapipilli. They had such great fear of the power of these goddesses that parents would not allow their children to go out during that period, to prevent their meeting them.

13. Under the sign of Ceytzeuintli, which they said was the sign of fire, they celebrated a great festival in honor of Xiuchtecutli, god of the fire, offering him great quantities of copal, and a large number of quails. They adorned his image with many kinds of paper, and with a great deal of rich ornaments. Among the wealthy people and those in power great festivities were held in their own homes, in honor of the fire, and they also prepared reunions and banquets. Under this sign solemn elections of chiefs and consuls were held and were celebrated in the fourth house of this sign with feasts, dances and gifts. After these celebrations were over, they immediately declared war on their enemies.

14. Under the sign called Ceatl they celebrated the feast of the goddess of the water in the first house of that sign. Her name was Chalchiuhtliycue, and festivities in her honor were celebrated by all those who derived their livelihood from the water, either by selling it, or in fisheries and any other trade they could secure with aquatic products. All such traders adorned her image during this festival, worshipped her, and made offerings in the house (oratory) called Calpulli.

15. The lords and chieftains, the nobles, and the wealthy merchants, were very careful in watching the sign, day and hour, under which a son or daughter was born to them, and they immediately went to inform the judicial astrologers of it, and to ask them about the good or bad fortune the new-born babe might have. If the sign was propitious, they had the child baptized at

once, and if it was adverse, they selected the most prosperous house of that sign where to baptize it. To this baptismal feast they invited their relatives and friends to be present at the christening, and gave them to eat and drink, and also asked all the children of the district (ward) where they lived. Baptism took place at sunrise in the house of the parents, and was performed by the midwife pronouncing many orations (prayers) and making a number of ceremonies over the child. This same festival is in usage today when their children are christened as far as it concerns invitations, eating and drinking.

16. As soon as parents considered that their son was of a marriageable age, they informed him that they wished to look for a wife for him, and he would thank them for their thoughtfulness and the care they took in getting him married. They at once spoke to the principal, whom they called Telpuchtlato, who was in charge of the youths, informing him that they wanted to marry their son, and asking him to approve of it. To this end they invited him and all the young men he had in his care, and, after having given them all food and drink, they made a speech. First they placed a hatchet for cutting down trees or splitting firewood before him. This hatchet was a sign that the youth was now taking leave of his companions because his parents wished him to marry; and so the Telpuchtlato left fully satisfied. After this, the parents chose the woman they were to give their son, and at once called the marriage-makers (match-makers) who were honest old women arbiters (mediators), and they were to go and speak to the parents of the girl. They went twice or three times to speak, and brought back the answer. In the meantime, the relatives of the girl conferred among themselves whether they were to give her to the youth, and then gave their consent to the marriage-makers. After this they looked for a very lucky day under a propitious sign, i.e., either the sign of Acatl, Ocumach, Cipactli, or Quauchtli. When any one of these was chosen the parents of the youth announced the date of the marriage to the girl's parents. They at once began preparations necessary for the

ceremony, food and drink as well as blankets and "cañas de humo" (hollow canes with incense in them), and many other things. Then they invited the chieftains and whoever else they wanted to have at the wedding. After the dinner, at which many speeches and other ceremonials were held, those of the bridegroom's house went to bring the bride from her home; this was done at night. She was conducted amid great solemnity, carried on the back by a matron. Ahead of her were carried two files of lighted torches. Around her, in front and back of her, went a great many people, until she reached the house of the groom's parents. There they placed the couple together close to the hearth, which was always in the center of a hall (large room), with a bright fire, the woman on the left of the man; the mother of the groom now clothed her daughter-in-law in a very beautiful "vipil" (sleeveless blouse), and placed close at her feet some very elaborate skirts, while the girl's mother covered her son-in-law with a very elegant blanket, fastening it on his shoulder, while at his feet she put an elaborate maxtli.[5] This done, certain old women whom they call titici tied a corner of the young man's blanket to the skirt of the girl's garment. Thus ended the wedding ceremonies, with a great many complements of food, drink, dances, executed afterwards, as is fully described in the corresponding chapter.

They had two more festivals which at times were at fixed dates, at times movable. They belonged to the latter class on account of their recurring every so many years, one being celebrated every four, the other every eight years. They could be called fixed because they had year, month and day positively designated; at the festival recurring every four years they perforated children's ears and held the ceremony of what they called "crespa," which means arrange (trim) the hair of children and teach them the handling of fire. The eight-year festival meant fasting for eight days previous with bread and water; they also held a dance at this feast, for which they dressed in the images or

[5] Maxtli—girdle or belt.

likeness of high personages, of birds, or other animals, saying that by so doing they searched for good luck, as we have explained it in the appendix of Book II.

As it happens with us, these movable feasts sometimes occurred on dates of feasts of their calendar.

THE ISLANDS OF TITICACA
AND KOATI

By ADOLPH F. BANDELIER

THE INDIANS
OF THE ISLAND OF TITICACA

Few, if any, of the present inhabitants of the Island of Titicaca
are direct descendants of the Indians who occupied it at the time
of the conquest. After Pizarro had established himself at Cuzco in
the latter part of 1533, he sent, early in December of that year,
two Spaniards to reconnoiter the Lake region, of which he had
already heard. The two scouts remained absent forty days and
returned with the following information:

"The two Christians that were sent to see the province of the
Collao delayed forty days on their journey, from which they
returned to the city of Cuzco, where the Governor was. They
gave him an account and report of everything they had learned
and seen, as will be related below. The country of the Collao is
distant, and far away from the ocean, so much so, that the natives
inhabiting it have no knowledge of it (the sea). The land is very
high, somewhat level and, besides, unusually cold. There are no
trees, nor is there any firewood, and what of the latter they may
use, is gotten by them in exchange of goods with those who dwell
near the sea called Ingri, and reside also along the rivers in the
lowland, where the country is warm; and *they* have firewood.
From these they obtain it against sheep and other animals and
vegetables; for the rest of the country is sterile, so that all sustain
themselves on roots of plants, on herbs, maize, and some little

From *The Islands of Titicaca and Koati* by Adolph F. Bandelier, The
Hispanic Society of America, 1910, pp. 1–127. (Footnotes and most illustrations deleted.)

meat. There are in this province of the Collao many sheep, but the people are so submissive to the lord to whom they owe obedience that, without his permission or that of the principals or governors that are in the country by his command, none are killed, and not even the lords and caciques venture to slaughter and eat any, unless it be with his license. The country is well settled because it is not destroyed through war as are the other provinces. Their settlements are of moderate size and the houses small, with walls of stone coated with earth (clay), and thatched with straw. The grass that grows in that country is sparse and short. There are a few streams, but small ones.

"In the middle of the province is a big lake about a hundred leagues in size nearly, and around this lake is the most peopled country. In the center of the lake are two small islands, in one of which is a mosque temple and house of the sun, which is held in great veneration, and in it they go to present their offerings and perform their sacrifices on a large stone that is on the island, called Thichicasa, which, either because the devil conceals himself there and speaks to them, or because it is an ancient custom as it is, or for some other reason that has never been found out, they of the whole province hold in great esteem and offer to it gold and silver. There are [on this Island] more than six hundred Indian attendants of this place, and more than a thousand women, who manufacture Chicca [chicha] to throw it on this rock."

After this first hasty visit by the Spaniards (either late in December, 1533, or in the first days of January, 1534), it is not impossible that Titicaca as well as Koati were abandoned by the Indians of Inca descent. Cieza states: "On large islands that are in the lake they (the Indians living on the shore) plant their crops and keep their valuables, holding them to be safer there than in the villages along the road." This was in 1549, fifteen years after the first visit.

What transpired during these fifteen years is vaguely indicated by various sources. Thus the name of the first Spaniard who visited the Island is given as Illescas, an officer of Pizarro. It is not clear, however, if Illescas was one of the first two explorers or whether he commanded a larger party sent *afterward* to seize the gold and silver supposed to have accumulated on the Island. A modern source, claiming to base on the earliest manuscript information, asserts that a visit to Copacavana was made by Gonzalo Pizarro in 1536, and that, on that occasion, the Indians were apportioned according to the system of "Encomiendas." If any reliance could be placed on the source alluded to, Diego de Illescas would have been at Copacavana in 1536, in company with Belalcazar and Pedro Anzurez de Campo-redondo, but it is well known that Belalcazar was in Ecuador at the time, and that Anzurez returned to South America in 1538!

In 1536 the Spaniards were blockaded at Cuzco by the Indians for ten months. Hence, while it might be barely possible that a small detachment had stayed on the lake, cut off from communication with Gonzalo and Hernando Pizarro, but on friendly terms with the Aymará Indians, it is very doubtful. No mention is made of it in any contemporaneous document at my command.

A work of considerable importance on Peruvian antiquities, but written more than a century after the conquest, by the Jesuit Father Bernabé Cobo, contains the statement that Francisco Pizarro sent three Spaniards to the Lake to visit the Island and take from it a statue, half gold and half silver, which they are said to have brought to Cuzco. If this is true, it must have happened *subsequent* to the *first visit*, else it would have been alluded to in the report from 1534. Nevertheless, Cobo favors the (then general) belief that the main ceremonial objects were, upon the coming of the Spaniards, concealed or thrown into the Lake. The Augustine Fray Alonzo Ramos, who was a resident of Copacavana at the same time as Cobo, but wrote fully thirty years before him, states: "To what we have already said about [the temple of] Titicaca we shall add that it was the most frequented one in the realm and with great riches, which, according to common belief, the Indians threw into the Lake when the first Spaniards entered the Island with the captain Illescas." Vizcarra affirms in regard to the Island of Koati: "And when the Captains Alzures [Anzures] and the Illescas, with the Franciscan Fathers, came to the peninsula [Copacavana], although they attempted it in 1536, they could not reach it [Koati] from lack of time, and because they thought it was, as well as that of the sun [Titicaca], deserted and waste." After the blockade of Cuzco had been raised and the bloody dissensions between Almagro and Pizarro terminated through the death of the former, Francisco Pizarro himself came to Cuzco in 1538, while his brothers Hernando and Gonzalo invaded the Collao with the avowed intention, says the treasurer Manuel de Espinall, of going to an island called "Titicacao," said to contain much gold and silver. Their attempt seems to have failed, for the younger Almagro, in his accusation against Pizarro (1541) accuses Hernando Pizarro of an attempt to hunt for the treasure *in the Lake*, in which attempt ten Spaniards were drowned! It shows that five years after the first visit the gold and silver believed to have existed at the shrines of Titicaca and Koati were already looked for in the waters of the lagune and *not* any more on the Islands. I am loath to admit as yet that any visit was made to the Islands between 1534 and 1538, and incline to the belief (until otherwise informed) that the *Quichua* attendants of the shrines, after secreting the principal fetishes, abandoned both isles, the Aymará Indians alone remaining. What the first Spanish explorers of Titicaca reported on the numbers of its Indian occupants (1600) must be taken with due reserve.

It appears, therefore, that the Islands were occupied, as a place of worship mainly, at the time of the conquest, and long previous, but that a part of the population abandoned it very soon after the first visit by the Spaniards. Information concerning the Island from times anterior to 1533 rests, of course, exclusively on tradition.

In 1550 Pedro de Cieza finished the first part of his valuable *Crónica del Perú*, in which he mentions folklore to the effect that "white men" with long and flowing beards had "once upon a time" inhabited Titicaca and were exterminated by (Aymará) Indians from the Collao. A contemporary of Cieza, and, like him, a soldier—Pedro Gutierrez de Santa Clara—has preserved what he claims to be genuine Indian lore, according to which the inhabitants of the Island, many centuries prior to the sixteenth, invaded the mainland and established themselves at Hatun-Colla, near Puno. According to the same source, the Inca tribe were originally Islanders and made war on the people of Cuzco, which warfare began about in the fourteenth century. I merely allude here to these very uncertain tales, having to treat of them in another chapter of this monograph and with greater detail. The same is the case with the (much better founded) statements concerning the occupation of the Island by the Inca, in the latter half of the fifteenth century, which will be discussed in the archaeological sections. Suffice it to mention here that at the time when the Inca first visited the Island they found it inhabited by Aymará of the Lupaca branch, or rather, who spoke the Lupaca dialect of the Aymará idiom. It seems that these were partly driven to the mainland, while some Quichua and a number of women established themselves, or were established, around the shrine and at other sites, chiefly for ceremonial purposes.

After the Spaniards had become complete masters of northern Bolivia, in 1538, it becomes difficult to trace the condition of the Island until the end of the century. On the map made by order of the Viceroy Don Francisco de Toledo in 1573 (herewith published) the "Embarcadero," or place where people from the Peninsula of Copacavana were wont to embark in order to cross over to Titicaca Island, is indicated; hence it may be the Island was inhabited at the time. From the same time (1571–1574) Juan Lopez de Velasco, cosmographer royal, conveys the information (obtained at second or third hand) that in the "great lagune of Chucuito, in the language of the Indians *Titicaca*," there are "many islands peopled by natives, who navigate it in their canoes and plant their crops on the islands, and keep in them, guarded as in a stronghold, the most precious things they have; and so, anciently, in the time of the Incas, there was a temple of the sun, great and very rich." While the Count de la Gomera was Governor of Chucuito (end of the sixteenth and beginning of the seventeenth century) he caused "all the uncultured Indians to be removed from the islands." Whether this measure was limited to the islands in the vicinity of Chucuito or whether it was also extended to Titicaca and Koati is not certain. At the close of the sixteenth century the Dominican Fray Gregorio Garcia, a resident of Peru and Bolivia for a number of years, describes the islands as deserted, which might indicate that they were depopulated under pressure of official measures. On the other hand, the Augustine Antonio de la Calancha, about thirty years later, published: "On the islands which its archipelago embraces, and especially on the largest one of Titicaca, there are great numbers of Indians, either as fugitives from the Doctrine, or on account of being troubled by the Corregidores and Caciques, or as fishermen for their own sustenance, and not a few of them in order to continue in their idolatrous practices." Thus, although the Island may have been abandoned for a number of years, at the close of the sixteenth and in the beginning of the seventeenth century, it was reoccupied afterward by Indians, but there seem not to have been any white settlers on it until the eighteenth century, or perhaps later. I have as yet been unable to find out if the Island was inhabited at the time of the great uprising of 1780.

The historical notices presented above are meager, but they indicate that few, if any, direct descendants of the Indians who occupied Titicaca in the early part of the sixteenth century can be looked for on the Island to-day. While the great majority of the Islanders are to-day Aymará by language, and regard themselves as such, it is not unlikely that Quichua, even Uro, and perhaps Chachapoyas elements are mixed with them, and the statement of the actual owners of Titicaca, that its present Indian population is of comparatively modern origin and has settled on it from various places, should not be lost sight of.

While the women on the Island are usually of the low stature of other female Indians, there are among them some of middle height and more slender than, for instance, the Pueblo Indian women of New Mexico. Among the men there are some tall and well formed figures, with pleasant faces; many are of low stature and have sinister countenances. It is not unusual to meet an Indian with a remarkably low forehead and abnormally elongated skull.

It is known that flattening of the forehead was carried on for at least half a century after the Spanish authorities had peremptorily forbidden the practice.

The Indians, not only of this Island but of the Puna in general, are rather a hardy race. Nevertheless, diseases are as frequent among them as among ourselves. With us, care is taken to keep the upper extremities of the body cool and the feet especially warm. The Aymará Indian goes barefooted, trudges for hours, nay for whole days, in the ice-cold waters of the Lake up to the knees, while on the head he carries a pointed woolen cap with earlaps drawn down, and a hat over that cap. Over his shirt or jacket he wears a poncho, more or less thick and more or less ragged and dirty, that reaches, when very long, as far as the knees. Thus only the upper part of the body is protected and the feet are bare. It is true that their feet gradually obtain a natural protection through the skin being thickened and hardened by constant exposure. Usually, the Indian wears a sandal of leather. Shoes or gaiters are worn only on festive occasions and are quite clumsy. The soles are about an inch in thickness, the heels three inches high, the uppers thick, often decorated with painted rivets and strings, and in the soles are ponderous nails with rounded heads. This festive foot-gear of the Aymará presents a striking but not graceful appearance.

The Aymará of Titicaca, and probably the whole tribe, suffer from colds, coughs and lung diseases. Protracted exposure to the cold waters, such as a long voyage on the Lake during stormy weather in an unprotected balsa, produces sometimes an ailment which we successfully cured with nitrate of potash. Skin diseases we found to be common on the Island. During our stay Mrs. Bandelier was besieged by men, women, and children begging for relief from what they erroneously call itch. All our supply of Peruvian balsam became exhausted, for, if applied together with sulphur, the treatment was invariably successful. This contagious disease began to show itself at the end of January, and by the middle of March over thirty of both sexes and all ages had been cured. It is certain that smallpox and measles occur, although we had no cases during our stay there. It is equally true that the former, especially, makes the same havoc among the Indians of Titicaca as among northern tribes. A number of less dangerous diseases have come under our observation and have usually yielded to the contents of our medicine chest, specially prepared at Lima. For consumption down to toothache, nearly the entire scale has been represented. A very common ailment is indigestion, produced by a happy combination of coarse food and excess of alcoholic liquids. Beside exposure to cold and moisture, the mode of living is the chief cause of the ailments to which these people are subjected. Their houses are mostly of stone, the more or less shaped blocks being laid in common adobe mud. They are usually of one room only, and I noticed the same distribution of the home into three buildings or more, which I had previously noted among the Indians of central and southern Mexico. A residence usually consists of at least three small rectangular and thatch-roofed buildings, each with its door and without any windows. One of these buildings is the kitchen, another is officially regarded as the dormitory, and there are one or more storehouses. This arrangement prevails in the Bolivian as well as in the Peruvian Puna. Around Juliaca and up the valley toward Ayaviri the numerous dwellings of the aborigines, each surrounded with several outhouses of almost the same size and shape, are scattered over the level expanse like so many tiny hamlets.

Living in close, low, and usually very filthy abodes is not hygienic. Furniture is limited to the most primitive. Instead of a bedstead, there is a so-called "gallo," or bench, made of adobe. On this bench the ponchos of the inmates are spread, and there they sleep, sometimes with a straw mat under the poncho. Not unfrequently the dormitory is united with the cooking-place, and then the family shares the room with numerous guinea-pigs, domestic fowl, or dogs, and even with swine of tender age.

In the kitchen of the hacienda buildings at Challa there dwelt the "Unya-siri," or Indian warden of the house, with his consort, a number of guinea-pigs, two white rabbits, and an occasional chicken. Chairs are not common, but still they are found and are invariably, as well as the tables, of the low kind so common ten years ago among the Pueblo Indians of New Mexico.

In the house of our "compadre" at Kea-kollu, where we spent a number of "picturesque" days, a table had been built with two ponderous stone slabs supporting a heavy stone plate. Such a home is not without some attempts at decoration. The walls have niches, and these niches sometimes contain a carved image and a few modest flowers. A saucer containing fat stands before the object of worship, and a burning wick timidly protrudes from the vessel. Crucifixes are not rare, although not generally displayed. Painted images we do not remember to have seen in Indian homes on the Island. It lies so utterly "out of the world!"

The valuables of the Indian are stored, or hidden away rather, in the store-rooms, and it is more than indiscreet to attempt to enter one of these. Hence a store-room is only known to us from the outside, or as far as the casually opened door permitted, in which case one or more of the family would surely block the way as thoroughly as possible. Mistrust is one of the leading traits of Aymará character, a mistrust which is partly the consequence of frequent abuses committed by political and ecclesiastical authorities. It is also due in part to the possible concealment, in such places, of objects of ancient worship and especially of sorcery. I would say here that the Aymará Indian is as mistrustful of his own people as he is of a stranger.

The kitchen furniture reduces itself to a hearth of clay, called "kere," provided with a firehole, and one or more holes on which to place cooking vessels. There are no chimneys or flues in Indian houses. As the brushwood is often green, or the substitute of táquia is used, the dingy place becomes filled with a pungent smoke injurious to the eyes. The cooking vessels are of clay mostly; an iron kettle or pan is regarded as a first-class treasure and stolen from the unsophisticated stranger as often as possible. The pottery is not made on the Island but at various places of the Puna, as, for instance, at Ancoraymes, on the northern shore of the Lake; and it is bought either at the Copacavana fairs or on an occasional voyage by balsa to that village or to Achacache. It may be said that the kitchen and household furniture of the Islanders, and inhabitants of the Puna in general, display the same combination of ancient and modern as that of the sedentary Indians of the southwestern United States and of Mexico, the preponderance being slightly in favor of modern implements. Ancient vessels are occasionally met with, but they are seldom well cared for. It is chiefly the larger jars that are preserved for the storing of grain and for the preservation of chicha.

The most important household utensil, from ancient times, is the grinding slab with its grinder, both of stone, called in common parlance, and in Peru and Bolivia, the *batán*. Father Cobo says of this indispensable utensil: "For grinding their corn and bread they have in their houses smooth and broad slabs on which they pour out a small quantity only, and when that is ground, as much again. They grind it by placing on this slab a stone made in the shape of a half-moon, about two palms in length and one in width, not round, but somewhat elongated, with three or four inches of edge. They take hold of the horns with their hands and, lowering and lifting alternately the arms, move it edgewise from one side to the other over the maize, and by means of this labor and difficulty grind it, as well as anything else, although now most of them use our mills. This instrument we have called batán . . . but the Indians call it 'maray,' naming the lower stone 'callacha' and the upper 'tanay.' "

The batán, whether ancient or modern, has nothing of the elaborateness of the "metate" used in Mexico and adjacent countries. It is simply a ponderous slab, unadorned and seldom even roughly shaped. Any suitable flat rock is selected for the purpose, but by preference an ancient batán is taken from some neighboring ruin. The crusher is usually a small oval boulder, picked up among the drift. Whereas the metate is worked on the incline, the batán is used in a horizontal position and indiscriminately for grinding red pepper, maize, dried meat, and quinua, or coffee when the latter can be procured. Mortars, ancient as well as modern (the latter manufactured at Viacha out of white stone), some with pestles and others with simply a rounded pebble, are frequently met with, and are used for grinding herbs and other condiments.

An Indian kitchen containing the hearth, several "galos," pots and pans, brushwood or táquia, and the batán, and occupied by a number of human beings, a colony of guinea-pigs, a dog or two, and the like, is one of the most crowded places on the globe.

Indian architecture in the Sierra, hence on the Island also, displays a marked tendency to exclusion of fresh air. The doors are not only low but even the sill is raised. Windows there are none, hence light is excluded as well as air, unless the door be open. I must say, however, that the same is the case in most of the hacienda buildings on the Puna. The rooms are much more spacious than those in Indian abodes and the ceilings higher, but the windows have no panes; they are closed with rude shutters, and he who must work during the day in these apartments has to open the door and sit in the humid cold, muffled in vicuña blankets and overshoes (if he has any), in order to be able to write or draw.

The constant cold prevailing in these regions is the main reason for excluding air, from the houses of the aborigines as well as from those of the better classes. Against this chilly air there is no way of protection, since there is no timber, hence no clean combustible, in the land. Both the Indian and the white are driven out of the house into sunshine, if there is any, and as long as it lasts. Should it be a rainy day, or at night, crowding is the only way for the Indian to obtain warmth, and if to that crowding the additional heat of a close kitchen can be added, life is rendered at least supportable. Leaving the door open, to let out the smoke or from force of habit, the Indian family agglomerates, either in the dark or by the dim light of a rare tallow dip until one after the other falls asleep. Usually the door of the dormitory is closed at night but rarely locked, although the doors of store-rooms are fastened. Then everybody slumbers, men, women, girls and children, on "gallos," on ponchos, covered or uncovered, but never undressed. The Indian sleeps to-day very much as Cobo describes it from early times: "Everywhere they sleep in the same clothes in which they go about in the daytime, except that the males take off the *Yacolla* and the women the *Lliclla;* and when they rise in the morning all the dressing they have to do is to shake and arrange their hair . . ." The dress of to-day still preserves some primitive features with the addition of breeches and sometimes a jacket as well as a shirt for the men, and of a chemise and skirts for the women. The ancient costumes are described as follows: Cieza de Leon mentions the pointed caps of the men, called by him "chucos," whereas "lluchu" is the name now given to them on the Island and on the Peninsula of Copacavana as well as at La Paz. Cobo, who gives the most detailed description, but who wrote nearly a century after Cieza, says of the costume: "Their dress was simple and limited itself to only two pieces, also plain and without lining or folds (plaiting); the men wear below, in place of breeches or underwear, a scarf a little wider than the hand and thin, and so tied around the loins as to give an appearance of decency . . . this they call *guara*, and only use it after they are fourteen and fifteen years of age. Over the *guaras* they put a vestment without sleeves or collar, which they call *uncu*, and we call it undershirt, as it has the cut of our shirts; and each one is woven separate, since they do not, as we do, weave large pieces and then cut off from these for their garments. The texture is like a piece of thick, coarse stuff, its width is three and a half palms, and its length two ells. The opening for the head and neck is left so that there be no need of cutting it open, and, once taken from the loom, all that is required is to fold it and sew the sides with the same thread with which it was woven, just as one sews a bag, leaving in the upper part of each side opening enough to stick through the arms. This garb commonly reaches as low as the knee or three or four fingers (inches) above it.

"The cape is less intricate. They make it of two pieces, with a seam in the middle, two and a quarter ells long, and one and three quarter ells broad. It has four corners or ends like a mantle or blanket, and for this reason we call it mantle, but the name which the Indian gives it is *yacolla*. They throw this over the shoulders, and when they dance, work, or do anything in which it might be an obstacle, they tie it with two ends over the left shoulder, leaving the right arm free. Beneath this mantle and above the underwear, they carry a bag or wallet hanging from the neck, named *chuspa*, one palm in length, more or less, and proportionately wide. This hangs down to the girdle below the right arm, and the strap to which it is hung passes over the left shoulder. This bag replaces to them our pockets. This is the common and usual costume of the males, arms and legs being bare, and this costume they make of wool in the mountains and of cotton in the hot lands."

Of the female dress the same author speaks as follows: "It consists of two mantles: one of these they wear like a tunic without sleeves, as wide above as below, and covering them from the neck to the feet. There is no slit in it for putting through the head, and they wrap themselves up in it in the following manner: they wrap the body in it from under the arms downwards, and pulling up the edges over the shoulders, they join and fasten them with their pins. From the girdle down they tie and cinch the body with a scarf, broad, thick and handsome, called *chumpi*. This tunic or wrapper is called *anacu;* it leaves the arms free and naked and it remains open on one side so that, although the edges overlap a little, when they walk they flutter and open from the *chumpi* or scarf down, showing part of the leg and thigh. . . . The other mantle is called *lliclla;* this is thrown over the shoulders and, gathering the edges over the breast, they fasten them by means of a pin. These are their mantles or mantillas, which come down as far as half the limb, and they take them off when they work or when they are at home.

"Their pins with which they fasten the dresses are called *tupus*, and they are very queer and as long as a third of an ell and less, and the smallest of half a span and as thick as small bones. At the top they have a thin and round plate of the same metal, as large as a *reál* of eight (half a quarter or twelve and a half cents), more or less according to the size of the *tupu*, with the edges so thin and so sharp, that they cut many things with them. Most of these *tupus* or *topos* have many trinkets of gold and silver dangling from the heads. In these pins they place their greatest pride. Anciently they were made of gold, of silver and copper; to-day the most of them are of silver with some carvings and paintings on the heads, made with special curiosity.

"To adorn their heads consists in carrying the hair very long, washed and combed; some wear it loose and others plaited. They tie it with a ribbon, more or less as wide as a finger, of many colors and striking, which they call *vincha*, that crosses the forehead. On the head they put a piece of very fine *cumbi*, called *pampacona*, and this piece of cloth they do not wear its full width, but folded, so as to be only one sixth of an ell wide. One edge comes down over the forehead and the other, twisting it around the head so as to leave the hair free on the sides, falls down over the back of the neck.

"On the chest, from one shoulder to the other, they used to wear necklaces of certain beads called *chaquiras*, which were made of bones and sea shells of various colors. They neither wore ear-pendants nor perforated their ear-laps."

Of the ancient costumes of the males, the pointed cap, poncho and breech-clout have remained. The pins and needles are also used. The men have adopted, besides shirt and jacket, a wide kind of breeches, open behind from the knee down—the so-called *calzòn*, known in Peru also as characteristic of the Aymará dress. A bright colored scarf, sometimes with striking designs, fastens this species of breeches about the waist, and the trousers are turned inside out when they are at work or in a specially bellicose mood. Scanty protection of the lower extremities, careless and unclean dress, and the pointed cap with the small, narrow-brimmed and round-topped felt hat, are, for the men, the essential components of an every-day Aymará costume on the Islands as well as along the shores of the Lake and on the Puna.

This costume is not very hygienic, in the climate in which it is worn. The houses are certainly not hygienic, nor is the manner of living. Custom and habit keep the Indian in the old road he still travels; although improvements have been made since the conquest, not only in dress but chiefly in household utensils and in implements. Thus the houses have doors, often of rawhide only, but still doors made to close and with wooden hinges, some also with hinges of iron. Lumber being an unknown quantity in the Puna, the Indian seizes upon every empty box in which the alcohol which furnishes him with most of his spiritual nourishment is transported, and with the aid of the few iron tools he has either bought or stolen, and a stone as hammer, he manufactures a door. Of the same material he occasionally makes a low table and perhaps an equally low stool with high square back, called by courtesy a chair.

All these are advances; and for their scantiness we must not blame too severely the Spanish colonist nor the former colonial government. I cannot sufficiently insist upon the extraordinary situation of the Spanish colonies. Importation was difficult, and transportation still more, to the interior of as secluded a region as Bolivia and the environs of its great Lake. Hence advances could be made but very, very slowly. If the Creole met with great obstacles, how much greater were they for the Indian who, besides, looked upon every innovation, every unknown and uncomprehended implement or source of comfort, with suspicion and superstitious aversion.

During primitive times, the Aymará Indians needed no other instrument in order to manufacture garments and dresses, or to mend them, than a needle which they called "ciracuna," made of a spine (thorn) as long as half a "geme" (five and a half inches), as thick as one of our darning needles, perforated at one end and very pointed. Copper and bronze needles ("yauri") were used also. To-day they have, on the Island and elsewhere, sewing needles, pack needles, metallic pins, and, at Sampaya on the mainland, as well as at Copacavana, the sewing machine. The maul of stone used for breaking clods of the often very hard soil is still in use; but the "chonta," a first cousin to the Mexican "coa," with a heavy blade of steel, has long ago supplanted the hoe of stone, copper or bronze. The wooden plough, drawn by treacherous bulls (not by cows), is in general use. Knives, forks, spoons, and ladles are of metal in many Indian abodes. Iron axes and hatchets, iron shovels, and occasionally planes, saws, bits and augers, are found in possession of the Indians and they know how to use them. Still the aborigine yet grasps a stone in preference to a hammer, and he *ties* in preference to *nailing*. He steals modern tools as diligently as he can, and no nail is safe from him, no end of rope or leather strap, even if they belong to a parcel or to a saddle, and if the removal endangers the safety of parcel or rider. But after he acquires such civilized implements and auxiliaries he does not take any care of them. The owners of Challa have repeatedly given tools to their Indians. The latter used them rather deftly, but after a year or so the saw was blunt and rusty, and the hatchet had lain in the mud so long that when a neighbor's offspring dug it out of the mire it became transformed into a harmless toy. Then they will beg or steal from a stranger's scanty supply of tools, to neglect these in turn, as soon as they have no immediate use for them.

This carelessness is exhibited toward everything. The Indian puts on a new shirt and wears it day and night until it is a disgusting rag; then he tries to get another one. Every article of clothing he serves in the same way. He likes animals, but does not give them any care. With very few exceptions, perhaps not a single one, the Indian houses are dilapidated. Sweeping with a very unhandy wisp of ichhu-grass is done mostly on the day previous to a feast, that is, only a few times each year. The accumulation of rubbish, it seems, propagates heat. Personal cleanliness is on the same level.

In addition to the improvements already enumerated, I have to mention, as an advance made since the Spanish occupation in articles of household use and furniture, the so-called gallo or sleeping platform of adobe. In olden times the family slept on the floor. The tile roof, not rare on the Island, is another improvement.

The Indians on the Island are not serfs. It would be more appropriate to call them "renters." In case of a sale they are not obliged to remain on the land. Those of the men who have lands in charge for cultivation cannot hire themselves out to others without permission of the proprietor; such as have no lands in charge may work for others, and it is not rare to find young men and boys, from the Island, at La Paz as servants or hired hands. The Indians have no real estate of their own, but occupy sites where their houses stand, and work little plots and fields for which they pay no direct rental. The compensation given the owners consists in:

(1) Cultivation of certain arable lands exclusively for the benefit of the owners, or, as it is called, for the "hacienda."

(2) Personal attendance, without compensation, at the houses of the owner, either when they dwell on the Island or at Puno, La Paz, or elsewhere. The men while performing such a service are called, "pongo"; the women, "mit'-áni."

(3) Other special services, such as selling of the produce ("Aljiri") at Copacavana, guarding the house ("unya-siri"), herding of sheep and cheese-making. These services are not entirely gratuitous, but compensated to a certain extent in products, that is, in sheep, cheese, milk, and the like. Money is neither received nor paid except when some of the products of the hacienda are sold, in which case the proceeds are received by the ilacata who keeps the accounts for the owners and settles with them and their "mayordomo," or overseer, who is the agent of the proprietors on the Island, although in the case of Challa he remains most of the time at Copacavana. Yumani has no mayordomo, as one of the owners resides there during fully one half of the year. The Indians are also obliged to transport the crops or products belonging to the hacienda to where the owners reside, or to Copacavana, which is the nearest market.

Of these four kinds of servitude only one, that of pongo or mit'-áni, may become vexatious. The pongos alternate every fortnight. Every fortnight a new set goes from the Island either to Puno, or to Copacavana if one of the family resides there, or to La Paz, or Sapahaqui, to attend at the houses of their landlords. This may become annoying at times, since it may fall upon one whose duties would lie nearer to home. But on the whole the proprietors of Titicaca treat their renters with a consideration akin to sacrifice of their own interests. This is especially the case in the working of the lands of the haciendas and in the gathering of crops. We had ample opportunity to convince ourselves of how much the Indians abuse the negligence of the owners, or rather their careless good nature; how little they did for the lands of the hacienda, and how the crops raised on them were stolen under the very eyes of the overseer. As for transportation of products from the Island, it is usually done by Indians who are called to Puno or other places of residence of the owners, hence it is not an extra duty, properly speaking.

According to Bolivian and Peruvian laws the Indian is, at least in theory, a citizen. Hence he might vote. Such an exercise of the "rights of a free and enlightened citizen" we have not had the pleasure of witnessing; but from descriptions it would be about as imposing an affair as voting in many parts of the interior of Mexico, where the Indian receives for his patriotic action a compensation that inevitably culminates in alcohol. The Indians from Titicaca would have to vote at Copacavana; but whether they exercise this right or not, and under what pressure, we have not yet been able to ascertain.

Communal tenure of lands was abolished in Bolivia, but the laws remained so far a dead letter. In the case of the Island, it is private property, and the Indians are only renters; there is no communal tenure, though some features of it remain. Thus every year in autumn (southern hemisphere) a distribution of plots for cultivation is made. On Titicaca, the ilacata proceeded to make this distribution, on the ninth of March, 1895, among the Indians pertaining to the hacienda of Challa. Every one who has a family, or requires land, is allotted a tract of tillable soil proportionate to his wants. This tract he cultivates for one year only. Then it is left to rest for a term of four years, while he receives in exchange a new plot that has been recuperating about that length of time. The rule is not the same in all localities. There are districts or valleys where lands rest three, seven or ten years. It results from this that, while the surface of the Island (wherever rocks do not protrude) appears to have been "anciently cultivated," that cultivation has been far from simultaneous. Only a small proportion was tilled at any given time, the other portions lying idle to recuperate. This system of rotation is a very ancient one, and there is no doubt it was general all over the Sierra long before the Cuzco Indians overpowered the mountain tribes. The lands on the Island may be classified as follows, starting from the basis that the entire real estate is vested in owners of originally Spanish extraction:

(1) Vacant expanses and pasturage, the latter used by the flocks of the hacienda, but the animals of the Indians obtaining their share of them with the knowledge and consent of the owners.

(2) Lands cultivated, for the exclusive benefit of the proprietors, by the Indians in common and without compensation.

(3) Individual plots distributed among the Indians annually and improved by them for their own benefit without payment of rent.

(4) The sites of the homes of the Indians which they occupy, without rent, as long as they please, or as long as they have no reason for abandoning their dwellings. Should they make a change, they can move to another site without being molested or compelled to ask for permission, as long as they do not inconvenience a neighbor or impinge on cultivated expanses or pasturages.

Thus the Indian has on the Island no real estate of his own, but he may exchange the plot annually allotted to him for cultivation for that of another Indian.

Political jurisdiction is vested in the Corregidor of Copacavana; and the courts of Bolivia rule in matters of serious crimes. The curacy of Copacavana is the ecclesiastical authority; but the Indians still maintain, as everywhere on the Puna and in the Sierra, an organization of their own, one handed down to them from pre-colonial times, and which is based upon the clan as a unit. The clan in Quichua as well as in Aymará, in Peru as well as in Bolivia, bears the name of "ayllu." It is the well-known consanguine cluster, all the members of which acknowledge an official and traditional relationship, governing themselves independently of other clans, while the tribe is but a shell, protecting and holding together a number of clans through common consent.

The rapid but irregular expansion of the sway of the Inca tribe of Cuzco did not modify these primitive organizations wherever conquered inhabitants were suffered to remain. The ayllus remained as before, as well as two larger groups, each of which embraced several clans. These groups existed at Cuzco as geographical divisions, called, respectively, Upper and Lower Cuzco—"Hanan" and "Hurin-Cuzco." Under the names of "Aran-Saya" and "Ma-Saya," analogous divisions are met with among the Aymará everywhere, and were found among them, together with the ayllu, by the Spaniards. At the present day the village of Tiahuanaco is divided into Aran-saya and Ma-saya, the former embracing what lies north, the latter what lies south, of the central square. In the older church books of Tiahuanaco the two "sayas" are noticed *occasionally*, the ayllu *always*. At present the ayllus are much scattered, not in consequence of depopulation, but of wider dispersion through intercourse. A number of Indian families settling in another village became there an ayllu named after the place they came from, a custom also observed in former times; thus there is an "Ayllu Tiahuanaco" at Coni, at the foot of Illimani. The Indians of Titicaca, at least those of Challa, belong (according to their own statement) to the cluster of Aran-saya of Copacavana. They are divided into two localized clans: the ayllu of Challa and the ayllu of Kea. About the organization of the Indians of Yumani I could not ascertain anything beyond that they have their own officers. They were even more reticent than the Indians of Challa. Agglomeration on haciendas has been a disturbing factor in original grouping and government. To-day the owners of haciendas believe that *they* appoint the Indian functionaries without consulting the wishes of their Indians. These officers are: An ilacata, an alcalde, and at least two campos. The ilacata represents the administrative power. He distributes the lands for cultivation. He receives the products of tracts cultivated for the benefit of the owners and oversees certain labors done in common. The alcalde is the executive officer. All cases of strife, conflict, acts of violence come under his jurisdiction. He also heads the men in case of warfare. So the former corresponds to the governor, the latter to the war-captain, of the New Mexico pueblos. On the Island these two principal officers are accepted rather than appointed by the proprietor on or about the first of January of each year; also the campos, who are subalterns and assistants, watching the fields and the manner in which they are attended, the housing of the crops, their transport, the dispatching of pongos, and the like. All these officers have their staffs of office, with silver heads if possible, but no distinctive costume.

I have said that the owners *accept* the officers proposed. The natives of Challa told me emphatically that there existed a council of old men, and that this council *proposed* the ilacata, alcalde and campos to be appointed each year. The existence of such a body was denied by the owners. Probably both sides were right, each from their own standpoint. A council certainly exists, but it does not propose the men of its choice *directly;* it elects them! We had proof of this while on the Island, in the fact that the Indians, among themselves, were quietly speaking of somebody as next ilacata, whereas the owner himself had not yet thought of any one. In cases of great importance a public meeting may be called, at which even women have vote and voice.

The term ilacata is an Aymará word, whereas alcalde is Spanish. We endeavored to find out how the alcalde was called in Aymará, but without result. In the documents concerning the great Indian uprising of 1780 and following years, of which José Gabriel Condorcanqui, or Tupac Amaru, was a conspicuous figure in the beginning, both the Indian alcaldes and the ilacatas are mentioned. Among northern Peruvian Indians, the *gobernadores* seem to represent the Bolivian ilacata. The alcalde was and is the police-magistrate of his tribe, or *comunidad,* hence he seems to be the counterpart of the *capitan á guerra* of the pueblos of New Mexico and northern Mexico; whereas the campos are *alguaziles* or constables, similar to the *tenientes* of northern village-Indians. That the alcalde is a leader in warfare was plainly shown on the 16th of March, 1895, when the Indians along the Peruvian shores had risen and were threatening Copacavana. It was the alcalde to whom the Corregidor of Copacavana gave orders to come to the relief with armed men, and similar orders were imparted to all the Indian alcaldes within the jurisdiction. The ilacatas remained quietly at home, and we were assured that they had nothing to do with the warlike preparations.

With the intermingling and shifting of clans, the changes wrought thereby and the formation of new ones, it is not easy now to detect *primitive* customs in regard to marriage, naming of children and interment. It seems certain, however, that marriage originally was *exogamous*, with descent in the *female* line. On the Island, regular marriage through the Church is officially required, but the Indians do not follow the precept. Baptism is more rigidly observed, and one reason for this may be the greater cheapness of the ceremony. Marriages are, according to the character of the parish priest, often expensive. The complaint raised against the clergy on that score is unhappily too well justified. It is true that with the advent of the Franciscans at the convent of Copacavana, a laudable change has taken place; still the Indians have remained rather loose in their marital relations, and little punishment is meted out to the unfaithful husband or wife. As to chastity, the natives are like Indians everywhere else, and like the population of these countries in general. Not a single marriage having been performed while we were on the Islands, we cannot give any details from personal knowledge. We, however, took part as godfather and god-mother in an Indian baptism, which was carried out strictly according to the rules of the Church. As presents, we had to give the mother (not to the father) chocolate, rice, sugar, two skirts—one for herself and another for the baby—and two chemises for the child. The father being the sheep herder of the

Island, we were excused from adding fresh meat to the gifts, but made up for it in the number of chemises.

We diligently inquired about aboriginal personal names, but were invariably told there were none, many personal names in Aymará having turned into family names since the conquest. That primitive ceremonies are yet secretly performed, both at marriage and at the birth of a child, is beyond all doubt, for we have seen too many evidences of the power sorcery and ancient ceremonials still exert over the Indian in every phase of life. But it is not possible, in a single year's contact, to gain the confidence of so reticent a tribe as the Aymará. In regard to burials we were more fortunate. In the first place, we witnessed at least a part of the burial of an adult at Challa; but saw only what can be seen, with slight modifications, among the New Mexico pueblos, in church. The body was wrapped in ponchos; but what transpired in the *churchyard* while the body was being interred, we were not allowed to witness. At Tiahuanaco, however, we were reliably informed that when a child dies, a vessel containing water, some food, and a small wisp or broom, are put into the grave with the body. The belief is that it takes the soul several days' travel to reach heaven, and that the broom is required for sweeping the road in order to reach the last resting place. While on the Island we were assured that on the death of an Indian peculiar ceremonies are performed around the body, and that when that body has been removed from the house, ashes are strewn on the floor inside the door-sill, and the house is locked from the outside. After burial the people examine the floor carefully. This is done by "old men," and seldom do they fail to discover foot-prints of men, women and roosters. The former are looked upon as prognosticating further deaths in the family, and the latter as indicating the presence of evil spirits whom they call "*devils.*" It is interesting to compare these practices with those in use among the pueblos as well as with ancient Peruvian customs mentioned by early chroniclers.

So far as our observation goes, organization, marriage and

other customs, on the Island, seem to be like those we saw and heard of at other places in Bolivia. There are local variations, but the main features are the same. In another work I shall record data obtained elsewhere in Bolivia, and that throw much more light on all these questions. For the present I confine myself to what we observed and learned on the Island and in its neighborhood.

If we resume the foregoing, we find (1) the same disposition of buildings constituting the Indian home as in central and southern Mexico; (2) a degree of development in art and industry about on a level with that of the New Mexico pueblos half a century ago; (3) communal tenure of lands; (4) a system of clanship antedating Spanish occupation, with indications that the original *gentes* may have partly disappeared, whereas new clans have sprung up, taking their names mainly from localities; (5) officers, elective in the clan, but under ostensible control of the government, and of the landowners where the Indians live on large estates, as on the Island; these officers corresponding to the governor, war-captain, and assistants of the New Mexico village; (6) marriage customs, officially regulated by the Church. Here I should add that in the seventeenth century the ayllu may have already lost control of marital rules, marriages becoming indiscriminately indogamous and exogamous. The distribution of estates depends upon the will of the parents, and there is not, as among the pueblos, as strict a division between what belongs to the mother and what pertains to the father; and yet it is asserted that the *wife* controls whatever is housed, or contained in the house! We noticed that we never obtained articles of the household, such as ancient pottery used in a kitchen, except with consent of the women. (7) Burial rites resembling those of the Mexican and New Mexico sedentary Indians at the present time.

The life of the Indian on the Island is seemingly monotonous. Agriculture is his chief occupation. He plants maize in October and harvests it in May. Barley is sown in January and February, and matures in May also. Potatoes, which are the important staple, are planted in August and September, so are the oca, and the quinua, but early potatoes are already harvested in January and February, whereas oca and quinua can only be gathered in May. This cycle of crops recurs with unvarying regularity year in and year out, and this is the narrow circle within which the leading occupations of the Islanders, and of the Indians in general, are kept alive. Personal service to the owners bears the same character of monotonous periodicity. But as these duties require absence from home, and at places where there is more to be seen and heard (as, for instance, La Paz and Puno), the Indian of Titicaca has become more wide-awake and crafty, more malicious, than many of the Indians of other localities of the Puna; his wits are sharper, and he is by no means the clumsy being as which he may appear at first glance. While at home, little sociability can be noticed. They hardly gather except on feast-days. Life is much the same as in a pueblo of New Mexico.

The young men associate more, and chiefly at night. Many of them, or of such as are married but still young, go on trading expeditions to Yungas, to the hot regions beyond the snowy Illimani. They take with them mules and donkeys laden with products, mostly chuñu and oca, also barley, and trade them off for coca, coffee, and sweet tropical fruit. These they sell either at Copacavana or on the Island, keeping a respectable lot for themselves. Such trips furnish food for discussion at home. An occasional voyage to the eastern Bolivian shore, to buy pottery and peaches, the former at Ancoraymes, the latter from the vicinity of Sorata, is another source of talk outside of the every-day treadmill. Gossip is as rank and rife among them as in any civilized community, and as the Aymará Indian is naturally of a quarrelsome and rancorous disposition, squabbles in words and deeds are not uncommon. For such dissensions there is always ample pretext. When crops are being gathered, stealing is diligently practiced. They are as dishonest towards each other as towards the owners of the Island, and we know of an instance of an old man, who had to sit up night after night in the bitterest cold and in the open field, to guard his potato crop.

During our stay we had occasion to heal a group of Indians, all of the cluster of Kea, who had ill-treated each other on the most futile pretexts. But the great occasion for displaying prowess is with their neighbors, the Indians of the hacienda of Yumani. The latter are as pugnacious as those of Challa and, although much less numerous, provoke hostilities now and then by trespassing upon their neighbors' lands. The results are regular engagements with slings and stones, women supplying the men with projectiles, which they carry in their skirts. A number are badly wounded and now and then some are killed, for the Indian is dangerously expert with the sling. Such engagements end invariably in the rout of the Yumani warriors, but still they are renewed annually. Among the Aymará, hostilities between villages are common occurrences, and a number of persons are killed every year in fights between pueblos or haciendas, or on festive occasions.

There is no school on the Island. An old man, who speaks Quichua as well as Aymará, teaches some of the children church hymns and Catechism in their own language. There is, as far as we could ascertain, one Indian, an old man, who is able to read and write. He does this lying on the floor, with his face down. His chirography is as original as his orthography is picturesque. Some of the Indians still preserve a kind of picture-writing. It is very difficult to obtain such pictographs. The Indians refuse even to exhibit them, and our tenders of money could not induce them to show us one of these curious pictographs. Their import is wholly religious; they are the Catechism, and church-prayers, pictorially represented. Nobody has, as yet, been able to secure a literal translation, but it seems certain that they all relate to church ritual and are of post-Columbian origin. For keeping their accounts with the hacienda, the Indians, on the Island as well as on the flanks of Illimani and elsewhere in the Sierra, still use a simple "quippu" or knotted string, also sticks with notches. We have seen the former in use at Llujo.

Councils are held on matters of interest to the whole community, but where and when we could not ascertain. The affairs of the little commonwealths on the Island are discussed, and Indians are by no means indifferent to the outside world either. We noticed, during our stay among them while the civil war in Peru was going on, with what interest the Indians followed the course of events and how surprisingly well informed they were of military movements. When Chilian troops once trespassed on Bolivian territory and an invasion of Bolivia by them was feared, we obtained the news through our Indians at Challa and at once noticed that the occurrence was not by any means a matter of indifference to them. While the Indian uprising along the Peruvian border continued and negotiations were being carried on secretly between the insurgents and the Indians on the Peninsula of Copacavana, we now and then noticed fire-signals on the mainland both west and east, and it was not very reassuring to see a response flaring up on the summit of Kea-Kollu, the most convenient height for that purpose on the Island. Of sign-language we have, as yet, not seen any trace.

The condition of the Indian of the Puna appears to be poverty, nay, indigence. One who arrives on the great central plateau and sees the Indian trundling along with bare feet or at best only with sandals, his body protected by a ragged poncho, following his donkey, as shaggy and uncouth as the master, or a llama; sees him devouring an unappetizing meal of chuñu and oca or roasted beans on the road, and sees the dingy, close, unclean home where the same kind of meal is taken, is led to deplore the fate of the aborigine. And yet, the Indians own more wealth in money than many of the landholders in Bolivia, but this money they hide most anxiously. Frequent spoliations, especially since the separation of South America from Spain, is one reason why the Indian hides his wealth. He keeps it for certain festive occasions, on which he lavishly spends for display in dances and in orgies. He hoards also for another purpose. The Indian is slowly accumulating even firearms. On the Island, revolvers are by no means rare, neither is ammunition. The disconnected state of Indian society, their segregation, maintained also after the Spanish occupation, render an uprising very improbable; but should they ever be able to coalesce, the situation of Bolivia and of the Peruvian Sierra might become exceedingly critical.

These are the main reasons why the Indian is so extremely anxious, as I have previously stated, to secure money. He uses it also as currency in his daily transactions. But there is a substance which he prizes even more, for certain reasons, than gold or silver, and this is *coca*. The dried leaves of *Erythroxilon Coca*, a product of the hot lands, are in many cases a greater incentive for the Indian to sell or to work than money. Such has been our experience elsewhere. Coca is, to the older men among them, more indispensable than food or drink. I need not treat here of the qualities attributed to this plant, whether real or imaginary; but its leaves are, if not another currency, like shell-beads among northern Indians, often a much surer resource than silver or gold. The use of coca is more common and more widely distributed among the male Indians than it was before the time of Pizarro, because the coca-plant was then cultivated to a limited extent only, and the coca-producing regions have become more accessible. What has been published about plantations of coca on Titicaca Island for the benefit of the Incas is, at best, very doubtful.

Both money and coca are indispensable to the Indians for *religious* purposes. As religious performances constitute an important part of their exterior life, and as their modes of thinking and the motives of their actions are dependent upon religious beliefs, I shall have to approach, though timidly, this important field as far as we were able to scrutinize it while on the Island of Titicaca and at Copacavana.

The Indian of Bolivia is a Catholic; at least nominally. He clings with utmost tenacity to his local church and certain sanctuaries, to the *images* they contain, and to every vestment and ornament. This attachment is manifested in the presence of the stranger and to any one who would endeavor to deride or profanate such objects. But, in case of a general uprising, I doubt very much (and in this I am confirmed by the opinion of reliable parish priests) whether the Indians would not return openly to a paganism which at heart they still profess and in secret actually practise. The great Indian rebellion of 1781 would have culminated in such a return. The Aymará Indian, especially the younger generation and the sorcerers, are fetish-worshipers to-day, while they follow the rites of the church also. The latter is done sincerely, inasmuch as the Indian attributes to these rites and ceremonies power in cases when the ceremonials of his primitive creed are powerless; in other words: he sincerely believes Catholic rites and prayers to be "big medicine" for certain things, whereas he still clings to the other, and with still greater tenacity perhaps. I can but repeat, on this point, what I have already published in regard to the tribes of the southwestern United States and of northern Mexico: "It is vain to deny that the southwestern Indian is not an idolater at heart, but it is equally preposterous to assume that he is not a sincere Catholic. Only he assigns to each belief a certain field of action, and has minutely circumscribed each one. He literally gives to God what, in his judgment, belongs to God, and to the devil what he thinks the devil is entitled to, for the Indian's own benefit. Woe unto him who touches his ancient idols, but thrice woe to him who derides his church or desecrates its ornaments." Substituting "Aymará of Bolivia and Peru" for "southwestern Indian," and this statement stands as well for South America as for those parts of the northern hemisphere about which it was written.

The Indian, so far as we could observe, firmly believes in a spiritual being—spiritual in the sense that it is invisible to his eyes—which being is the Christian God, "Dios" or "Dius," and for which he has, at least on the Island, no other name. The Indian professes great devotion to the patron saint of his chapel, and on the Island "Our Lady of the Light," the miraculous image of Copacavana, certainly stands higher in his estimation than the invisible "Dius." He attends church nearly every Sunday. The balsas that cross to Yampupata and recross, are filled with men, women and children on Saturdays, who go to pray at the sanctuary of "Nuestra Señora de Copacavana," and at the same time to sell their products at the Sunday fairs. They make vows, and discharge the obligations thereby incurred; they are anxious to have their children baptized; they sob and howl and sigh at church in a heartrending manner, and if they can steal a piece of the *hostia*, it will invariably be used for some medicinal, that is, witchcraft, purpose. At Tiahuanaco we were told that the Indians believe that when a child dies unbaptized it returns to the body of the mother, causing it to swell, a process which they call "limbo," and to prevent this they use the *hostia*. They confess themselves regularly for some years, then again drop the "habit." They regard God and the saints usually as beneficent or rather as useful. Certain diseases, however, are attributed to an ill wind produced by God, and others to an ill wind due to some saint; hence the "pacha ayre" and the "santo ayre." In some districts or villages, no image of a saint is tolerated in their houses, out of dread of that "ill wind" of the saints. Of retribution after death they have, as far as we could ascertain, no idea. Of the existence of evil spirits they are firmly convinced. On the Island, it is "Supay" who sweeps over the land in the hail-storm, and when their crops are destroyed by hail they say that Supay has preyed on them with his hordes of other fiends. How often were we, at night, startled by the lugubrious sound of the "Pu-tu-tu," a cow-horn, which the Indians blew on the approach of clouds threatening hail, in order to oblige Supay and his associates to take another course in their devastating career. At Tiahuanaco and vicinity it is "Anchancho" who plays the part of the spirits of evil, and when they fear his approach in a threatening storm, they also blow their pu-tu-tus and shout at the top of their voices: "Pass on, pass on!" On the Island, there seems to be greater indifference than on the mainland toward some church practices, as, for instance, they care very little for an official blessing of the crops. Mass, however, is *exacted* by them on the feast day of their patron saint. When the agents of the owners of Challa, through a very ill-timed measure, attempted to prevent the usual celebration on the twenty-fifth of July of 1895, our intervention alone prevented a serious outbreak. We noticed, however, that it was more the opportunity of celebrating the day with dances of old and immoderate drinking that would have been missed than the religious ceremony.

We could not detect, in the midst of the host of witchcraft practices and reminiscences of ancient beliefs, any preference to a worship of either *sun* or *moon*. The definition of Indian fetishism given by Mr. Cushing applies also to the Aymará: "The A-shi-wi, or Zuñis, suppose the sun, moon, and stars, the sky, earth, and sea, in all their phenomena and elements, and all inanimate objects, as well as plants, animals, and men, to belong to one great system of all-conscious and interrelated life." One thing struck us, namely, the belief that both sun and moon were *created* beings, and this is primitive belief, anterior to influences of a Christian origin. What, however, the Aymará of the Island pays particular attention to are the "Achachilas," literally "grand-fathers," spirits, dwelling at all conspicuous places, in all striking objects, and who are supposed to exert a constant influence upon man. This belief in the "Achachilas" is nothing else but the fetishism so well characterized by Mr. Cushing, and which I have traced among every Indian tribe with which I came in contact.

Every conspicuous object in nature is believed, by the Aymará, to harbor its own spiritual nucleus or essence, that plays an active part in the life of its surroundings, man included. This Indian conception may be illustrated by examples that came under our observation. While we were at Challa, the Indians received orders to tear down some walls forming the southern side of a court, and to erect on the site a store-house of adobe. The first part of this work was performed without any ceremony, and this greatly incensed the warden or "unya-siri" who happens to be one of the leading medicine-men on the Island. He chided the workmen and insisted that, in order to prevent disaster to the new edifice, they should, before proceeding to demolish the walls, have burnt incense in each of the four corners; should have prayed (begging forgiveness) in each corner, and finally, in the center, prostrating themselves, kissing the earth and looking up to the sky, with both hands raised in prayer. On the following morning the foundations of the new structure were to be laid, and for that purpose they had, the night before, prepared as many tiny bundles as there were corners, and an extra one for the center. Each bundle contained: The fetus of a llama, the fetus of a pig, a piece of llama-tallow, leaves of a plant not found on the Island and called by them "uira-ko-ua," and *coca* leaves. These bundles are prepared by men only, and at night, and the parties are chosen the evening before by the ilacata, which shows that this officer has certain religious functions also. When all the workmen had gathered on the site, the one who directed the work, the *maestro,* or architect (a plasterer from the Peninsula of Copacavana), spread before him a "llik'lla," or square piece of embroidered cloth, made like a poncho, but smaller. Every Indian took three coca leaves, arranging them in the shape of a trefoil, and deposited them on the llik'lla, while the master of ceremonies was pronouncing the following prayer: "Children, with all your heart, put coca into your mouths [each took a mouthful of coca-leaves]; we must give to the virgin earth, but not with two hearts; with one heart alone." After this ceremony they set to work. In the afternoon when they had again gathered they all took off their hats, and the director said: "Children, we shall ask of God (Dius-at) and of the Achachila and the grandmother, that no evil may befall us." Then they buried the bundles, in each of the four corners and in the center, adding to them "aji" (red pepper), sugar, and salt. After this the master again spoke as follows; "Let all of you together take coca [they put coca into their mouths], throw coca on the ground [upon this they began to scatter coca into the trench made for the foundation], give them their dues!" The old men responding: "Dius pagarat-kat, uauanaka!"—May God reward you for it, children! After this they threw earth on the bundles. In this ceremony the Christian God and the fetishes are both appealed to. The articles offered in sacrifice represent olden as well as modern times. Thus the llama-fetus and llama-tallow, the "uira-koua" and the coca are ancient, the others are modern.

The above ceremony of invocation and sacrifice is called "tincat" (giving the "tinca"), and it is practised on almost every similar occasion. While we were excavating at Kasa-pata, a new house was erected near this site, and we were told that the same sacrifice had been performed before work was begun. On the first day, all the men who took part in that "house-raising" wore wreaths of flowers around their hats and caps. At Tiahuanaco we were assured that house-building is a communal undertaking of the ayllu, or of those of its members that are related to the family for which the building is erected, and that the only compensation for such assistance is chicha and food. The custom is undoubtedly primitive.

Another ceremony, which we only partly witnessed, however, took place on the Island during the days of Carnival, February 24th, 25th, and 26th of 1895, and it is annually repeated. Already on the 24th preparations were going on in the practice of the drum here and there. On the following day, the Indians of Challa with the alcalde at their head brandishing a Peruvian flag, and with his hat, as well as those of most of the other participants, wreathed with flowers, went in procession, to the sound of drum and flute, to the fields at "Kea," there to exchange, for about half an hour, throws of peaches with the people of that settlement, and offer to the *soil* the tinca above mentioned. They burned this offering, burying the ashes in the fields with appropriate invocations, and sprinkling the ground with alcohol and red wine. Afterward they dug out small quantities of whatever fruit had been raised, which was taken home to be kept until the following season. The idea is, to give to the earth (which also is "Achachila") a remuneration or compensation for its favors. The most instructive examples of Achachila worship that we were allowed to witness were those performed previous to our excavations for antiquities, and without which no such work is expected to be successful. We had to go through this ordeal at three different places—on Titicaca, on Koati, and at Cachilaya, near Chililaya, on the mainland. I shall limit myself to a description of the performances on Titicaca, as the others showed but slight variations.

At the laying of the corner-stone, the architect or superintendent officiated, but for the ceremony initiating excavations a medicine-man, or shaman, was required. At Challa we had the desired dignitary at the very house of the hacienda and in the person of its unya-siri, or warden, Manuel Mamani. He informed me (my wife was at first excluded from the deliberations, though afterward she was permitted to see some of the preliminaries) that the articles needed for the conjuration were: *Coca, uira-koua*, llama-tallow, the two fetuses, a piece of the skin of the "titi," or wild-cat, grape-brandy, wine, and especially "mullu." For this ceremony the latter is a fetish of white alabaster representing a bull or cow, and resembling, both in color and in shape, certain well-known fetishes of New Mexico. The fetuses could not be procured, but the other substances were ready on the day appointed, and in the afternoon a walk was taken with the conjurer to two of the places where we intended to begin, Kasapata, and the pasturages of Ciria-Pata. There, Manuel Mamani squatted on the ground, took off his hat, and greeted the "Achachilas" as follows: "Good afternoon, Achachilas: *Kasa-pata Achachila, Llak'aylli Achachila, Chincana Achachila, Calvario Achachila, Santa Maria Achachila, Ciria-Pata Achachila!* We have greeted all of you whom a *viracocha* [the common designation for a white stranger] has sent me to greet; for him [on his account] I have come, as he cannot speak to thee. Forgive me for asking of thee a favor." Then he took coca, made two trefoils of coca-leaves and placed them into as many balls made of llama-tallow (untu), wine, uira-koua, a piece of cat's fur, and mullu, rasping with his knife from the alabaster fetish. Then making two holes at some distance from each other, he placed one of the balls in each of them, covering the hole with a stone. This was an "official notice" to the Achachilas of the main ceremony that was to take place the night following. Ordinarily, this preliminary is performed the evening before, and the sorcerer then goes to dream about the most eligible spot. The Aymará believes in dreams as firmly as all other Indians; but in our case the dreaming part was deemed unnecessary, as we had already determined upon the locality. After nightfall, Manuel stealthily crept into our rooms. Squatting by the side of a candle he formed twenty balls like those he had made in the afternoon, with the addition, however, of brandy. He also made two larger ones, in the center of which he placed, in lieu of the usual trefoil, a bunch of coca-leaves. With these twenty-two pellets, the remainder of a bottle of brandy, and a bottle of red wine, our procession of conjurers crawled up to Kasa-pata in the darkness of the night, over cliffs and slippery rocks, and with more than one tumble. The greatest care was taken to avoid dwellings, and a secluded spot selected for the operation. The medicine-man repeated the formula of the afternoon and sprinkled wine and afterward brandy in the direction of each of the six Achachilas named, saying: "All thy presents I have now brought." With this, he counted out the twenty balls one by one, each being counted as a *quintal*, or hundredweight, and adding: "Thou hast to give me with all thy heart." Then a fire was built, and the twenty balls were placed on it. Manuel threw into the flames a substance which he refused to show us and which caused the fire to spit and to crackle. At this sound everybody had to run off a short distance while he exclaimed; "The Achachilas are eating!" After the fire had gone out he returned to the place and covered it with stones. Then he went with the two larger balls to another spot and dug a hole, saying: "The virgin earth is now invited, here is thy burial of treasure," and placed both balls into the hole. "The very things of the Inca thou hast to bring forth. Now, with thy permission we will take leave. Forgive me." With this the performance was at an end and we groped our way back, over the steep and wet rocks, without a single star on the dark firmament. By midnight we were home again, bruised and tired, and the next morning, the Indians, satisfied that we had the "Achachilas" in our favor, went to work, convinced that the yield would be abundant. Nevertheless at noon on the following day, while our laborers took a recess for lunch, another medicine-man among them poured out wine and alcohol in the direction of the six Achachilas, after each one of the laborers had taken a pinch of coca, and said: "Achachila, do not make me suffer much work, we are those who work under pay; to this viracocha thou hast to return what he paid to us, for this thou art beckoned [invited]." If an Indian is offered a glass of wine, or whenever he partakes of their favorite beverage, alcohol diluted to about sixteen or seventeen degrees, he first pours out a little, as libation. The well-known offering by the Peruvian and Bolivian Indians, at the "apachitas," is also to the spirits. Every pass, and the mountain peaks around it, are "Achachilas," and every Indian places a stone and some coca leaves in a corner or spot along the trail in order to influence the spirits in his behalf. The next one adds *his* votive offering, and thus heaps of pebbles and leaves gradually accumulate. They have their counterparts in the "tapu" of the New Mexico Tehuas, the little stone heaps around many of the pueblos in general, and in the Apache reservation of Arizona. According to pueblo inter- pretation, each stone lying on twigs in one of these heaps sig- nifies a prayer. The Quichuas and Aymarás claim it to be a sacrifice. A sacrifice is always accompanied by a wish, whether expressed in a formal prayer or not, hence the fundamental idea is the same in South America as in the southwest of North America.

From what precedes it is clear that the number of Achachilas is immense. Every summit, every gorge, every spring, in short, every site more or less prominent is thought to be inhabited by such a spirit. Meteorological phenomena also are included, such as lightning, the rainbow and the clouds. One of their devices for rain-making consists in "calling the rain-clouds." It resembles the pueblo practice of invoking the "Shiuana" and beckoning to them to come. Near Tiahuanaco, there is a height whither the Indians repair whenever they need rain, to sacrifice coca and to call the clouds. The rainbow ("kurmi") is Achachila, and at Tiahuanaco they forbid children to gaze at it lest it might kill them. In short, the Achachilas are the "Guacas" or "Huacas" of Peru; they are analogous to the "Shiuana," and "Kopish-tai" of the Queres, and to the "Ojua" of the Tehuas, in New Mexico.

Whether the Indians have other fetishes besides the "Mullu" above referred to, I am unable to tell. All our endeavors to elicit information on that score were in vain. The queries were eluded, not answered.

Where the idea prevails that nature is occupied by a multitude of spiritual individualities more or less potent, it results that whatever man suffers, be it from disease or through accident, is attributed to evil *spiritual* agencies. In many instances there is a singular blending of ancient with Christian notions. Thus, at Tiahuanaco, we were informed that, when lightning strikes a house, it is abandoned for the day and night following, for they believe that "Santiago" (Saint James) has stumbled or made a mistake. The doors are draped in black. The next day twelve boys, personifying the twelve apostles, are fed in the building. Once the meal over, these boys go home *without looking back;* if they turn around to look, lightning will strike one of them soon after. After their departure, the owner of the house and his wife return accompanied by a shaman, or medicine-man, who, after joining their hands, covers their heads with a black poncho and utters a prayer to "Pachacamac" (I have my doubts about this word) in behalf of the future safety of the house. To this prayer the sorcerer replies in a changed tone of voice explaining the lightning-stroke as a mistake that shall never occur again. Huge stones are dreaded as swallowing people occasionally. When the priest of Tiahuanaco once found it advisable to have such a stone removed, he obtained assistance only with the greatest difficulty, and after its removal the Indians sacrificed coca and alcohol to appease "Anchancho" and induce him not to take revenge upon them for the removal.

In the valuable essay on Zuñi fetishes already quoted, Mr. Cushing says: "In this system of life the starting point is man, the most finished yet the lowest organism, actually the lowest, because the most dependent and least mysterious. In just as far as an organism, actual or imaginary, resembles his, it is believed to be related to him, and correspondingly mortal. In just as far as it is mysterious is it considered removed from him, further advanced, powerful and immortal. It thus happens that the animals, because alike mortal and endowed with similar physical functions and organs, are considered more nearly related to man than are the gods; more nearly related to the gods than is man, because more mysterious, and characterized by specific instincts and powers which man does not of himself possess."

The truth of this is also exemplified among the Aymará. They attribute to animals not only the gift of presage, but also the faculty of *intercession*. Innumerable are the beliefs in manifestations of evil omens. The owl, that unlucky bird, one of the most slandered in this world, must, of course, head the list, especially the large species or "urcu" (*Bubo magellanicus*). But the smaller *lechuza* are also noted for the ominous significance of their cry. When Indians see an owl flying in the night they throw salt at it with the left hand. Domestic fowl also play a conspicuous part. Whenever a hen crows like a rooster, or a rooster cackles like a hen, or when a rooster crows at the hour of evening prayers, it is a bad omen and the bird is forthwith killed. On the mainland, a little bird which they call "tiolas" is much dreaded, being charged with the disagreeable habit of taking away the "fat of the heart" while flying past a person, and thus causing his or her death. Another very unpopular bird is called "cochi-pachi," and its voice bodes no good. Among quadrupeds, the skunk and the fox are, on the mainland, suspiciously watched, and if a fox crosses our path accidentally, we had better prepare for ill luck. Among domestic quadrupeds it is the guinea-pig or cuy, formerly, at least, much used in sacrifice and divining. In case one of these lively creatures whines at night or chuckles, it is killed at once and its body thrown away, as it is a *conejobrujo* (rabbit-witch) and will carry sickness into the family. The barking of dogs in a dark night is also an evil omen. The alcalde of Challa, a man not by any means gifted with an exalted imagination, and still less a coward, when returning from our room to his home one dark night, was terribly frightened by the sudden barking of the dog of the hacienda. He swore he would never visit us any more after sunset, as the dog had seen a ghost, and he thought to have noticed a dark figure near our door.

Belief in *fabulous* animals is also current. If the "marine monster" previously mentioned should not, in course of time, prove to be some large aquatic animal, we may classify it among the mythical beasts, although the belief in its existence is of rather recent origin. The fabulous animal most generally believed in, however, is the *carbuncle*. As everywhere else, the "carbuncle" is described as a cat, having on its forehead a blood-red stone which shines at night. On the Island it is confounded with the titi, and that name is also given to it. We were told that the carbuncle dwelt in the snows of the high peak of Sajama, near Oruro, and impeded approach to the summit of that mountain.

Spiders are used, by some sorcerers, for prognostics. From the movements of the legs of the insect, the diviner draws his inferences, in a similar manner as the Opata Indians of Sonora prognosticated from the motions of the cricket.

We lack yet most of the information desirable in regard to the role of animals as *intercessors*. But we were positively informed that the group of dancers called "Chayll'pa," and of which I shall hereafter speak, have among other duties that of *conjuring drouth*. They go to the summit of the height called Calvario, which is denuded of all vegetation, gather small stones and throw them into the Lake. But they also catch toads and throw them into the water, there to intercede for rain. Among the objects of stone found on the Island, on the Peninsula of Copacavana, and chiefly on Koati, are frogs of stone, and we diligently inquired of the Indians whether these had been perhaps rain-intercessors after the manner of those used by the pueblos to-day. We never received any other but an evasive reply.

Another indication of intercession by animals is found in the dance called chacu-ayllu, or chokela, danced by the Chayll'pa. In this dance the vicuña plays the same part as, in symbolic dances of the pueblo Indians, the eagle, the deer, and the mountain-sheep. The chacu-ayllu is an ancient ceremonial, the signification of which as a "hunter's-dance" is no longer understood.

The Chayll'pa, whenever they appear in full costume, wear the skin of a young vicuña, head included, hanging down their backs. The "Kena-Kena," another group of dancers, wear a sleeveless jacket made of the skin of a jaguar. Animal forms are also represented in the fetishes called "Mullu," so extensively peddled

about the country by the curious guild of Indian medicine-men
and shamans known as "Callahuaya."

The Callahuaya speak the Quichua language. Their home is the
province of Muñecas, east of the Lake, which province is partly
inhabited by Quichua-speaking aborigines. On the Island they are
sometimes called Chunchos, but they have nothing in common
with these forest Indians except inasmuch as they pretend (and it
is probably true) that some of their medicinal herbs are gathered
in the *montaña*, or forests, where the wild tribes (often called
Chunchos *collectively*) dwell and roam. The Callahuayas are
great and intrepid traveling peddlers; they extend their journey-
ings to the eastern as well as to the western seacoast, and one is as
likely to meet a Callahuaya in Buenos Ayres as to find him
offering his wares at La Paz, Copacavana or on Titicaca Island.
Their costume differs from that of the Aymará, in that they
wear pantaloons and broad-brimmed hats. A poncho with more
or less intricate patterns, and always dirty, falls down from the
neck as far as the knee, over the usually dilapidated breeches.
Two big bags, like saddle bags, and a wallet with coca and other
ingredients, handsomely woven, but stiff with grease, complete
the official costume of the wandering Callahuaya. We met them
everywhere. Between Puno and Sillustani we saw these quaint
figures walking single file, wending their way in silence from
Indian village to Indian village, from isolated dwelling to isolated
dwelling, everywhere tolerated and everywhere received with
undemonstrative hospitality. A close study of the Callahuayas at
their home is much needed, and would reveal a host of interesting
details on aboriginal medicine and witchcraft. As yet we can only
speak of these singular and enterprising peddlers from what we
saw of them far from the district which they inhabit.

Objects peddled by the Callahuayas are mostly herbs, but these
are not all indigenous. We bought, from a Callahuaya who came
to the Island and offered his wares at Challa, the following
remedies: (1) Against *melancholy:* "*yerba de amante*"; (2)
against *rheumatic* cold: "*uturuncu*," to be rubbed in; (3) against
headache: "*yerba de Castilla*" and *sternutative powder of*

hellebore. Hence, of these four substances, at least one came from some druggist. That such was the case was further proven by the fact that the Indian wizard himself called the powder *rapé.*

There is no doubt that the Callahuaya had other medicines, more efficient and certainly indigenous, but these he was careful not to show us. He was very soon taken in charge by some of the Indians of Challa and remained several days on the Island, without showing himself any more about the hacienda buildings. But—and this seems to be the principal treasure in which the Callahuayas deal—he had for sale a number of fetishes made of white alabaster. This mineral is said to be abundant in the region of Charassani, where the Callahuayas are at home. We purchased such of them as he showed us, and they were all sent to the Museum. One represents a snail, others clenched fists, and these are said to create contentment and give wealth. They were all besmeared with llama-tallow, "untu," the same substance that is indispensable for incantations. Other accessories were gold and silver tinsel, and red and black beans. These fetishes are sold not only to the Indians (and perhaps less to these), but to mestizos, and even to whites occasionally, as faith in the cures and supernatural gifts of the Callahuayas is very common and deeply rooted in all classes of society, though seldom confessed.

We certainly saw only such fetishes as the Callahuaya deemed safe to exhibit, and not the most interesting ones. The latter are more particularly called Mullu, and are of ancient origin and use. The word is Quichua, but has been adopted into the Aymará language. A Mullu is usually an animal figure, like the one used by Manuel Mamani in the ceremonies preceding our excavations. It is "good" for a great many things, and the Callahuayas also sell, secretly, *human* figures. We sent to the Museum a small one, found on the surface of the slopes of Ticani, and of a whitish stone apparently arenaceous. When I showed this figure to one of the wizards on the Island, his eyes sparkled, and he displayed intense desire to obtain it, saying: "If it were Callahuaya, then it would be worth a great deal!" This significant remark caused us to interrogate him cautiously, and thus we ascertained that fetishes in the form of men and of women are still in use. We further found out that, while the *white* fetishes served for *good* purposes, the Callahuayas had fetishes of *black* or at least dark-colored stone, which were used for *evil sorcery*. Here our inquiries came to an end, as Mamani denied any knowledge of "black art."

Accessory information, however, was obtained in another way. A friend of ours, the Franciscan Father Juan Mariscal, on one of his intrepid tours among the then rebellious Indians of the Peruvian boundary, saw a whole arsenal of implements for witchcraft, which he tried to secure for us, but the owner refused to give them up. Our friend could barely more than glance at them. He noticed, however, human figures and other strange objects of wood and stone, and also of rags, but was not permitted to examine them closely as soon as the party having them in charge understood the priest's intention. On the hacienda of Cusijata, a short distance from Copacavana, a number of objects for evil sorcery were found, previous to our coming to Bolivia. One of the chief means for mortally hurting anybody through witchcraft is, to make a human figure out of grains of Indian corn, and pierce it with thorns. In order to separate a loving couple, two such figures are tied together with hairs (not fur) of a cat, and buried, with a live toad alongside of them.

It will be noticed, that not only is witchcraft (good and evil) extensively practiced among the Indians of Aymará stock, hence on the Island also, but that they have *symbolic* figures, of which, however, we saw very few. But any one visiting Bolivia can, if he looks at the roofs of Indian houses, at once descry a primitive symbol placed there alongside of the crosses with which nearly every gable of an Indian home is decorated. This symbol is a *snake*, and represents *lightning*. We had noticed this figure without seeing in it more than an accidental ornament until at Challa the chapel of the hacienda was being repaired. Its low tower had been finished; the cross alone was lacking. To humor the Indians, we promised to obtain a cross at Copacavana, of iron or brass, and donate it to them. As our trip to Copacavana became delayed, our servant (a Bolivian mestizo, who afterward gave us untold trouble through his intemperance and dishonesty) volunteered to make such a cross, with the aid of our carpenter's tools, out of an old box unserviceable for packing, and an aged tin can. He kept his promise and, on completing the ornament, stated that he would have to add two figures of *snakes*, to be fastened diagonally over the cross. Upon asking the wherefore of this, we were told, by him as well as by the Indians, that the snake was a protection against lightning, and its symbolic picture. Figure shows the symbol in the text.

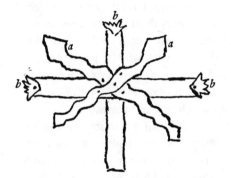

Cross and Snake, the latter symbol for lightning, common on the gables of Indian houses on the Bolivian Puna.

a and a is the symbol for lightning, and intended to represent a snake.

b, *b*, *b*, are called hands (*manos*) and also stand for lightning. As far as I could understand, the snake rather represents the downward ray, or thunderbolt.

The snake symbol is the more singular since that reptile is rarely met with on the high and cold table-lands, the only striking species being the aquatic "yaurinca," already mentioned.

There can be no doubt that the dances of the Aymará are symbolic, although in many cases their true significance is now only known to a few Indians. Their dancing is clearly a *religious* act, and if the performances are accompanied by demonstrations of boisterous delight and by excessive imbibing, this does not militate against their intrinsically *serious* character. The orgies into which nearly all, if not all, the Indian dances degenerate are not the result of degradation and growing viciousness since the advent of the Spaniards, as is often pretended; they are ancient customs, in which the intemperance displayed takes the character of *libations*. It may be that the Indian of the Puna dances for mere enjoyment also, but we know that every religious festival, and every public celebration in general, is accompanied by Indian dancing. The variety of dances is great, among the Aymará as well as among the Quichua. Some of these are common to all districts; many are danced only in certain localities. Some are performed at long intervals of time, others on every occasion, for reasons which only a protracted study of the Aymará will reveal, a study that, like the work of Mr. Frank H. Cushing among the Zuñis, of Dr. Washington Matthews among the Navajos, and of Miss Alice Fletcher among tribes of the central plains, must be carried on with much tact and patience.

It was not possible during our stay in the Lake basin and on certain islands to penetrate deeply into the nature of ceremonies identified with the innermost nature of the Indian and his most hallowed reminiscences. I can present, therefore, but an incomplete *introduction* to the subject. The Aymará are much more reticent on these points than northern tribes. Besides, the true meaning of many dances is either lost or known only to few, and these few are just those whose confidence it is most difficult to gain.

Comparatively few dances are performed on the Island, and these are also danced at Copacavana. Hence what I shall say in regard to the Island will apply to the Peninsula, so far as ascertained. We heard that others are performed at Copacavana besides, and have no reason to doubt it. They differ from those of the pueblo Indians. The procession, sometimes men alone, sometimes men and women, files in with less regularity, and with a step that is rather a clumsy trotting. As there were always several groups dancing at the same time and changing places with each other, it was very difficult to watch the figures. Each group of dancers has a number of musicians, who do not, as in New Mexico, stand still and play their discordant and noisy instruments, but join the others in the dance. The figure is, sometimes, a meandering back and forth in single file; generally, however, and when there are women in the group, they describe a circle, with one man or a pair in the center whirling about like tops, the women especially. We have often wondered at the length of time a woman, encumbered with her many skirts and the bundle of blankets on her back, can endure that vertiginous gyration. The dancer often falls to the ground, and while it is sometimes from intoxication, it is also from sheer dizziness. No better idea can be gathered of the general character of these performances than at one of the great festivals at the sanctuary of Copacavana, for instance on the first and second of February. We went to Copacavana on the day previous and when, on the picturesque trail from Yampupata to the village, we descended into the bottom by the Lake-side, loud shouting, singing, the rumbling of big drums, and firing of muskets was heard. Ahead of us on the road, a procession of white figures with gaudy head-dresses was moving toward the village. They were dancers going to the festival. In front walked the "Chunchu-sicuri," their heads adorned with tall umbrella-like contrivances, each of the canes composing the frame carrying a tuft of red, yellow and green plumes. This head-dress is light, but at least three feet high. All these dancers were men. They wore the gray and laced jackets so common on the markets of La Paz, and over them a sleeveless bodice of jaguar-skin similar to a cuirass. A skirt, made of white cotton and nicely plaited, sometimes stitched handsomely, floundered about their limbs. The leaders carried the Bolivian tricolors and lances, and their head-dress consisted of a stiff hat, with three tiers of parrot plumes, in the national colors: red, yellow and green. The noise made by this group, with flutes and drums of all sizes and descriptions, frightened our animals, although they were old and decrepit. Following the Chunchu-sicuri, a second procession wended its way to the village. This was the ancient and honorable cluster of "Chirihuanos." Their dress consisted of the usual festive garb of the Aymará: jacket, trousers, white shirt, and an occasional vest. Over these was draped a white mantle, graceful when new, but already much worn. Over this mantle a broad band of parrot feathers, beautifully worked, was fastened as on a drum. On the head they wore a black hat, but this post-Columbian head-gear was disguised by a profusion of mostly drooping plumes, white and red. With the first of these two groups a few women jogged along, joining in the discordant shouts and arrayed in their most select accoutrements: a number of gaudy skirts and the little bundle of blankets on the back. These women accompanied the Chunchu-sicuri, the Chirihuanos not allowing women to dance with them. Forcing our animals past this noisy procession, we reached Copacavana and saw the devotion with which each cluster approached the sanctuary. They were admitted to church to offer their respects, and, upon sallying from it, began to dance, pound their drums, and blow their flutes in each of the four corners of the square or *plaza* successively. It may not be out of place here to give an idea of the appearance of this square on the evening before the festival.

At each of the four corners, which are also the four entrances, an altar had been erected. Two poles, about twenty feet in height, were set into the ground and decorated with colored cloth and ribbons, and connected, on the side towards the street, by blankets and ponchos stretching from one pole to the other so as to form a background. This background was further supported by two intermediate poles. At right angles to the former were set on each side two other masts of equal height, and these sides were also closed, leaving open only the front. In the quadrangular recess thus formed stood the altar, simply a table covered with cloth, blankets, or ponchos, on which the image is placed, and loaded with offerings and ornaments, sometimes of the crudest kind. Across the opening, from pole to pole, ropes are stretched at a considerable height above the ground, and from these ropes dangled silverware, sometimes of great value; plates, trays, cups, all from the early times of Spanish colonization, massive, and of quaint workmanship. Between them hung purses filled with money, ancient coins, spoons, in short, all that could be used for representing metallic wealth. We have seen some very remarkable pieces, that would be worthy of any museum of colonial antiquities. These treasures are the property of private individuals, sometimes of Indians, who keep them carefully concealed between festival and festival. There are also parties who loan or rent their plate for such occasions.

The four altars, although alike in the main, vary in details. In front of them gather the Indian dancers, one group after another; they bow to the image, and then dance to the sound of their wretched instruments, finally in the center of the square also. None of these dances can compare with those of the New Mexico pueblos for symmetry. Everything seems to be carried on in a much looser way. Already on the evening before the festival the Indians begin to drink, and only the nature of the beverage has changed since ancient times; alcohol, diluted from forty degrees to sixteen or seventeen, taking the place of the primitive chicha. During the night, one or several trusty Indians keep watch at each of the altars. To keep awake, they drink, play the flute, and the dancers return to the plaza from time to time to repeat their performances and to disturb the slumbers of the inhabitants with their horrid noise. As, late in the evening, new groups come in, they add their din to that of their predecessors, so that the first night, or rather the night before the feast, is already a torture on account of the truly infernal uproar. The musical instruments of the Aymará are more varied than those of the pueblos. They have a great variety of drums, from the smallest to the largest, and from the most ancient type, similar to the tambourine, to the military drum, big and small. The Panflute, called in its tiniest form "kena-kena," and in its tallest (nearly of the size of a full grown man) "zampoña," is most numerously represented. Nearly every Indian carries a clarinet-like instrument or a fife as his constant companion when traveling. These instruments, on a great feast-day, are represented by hundreds, and each group of players blows and beats as hard as possible, regardless of harmony with the tune executed by their next neighbors.

The second day of February was the great day of the festival. At daybreak hosts of dancers poured into the square, and the fifes, kenas, zampoñas, and drums made a deafening noise. The members of each group first knelt on the steps at the entrance of the churchyard and then filed into church, taking off their head-gears. Upon returning to the square, they began their noisy performances at the corners and in the center. The following groups of costumed dancers made their appearance: (1) The Kena-kena, or Kenacho. These were the most numerous, and all able-bodied young men. With them came a number of women and girls. The costume of the men is striking: a short jacket of cloth, black or brown or gray (the latter hue predominating), cut square above the waist and mostly with braids across the breast; the usual breeches, and beneath them often drawers with common white lace. All wear over the jacket a tiger- (jaguar-) skin in the form of a cuirass. Many of them also carry a broad band like a talbart of red, green and yellow parrot-plumes, and on the head a narrow-brimmed black hat of felt or plush, surmounted by an arch of plumes. From the band of this hat dangles, down the back, a train of tinsel, ribbons, and small mirrors. Nearly every Kena plays his fife, never the Pan-flute, and many have drums. (2) The Chayll'pa. Their distinctive dress consists in a white cotton mantle hung edgewise across the shoulders, one of the ends reaching nearly to the knee, and over this mantle, the skin of a young vicuña, its head provided with eyes of glass, and profusely decorated with tinsel, ribbons, and tiny mirrors. A black felt hat with a load of drooping plumes, red and white, and a crown of similar plumage completes the costume. (3) The Chirihuanos (already described). Each is provided with a big drum. (4) The Inca-sicuri. Costume: velvet, cloth and silk, gold and silver embroidery, imitating the supposed dress of the Incas, and clearly of colonial origin. (5) The Chunchu-sicuri (already described). They all beat small drums and play flutes or fifes.

There are two bands of these each with a leader, whose distinctive mark is a hat with a triple row of bright plumes, and a long spear or lance which he brandishes sometimes quite offensively. (6) The Chaca-na-ni. They dance along with the Kenacho, and wear the same costume, without tiger-skins.

Add to these groups a great number of independent performers, male and female, in festive Indian dress, and hosts of spectators, hundreds of big and little drums, hundreds of flutes, from the tiniest to the biggest, and perhaps more fifes yet, the instruments rumbling, thundering, rattling, screeching, howling and screaming, without any regard to rhythm or harmony; hundreds of ugly voices singing monotonous melodies; now and then, here and there, a yell or a whoop; all the performers more or less intoxicated and drinking harder and harder towards nightfall—the scene is indeed very picturesque, very strange and brilliant in hues; but at the same time the din and uproar is so deafening, so utterly devoid of the slightest redeeming feature, that it forms one of the weirdest and, at the same time, most sickening displays imaginable. Once started, this moving crowd, ever changing like a kaleidoscope, keeps on the distressing roar, night and day without intermission, for never *less* than two days and two nights, sometimes as long as *a whole week!* We had the excruciating "pleasure" of enduring three of these festivals at Copacavana, the first of which lasted three days and as many nights, only interrupted by hard showers. The second and third were continued for three days, but the nights were less noisy. At Tiahuanaco, however, the festival lasted *five days and four nights,* the din *never ceasing during that time.*

The Aymará dances which we have seen lack, as stated, the decorum of pueblo dances. Hence, much of their original symbolic character appears to be lost. They all degenerate into an orgy, drunkenness prevailing among both sexes after the first afternoon. Once at this stage, the naturally quarrelsome character of the Aymará crops out and most Indian festivals in Bolivia end in bloodshed. It may even be said, that no Indian festivity is satisfactory without one or more homicides. Feuds between neighboring haciendas are often fought out on such occasions, for the Indian often carries, besides his sling (for which the women provide round pebbles in their skirts), a dangerous weapon in the shape of a whip terminating at the upper end of the handle in a small tomahawk of steel. Whenever such fights take place it is not rare to see men swallowing the brains oozing out of the fractured skulls of the wounded, and women dipping chuñu in the pools of blood, and eating it, when well soaked, with loathsome ferocity.

Two peculiar performances took place on the second of February at Copacavana. One began before sundown, causing the uproar to subside somewhat for about an hour. Two processions marched into the square from opposite sides. Each was headed by a litter of wood borne on the shoulders of four or six Indians.

On each litter, and on an old carved chair decorated with boughs and other cheap ornaments, sat an "Inca," that is, a young Indian in the toggery of the "Inca-sicuri," and armed with a sling. When the two files met, both "Incas" rose in their litters and a dialogue began, treating of the historic strife between Huascar and Atahuallpa and abounding in challenges and insults; one of the "Incas" personifying Huascar, the other Atahuallpa. From words they came to throws with slings, pelting each other with roots instead of stones. The action was quite lively and lasted until one of the "Incas" gave up, considerably bruised and bleeding. After the combat, both stepped down from their litters and mingled with the crowd, dancing side by side. This performance is, of course, post-Columbian. It is one of the many semi-theatrical performances invented as a substitute for the idolatrous and often obscene primitive ceremonials.

The other took place after nightfall and in the darkest corner of the square, where not even the numberless firecrackers, rockets, and other luminous displays shed a spark of light. It was the "Mimula," an ancient round dance in which both sexes take part, and which is now only performed at night. Hence we could not discern any particulars, beyond a number of figures moving about on a small space and to some indifferent tune that did not even seem to be primitive.

None of the groups of dancers heretofore enumerated have, like the New-Mexican pueblos and the Yaquis of Sonora, their particular jesters or clowns. But clumsy mimicries were executed, during the day, by mestizos wearing masks. There is a special group of clowns that appears on the scene everywhere and at every festival, even in public processions at La Paz. These are the "morenos"; not Indians, but mestizos, "cholos," young men who are not unfrequently paid for their performances. We saw them first at La Paz, afterwards at Tiahuanaco, and lastly at Copacavana. The dress of the morenos is usually very costly, being the costume of the eighteenth century, bright-colored frocks of velvet or silk, richly embroidered with gold and silver, vests to fit, knee-breeches, hats, and low shoes and masks, hideous rather than comical. With them go small boys wearing ugly masks of devils, and frequently a condor, that is, a performer arrayed in the plumage of that bird and with a mask imitating its head. If the morenos were less addicted to hard drinking, their pranks and jests might be more palatable. At Copacavana, however, they performed in a rather dignified way. Their costumes were plainer, and each played a small flute or fife. They evidently have nothing in common with the primitive dances of the Indians.

At Tiahuanaco, the Indian dancers belonged to the plain "Sicuri," distinguished from the others by a towering head-dress of gray plumes of the American ostrich, and to the Kenacho, with some Chacanani. The Kenacho had in their company women who wore peculiar hats. At Copacavana female performers wore simply their "nice" clothes, and each had the characteristic bundle slung around the neck. We have not, as yet, been able to obtain a *satisfactory* explanation of this custom, which seems to be ancient.

On the Island of Titicaca, the 25th of July, feast of the patron saint of Challa, could be only partially celebrated. But we coaxed the Indians into dancing during the afternoon. Before noon a group resembling the Chirihuanos in costume, but called "Pusi-piani," came to the chapel to dance and play their fifes and drums before the building. The Chayllpa followed, and later on, besides these two clusters, the Kenacho and the Chacanani presented themselves. Within a very short time the courtyard of the hacienda was filled with dancers, with or without official cos-tume, and with the same din and uproar, though proportionately less, than at other places and larger gatherings. The wonted dis-regard for symmetry and harmony prevailed, showing that dis-cordant noise and irregular motions are inherent to most aboriginal dances of Bolivia; those of Peru we have not yet witnessed.

The existence of numerous groups of dancers, groups that are *permanent associations* and represented over a wide range of territory in villages, communities, and on estates, leads to the inference that there might exist, among these Indians, a special organization controlling these associations and upholding them in the midst of slowly encroaching civilization. But to obtain an insight into this organization is as difficult as it was among the Indians of New Mexico, until the classical researches of Mr. Cushing removed the veil with which the aborigine shrouded his *primitive religious customs*. The study of these features is an enormous virgin field, that claims the attention of students. We found the Aymará as reticent on such topics as any other Indian tribes and even more difficult of approach. Proficiency in their language is, of course, the first condition, and this we had not yet been able to acquire. Besides, with the exception of a few com-munities, who still live according to ancient customs, long resi-dence and familiarization with the Indians in Bolivia may not be even as profitable as in the North. Adoption in an Aymará tribe is out of the question for several reasons: First, there is among the Indians, bitter hatred against all that are not of their stock. An ethnological observer would be at once liable to suspicion as a spy; for the Aymará has many things to conceal from the white man. The local authorities and the landowners themselves are likely to take umbrage at investigations, the purpose of which many would fail to understand, and hence misconstrue. Furthermore the Indian himself has changed many of his customs, and it is a question how far a life of sacrifice and privations could be rewarded, *except* in places where the Aymará preserved most of his primitive habits through *rigid seclusion*. There are a few communities where a discreet and practical student might do important ethnologic work.

Besides the dances mentioned, we have heard of a number of others which it did not fall to our lot to witness. At Llujo on Hallow-eve, the Indians, unbeknown to us, danced the "Auqui-auqui" at their chapel. It was accompanied by prayers and offerings to the deceased. The people were pining for rain, and they believe that, when the bones of the ancient inhabitants are disturbed, drouth follows. We had begun our excavations, and the Indians were mortally afraid of the consequences. On the night, however, of the day mentioned it began to rain and thereafter rained abundantly. The Indians thus became reconciled to our doings, and we never had better laborers and more willing ones than at Llujo. Whether the auqui-auqui had anything to do with their intercessions we could not ascertain. That the chacu-ayllu is a rain-dance was at least *not denied* by our old wizard on Titicaca Island.

The first indication of an organization, are the officers called "Irpa," in Spanish *maestros de bayles* (literally, teachers of the dances). These officers, according to what was stated to us at Tiahuanaco, are appointed for *life*, but on Titicaca we were assured, by the Indians themselves, that the irpas are selected for each dance (by whom they did not say), and that every band of dancers is divided into two groups, each with its director; one group representing Aran-saya and the other Ma-saya. At Tiahuanaco it was asserted that each of these clusters danced on its own side of the square, the Aran-sayas on the north, the Ma-sayas on the south, and that if one section trespassed upon the ground of the other, bloody conflicts would ensue. We noticed such a division in church, but at the dances the confusion became so great, at Tiahuanaco as well as at Copacavana, that it was impossible to ascertain anything. The Indians of Titicaca belonging to the cluster of Aran-saya of the Peninsula of Copacavana, there could be no division on the Island. The irpas are not remunerated for their work. It is an honorary office, as well as that of "alférez," banner-bearer, or godfather to the festival, an introduction from colonial times.

The dances of the Aymará being a part of their *primitive* religious ceremonies, and but superficially connected with the church, any association directing and conducting them must be a part of their *primitive* religious organization. I need not allude here to church-officials among the Indians, like the *fiscales*, but there is *one* office, at least, connected with the church, and little noticed, that possibly recalls certain functionaries among northern Indians who are more particularly keepers of *ancient* beliefs and rituals. We first heard of this office on Titicaca. It is called *Preste*, and its incumbent was an old man, acknowledged to be a potent wizard. It was whispered that he was a lineal descendant of the ancient "gentiles," or "Chullpas." This preste is appointed, by the Ilacata and the old men, or *mayores*, for five years. His duties consist ostensibly in caring for the church, and overseeing preparations for feasts and the like; hence our aged friend Mariano Muchu, the preste of Challa, wandered to Copacavana as frequently as it was *indispensable on account of these duties*, but not oftener, and not out of devotion. We were assured by one of the other shamans that this preste had also the obligation of *doing penance for his people!* I give these statements as we received them, and do not guarantee their veracity, although the same office was mentioned to us at other places.

The existence of wizards, sorcerers, and medicine-men among the Aymará Indians, has been frequently mentioned in the preceding pages. It was natural that, once informed of their existence, we should endeavor to obtain as much information as possible in regard to them; and it is easy to believe that this was a very delicate and difficult task. On general principles, and from what I had seen among the Peruvian Indians, we were prepared to find the shamans in Bolivia also, and the first somewhat detailed statements in regard to them were obtained at Tiahuanaco, though not from Indians. There, the term *brujo* (sorcerer) appeared to be a household word applied to all Indian medicine-men. There also we were told of the belief among the Indians that bones of dead "gentiles" could be introduced into the bodies of persons through evil witchcraft and taken out by some *brujo* through *sucking!* Later on, in the course of conversation with people of the country who spoke Aymará and appeared well versed in the customs of the Indians, we were informed that the titles of those who officiated as diviners were "Layka" and "Yatiri." Some become "Yatiri" because they have been struck by lightning and survived, therefore looked upon as endowed with supernatural gifts; a belief mentioned by older chroniclers and prevailing all over the mountainous districts of Peru. We were assured that the layka consulted the coca, throwing its leaves like cards or dice when they wanted to discover hidden, lost, or stolen property, and that they also used playing cards. One of their performances was described to us as follows: The layka gather at night in some house and begin to drink. At midnight the light is put out, after previously consulting the cards, and then the owl ("jur-cu," or "urcu") is called. The bird answers at once, and its cry is interpreted by the wizards as confirming the conclusion at which they arrived by means of the cards.

On the Island of Titicaca, compelled to live for months with the Indians, we obtained more precise data. The incantation to which we consented in order to obtain an idea of such cere-monies, led us to know that Manuel Mamani, warden of the hacienda buildings (unya-siri), was one of the chief layka on the Island. Toward the end of our last stay at Challa he acknowl-edged it. But direct questioning in regard to his art and rank among the wizards proved useless. It made him offish and caused him to avoid, for a time, the familiar evening talks at our room. Neither gifts of coca nor of money could prevail upon him to speak. With other Indians the result was still worse. The preste, who had been pointed out to us, and by Manuel Mamani himself, as a very powerful shaman, shunned us from the moment he suspected we might interrogate him. Hence it was only through very indirect methods, and by comparing indications thus secured with statements freely made by whites and mestizos, that we were finally able to learn something. We found out that there were at least three principal wizards on Titicaca, and that (this from their own confession) they were subordinate to medicine-men of higher authority residing at Sampaya on the Peninsula of Copacavana. But it was also stated, and by Indians, that at Huaicho there resided some powerful magicians whom they obeyed. This would indicate that the religious organization of the Aymará of that region is independent of the two partialities of Aran-saya and Ma-saya. Among some of the whites and mestizos, a certain Indian family [and particularly one man], residing at Tiquina, was in very bad repute, as mighty sorcerers dreaded on the Peninsula, the Islands, and on Peruvian territory adjacent to Copacavana. But we found out, through the Indians themselves, that although that personage was indeed a noted shaman who frequently abused the credulity of mestizos and even of whites, his influence was not so great with the *Indians*. Casual observations, hints caught here and there, the testimony of residents at Copacavana and Puno satisfied us that the influence of the shamans is as great among the Aymará as among northern Indians, and that it amounts to nearly absolute control of their actions and thoughts. We became convinced that among these wizards there is a proper organization, that there are degrees of rank, that some limit their performances to a certain sphere, others to another. On the evening of our last day at Challa we obtained, at last, some positive information. The Indians had been celebrating, and at our expense, which we readily allowed for obvious reasons. On the day before, two of the highest medicine-men from Sampaya, as it was afterward acknowledged to us, came to Challa under pretext of a friendly visit, and in the forenoon (while the aborigines were still undecided whether they would rejoice or do mischief) the Indians gathered around these wizards to see them consult the coca. We were not allowed to look on. The response must have been favorable, for our offers to defray the expense of the celebration were accepted, and the dances took place in the afternoon. At night the house-warden, being moderately intoxicated, called at our room to receive his gift of coca, and we found him inclined to intimate talk. We approached him first on the subject of the dances and elicited the following information, which I consider mostly reliable; but while it is probably true in regard to the Island and Copacavana, there may exist variations elsewhere.

Manuel Mamani of Challa, our informant, stated that among the inhabitants of Titicaca the following dances and groups of dancers exist: the Mimula, which is seldom performed; the Pusipiani, the Chacanani, the Chayllpa.

These four groups he distinctly and emphatically declared to be *ancient* and *primitive*. The Mimula and Pusipiani, he further asserted, were branches of the *highest of all*,—the Chirihuanos,— which were not on the Island, but had their headquarters at Sampaya, their leaders and highest shamans being layka from the Mamani family.

Besides these five *ancient* groups, there were the following more *modern* ones: The Kenacho, or Kena-kena; the Sicuri, the Inca-sicuri. The latter three clusters he represented as being less important. His statement as to the Chirihuanos being the oldest and the last three named the most recent and least important, was repeated to us, spontaneously, by Dr. del Carpio, the owner of Koati, who has good opportunity of securing information, since the headquarters of the Chirihuanos are in the near neighborhood of his property.

We could not elicit from our Indian other information in regard to the Chirihuanos, Mimula and Pusipiani. As he himself belonged to the last-named, hence to a branch of the Chirihuanos, it is evident that he did not wish to talk "out of school." But in regard to others he was more communicative, as the Indian always is about matters that do not directly concern him.

He told us that it was the duty of the Chacanani "to fight," and that the Kenacho, or Kena-kena, have the same office, but as a recent and "younger" branch of the Chacanani. The Chayllpa he represented as being *hunters*, hence they dance the chacu-ayllu. But he also stated that the Chayllpa are charged with the duty of "making," or procuring, *rain*, by using frogs and toads as intercessors, and by collecting little stones on the rocky summit of the Calvario and throwing them into the Lake. In addition to these duties, the Chayllpa are expected to "make peace when the Chacanani and Kenacho begin to fight."

Assuming the above statements to be true (and from our present knowledge I must regard them as true in the main, at least so far as concerns the Island), these different groups of dancers form as many *esoteric societies*. Upon being closely interrogated on their origin, our informant gave evasive answers, repeating, however, that the layka of Sampaya were the heads of the Chirihuanos; that he himself, as Pusipiani, was the leader of the latter on the Island (there may have been some exaggeration in this); and that initiation in any of the clusters depended upon the pleasure of the "old men" exclusively. We asked several times whether the parents of a child might, through some vow, or pledge, destine that child to become a member of any society of dancers. He either did not understand the query, or was wary enough to suspect the true import of it: at all events he emphatically asserted, that neither the parents nor the party himself could decide or choose. But he also made the somewhat strange statement that the "old men" had power to transfer from one group to another!

There is much in this that recalls the esoteric societies discovered by Mr. Cushing among the pueblo Indians of New Mexico, which certainly existed among the ancient Mexicans and other tribes. Thus the Chacanani and Kenacho appeared to be the *warriors*, the Chayllpa, the *hunters*. I mention such analogies only as hints, and as problems for further careful investigation.

At all events, the existence of these groups, their organization and duties, are kept very secret. That their functions are connected with beliefs and rites antedating Spanish times, appears manifest. Not only the performances of the Chayllpa as pro-

curers of rain, but other features indicate this. While the manufacture of costumes and toggery is partly carried on in broad
daylight, the days and nights preceding a big dance are marked
by doings to which outsiders are not admitted; the layka are, at
such times, often absent from their homes or at least are not
accessible to strangers. The dance itself seems to be but the *display*, not the *object*, of the performance. Its connection with
festivals of the Catholic church is a veil under cover of which the
Indian performs ancient ceremonies. These embody ethnologic
features of great antiquity and considerable interest. I can only
urge the necessity of studying the aborigines of this part of South
America according to the methods so successfully employed
within the last twenty-five years among northern Indians.

The great variety of shamans scattered over Bolivia among the
Indians of all tribes and stocks, as well as among all Indians of
Peru, renders their classification difficult. On the Island, there
was a shaman over whom a cloud seemed to hover. He was
mentioned as being "chama-kani," and regarded with mistrust
because he had "dealings with the owl." We tried to ascertain
whether the medicine-men, the healers and curers proper, or
doctors, so-called, were distinct from the diviners or prophets. It
struck us that our medicine chest and the household remedies of
my wife were so frequently put in requisition, and that even the
layka Manuel Mamani preferred to ask for *our medicaments*
rather than, at least openly, use remedies of his own. It seemed as
if he had no knowledge of aboriginal medicine. Still this same
man, who usually accompanied us and particularly assisted Mrs.
Bandelier in her gathering of medicinal plants, displayed on such
occasions a very intimate acquaintance with herbs and their
application in sundry cases. His knowledge was indicated by
what he refused to tell or avoided to acknowledge, as well as by
what he freely told. Thus we learned, from other sources, of
plants which we saw and of which *he* refused to give even the
names. On the other hand he revealed to us, unconsciously, many
strange beliefs and customs, relating to medicine. Whenever one
of us accidentally hurt himself by falling against a stone, he

would enjoin us to take a small piece of the rock, reduce it to powder, dilute it with water, and drink it, lest the same rock might hurt us again. He it was who told us about the ailment called "larpata," a child's disease, caused by the sight *of a corpse.* In the list of medicinal plants sent in by my wife, a number of species used in *witchcraft* are noted. Whatever remains of the aboriginal practice of medicine among the Aymará is kept secret, and this is doubly strange, since the more suspicious "art" of foretelling by means of the coca is practiced by Indian sorcerers, not for Indians, alone, but frequently for the benefit of mestizos as well as of whites. Singular coincidences of prophecy with fact have been related to us. These oracles and the manner in which they are obtained further illustrate belief in the "Achachilas," so often mentioned here. The conjurer takes certain coca leaves, perfect in form, which, when thrown, fall with the lustrous side upward. Such leaves are to represent the "Achachilas," of the localities where the object or subject of the consultation is at the time, or where a certain action takes place directly connected with the matter at issue. We know of an instance where the object of the performance was to obtain information in regard to military movements connected with political disturbances in Peru and Bolivia. The consultation of the coca took place at Copacavana, and the shaman was an Indian of that Peninsula. He selected three coca leaves as representing, respectively, La Paz, Arequipa and Puno, the first through the "Achachila" of *Illimani,* the second that of the *Misti,* and the third of some height near Puno. That most of the diviners or layka are imposters cannot be affirmed. They to a great extent are sincere, but at the same time there are some who abuse credulity, especially of those who are *not* Indians. Upon the Indian mind these predictions, or oracles, exercise an astounding influence, much greater than a wonderful cure. Hence the diviners, among the Aymará, assume a position superior to that of the medicine-men. Our later investigations have fully established that the shamans are, among the Aymará, organized into several main esoteric clusters. But it is not the place to enter into details of researches carried on after our work on the Islands, in other sections of Bolivia.

That the Indian punishes evil sorcery as cruelly as he bows slavishly to what he considers *legitimate* magic art, applies in full force to the Aymará. When the Indians of Yunguyu broke out on the Peruvian frontier, they sacked the house of the Governor, a white man. On that occasion they discovered two innocent *dolls*, but they had been hidden beneath the floor. It satisfied the natives that they were *objects of black sorcery* and raised their fury to such a pitch, that the house was actually *torn to shreds*. We saw the wreck soon after, and I never saw such complete annihilation through the hand of man. In 1893 an Indian on the Island, well known to us, took it into his head that a certain woman was a dangerous witch. He seized the unfortunate on a favorable opportunity, thrust her into a burning brush pile until she was completely roasted and then—*ate her up!* Acts of cannibalism, by the way, are not uncommon among the Aymará of Bolivia, and many of them are well known to the authorities who, however, either deny or confess they are impotent against such customs. Where an Indian stock has preserved so many of its ancient customs and beliefs, it is natural to suppose that authentic traditions, mythical and historical lore, are still to be gathered. Since the Aymará possess an esoteric organization like that found among the aborigines of the North American southwest, it is chiefly among their *esoteric clusters* that we must look for ancient historical lore.

FROM

THE MYTHS OF THE NEW WORLD

A TREATISE
ON THE
SYMBOLISM AND MYTHOLOGY
OF THE
RED RACE OF AMERICA

By DANIEL G. BRINTON

CHAPTER I

GENERAL CONSIDERATIONS
ON THE RED RACE

Natural religions the unaided attempts of man to find out God, modified by peculiarities of race and nation.—The peculiarities of the red race: 1. Its languages unfriendly to abstract ideas. Native modes of writing by means of pictures, symbols, objects, and phonetic signs. These various methods compared in their influence on the intellectual faculties. 2. Its isolation, unique in the history of the world. 3. Beyond all others, a hunting race.—Principal linguistic subdivisions: 1. The Eskimos. 2. The Athapascas. 3. The Algonkins and Iroquois. 4. The Appalachian tribes. 5. The Dakotas. 6. The Aztecs. 7. The Mayas. 8. The Muyscas. 9. The Quichuas. 10. The Caribs and Tupis. 11. The Araucanians.—General course of migrations.—Age of man in America. —Unity of type in the red race.—Mythological parallels.—Bibliographical note.

When Paul, at the request of the philosophers of Athens, explained to them his views on divine things, he asserted, among other startling novelties, that "God has made of one blood all nations of the earth, that they should seek the Lord, if haply they might feel after him and find him, though he is not far from every one of us."

Here was an orator advocating the unity of the human species, affirming that the chief end of man is to develop an innate idea of God, and that all religions, except the one he preached, were examples of more or less unsuccessful attempts to do so. No

From *The Myths of the New World* by Daniel G. Brinton, David McKay, Philadelphia, Third Edition Revised, 1896, pp. 13–82; 257–303; 329–345. (Footnotes partially deleted.)

wonder the Athenians, who acknowledged no kinship to barbarians, who looked dubiously at the doctrine of innate ideas, and
were divided in opinion as to whether their mythology was a
shrewd device of legislators to keep the populace in subjection, a
veiled natural philosophy, or the celestial reflex of their own
history, mocked at such a babbler and went their ways. The
generations of philosophers that followed them partook of their
doubts and approved their opinions, quite down to our own
times.

But now, after weighing the question maturely, we are compelled to admit that the Apostle was not so wide of the mark
after all—that, in fact, the latest and best authorities, with no bias
in his favor, support his position and may almost be said to
paraphrase his words. For according to a late writer whose work
is still a standard in the science of ethnology, the severest and
most patient investigations show that "not only do acknowledged
facts permit the assumption of the unity of the human species,
but this opinion is attended with fewer discrepancies, and has
greater inner consistency than the opposite one of specific diversity."[1] And as to the religions of heathendom, the view of St.
Paul is but expressed with a more poetic turn by a distinguished
philosopher when he calls them, "not fables, but truths, though
clothed in a garb woven by fancy, wherein the web is the notion
of God, the ideal of reason in the soul of man, the thought of the
Infinite."

Inspiration and science unite therefore to bid us dismiss as
effete the prejudice that natural religions either arise as the
ancient philosophies taught, or that they are, as the Dark Ages
imagined, subtle nets of the devil spread to catch human souls.
They are rather the unaided attempts of man to find out God;
they are the efforts of the reason struggling to define the infinite;
they are the expressions of that "yearning after the gods" which
the earliest of poets discerned in the hearts of all men.

Studied in this sense they are rich in teachings. Would we

[1] The theory of "monogenism," or the specific unity of Man, is now
adopted by most anthropologists.

estimate the intellectual and æsthetic culture of a people, would we generalize the laws of progress, would we appreciate the sublimity of Christianity, and read the seals of its authenticity: the natural conceptions of divinity reveal them. No mythologies are so crude, therefore, none so barbarous, but deserve the attention of the philosophic mind, for they are never the empty fictions of an idle fancy, but rather the utterances, however inarticulate, of an intuition of reason.

These considerations embolden me to approach with some confidence even the aboriginal religions of America, so often stigmatized as incoherent fetichisms, so barren, it has been said, in grand or beautiful conceptions. The task bristles with difficulties. Carelessness, prepossessions, and ignorance have disfigured them with false colors and foreign additions without number. The first maxim, therefore, must be to sift and scrutinize authorities, and to reject whatever betrays the plastic hand of the European. For the religions developed by the Red Race, not those mixed creeds learned from foreign invaders, not the old myths as colored and shot with the hues of Aryan and Semitic imagery, are to be the subjects of our study.

Then will remain the formidable undertaking of reducing the authentic materials thus obtained to system and order, and this not by any preconceived theory of what they ought to conform to, but learning from them the very laws of religious growth they illustrate.

The historian traces the birth of arts, science, and government to man's dependence on nature and his fellows for the means of self-preservation. Not that man receives these endowments from without, but that the stern step-mother, Nature, forces him by threats and stripes to develop his own inherent faculties. So with religion. The idea of God does not, and cannot, proceed from the external world, but, nevertheless, it finds its *historical* origin also in the desperate struggle for life, in the satisfaction of the animal wants and passions, in those vulgar aims and motives which possessed the mind of the primitive man to the exclusion of everything else.

There is an ever present embarrassment in such inquiries. In dealing with these matters beyond the cognizance of the senses, the mind is forced to express its meaning in terms transferred from sensuous perceptions, or under symbols borrowed from the material world. These transfers must be understood, these symbols explained, before the real meaning of a myth can be reached. He who fails to guess the riddle of the sphinx, need not hope to gain admittance to the shrine. With delicate ear the faint whispers of thought must be apprehended which prompt the intellect when it names the immaterial from the material; when it has to seek amid its concrete conceptions for those suited to convey its abstract intuitions; when it chooses from the infinity of visible forms those meet to shadow forth divinity.

Two lights will guide us on this venturesome path. Mindful of the watchword of inductive science, to proceed from the known to the unknown, the inquiry will first be put whether the aboriginal languages of America employ the same tropes to express such ideas as deity, spirit, and soul, as our own and kindred tongues. If the answer prove affirmative, then not only have we gained a firm foothold whence to survey the whole edifice of their mythology; but from an unexpected quarter arises evidence of the unity of our species, far weightier than any mere anatomy can furnish, evidence from the living soul, not from the dead body. True that the science of American linguistics is still almost in its infancy, and that an exhaustive handling of the materials it even now offers involves a more critical acquaintance with its innumerable dialects than I possess; but though the gleaning be sparse, it is enough that I break the ground.

Secondly, religious rites are unconscious commentaries on religious beliefs. At first they are rude representations of the supposed doings of the gods. The Indian rain-maker mounts to the roof of his hut, and rattling vigorously a dry gourd containing pebbles, to represent the thunder, scatters water through a reed on the ground beneath, as he imagines up above in the clouds do the spirits of the storm. Every spring in ancient Delphi was repeated in scenic ceremony the combat of Apollo and the Dragon, the victory of the lord of bright summer over the demon of chilling winter. Thus do forms and ceremonies reveal the meaning of mythology, and the origin of its fables.

Let it not be objected that this proposed method of analysis assumes that religions begin and develop under the operation of inflexible laws. The soul is shackled by no such fatalism. Formative influences there are, deep seated, far reaching, escaped by few; but like those which of yore astrologers imputed to the stars, they potently incline, they do not coerce. Language, pursuits, habits, geographical position, and those subtle mental traits which make up the characteristics of races and nations, all tend to deflect from a given standard the religious life of the individual and the mass. It is essential to give these due weight, and a necessary preface therefore to an analysis of the myths of the red race is an enumeration of its peculiarities, and of its chief families as they were located when first known to the historian.

Of all such modifying circumstances none has greater importance than the means of expressing and transmitting intellectual action. The spoken and the written language of a nation reveals to us its prevailing, and to a certain degree its unavoidable mode of thought. Here the red race offers a notable phenomenon. Scarcely any other trait, physical or mental, binds together its scattered clans so unmistakably as this of language. From the Frozen Ocean to the Land of Fire, with few exceptions the native dialects, though varying endlessly in words, are alike in certain peculiarities of construction, certain morphological features, rarely found elsewhere on the globe, and nowhere else with such persistence.

So foreign are these traits to the grammar of the Aryan tongues that it is not easy to explain them in a few sentences. They depend on a peculiarly complex method of presenting the relations of the idea in the word. This construction has been called by some philologists *polysynthesis;* but it is better to retain for its chief characteristic the term originally applied to it by Wilhelm von Humboldt, *incorporation* (Einverleibung).

What it is will best appear by comparison. Every grammatical

sentence conveys one leading idea with its modifications and relations. Now a Chinese would express these latter by unconnected
syllables, the precise bearing of which could only be guessed by
their position; a Greek or a German would use independent
words, indicating their relations by terminations meaningless in
themselves; a Finn would add syllable after syllable to the end of
the principal word, each modifying the main idea; an Englishman
gains the same end chiefly by the use of particles and by position.

Very different from all these is the spirit of an incorporative
language. It seeks to unite in the most intimate manner all relations and modifications with the leading idea, to merge one in the
other by altering the forms of the words themselves and welding
them together, to express the whole in one word, and to banish
any conception except as it arises in relation to others.[2] Thus in
many American tongues there is, in fact, no word for father,
mother, brother, but only for my, your, his father, etc. This has
advantages and defects. It offers marvelous facilities for defining
the perceptions of the senses with accuracy; but regarding everything in the concrete, it is unfriendly to the nobler labors of the
mind, to abstraction and generalization.

In the numberless changes of these languages, their bewildering
flexibility, their variable forms, and their rapid alteration, they
seem to betray a lack of individuality, and to resemble the vague
and tumultuous history of the tribes who employ them. They
exhibit at times a strange laxity. It is nothing uncommon for the
two sexes to use different names for the same object, and for
nobles and vulgar, priests and people, the old and the young, nay,
even the married and single, to observe what seems to the European ear quite different modes of expression. Their phonetics are

[2] The term *polysynthesis* refers properly to the external form of the expression, *incorporation* to the linguistic process itself. Incorporation was
fully defined and illustrated by Wilhelm von Humboldt in his celebrated
essay prefixed to his work on the Kawi language. The assertion repeatedly
advanced by writers superficially acquainted with the process that it is the
same as agglutination, or a form of it, proves that they are not familiar with
the subject. Incorporation may exist without polysynthesis, as is the case in
the Otomi and various other American tongues.

fluctuating, the consonantal sounds often alternating between several which in our tongue are clearly defined.

Families and whole villages suddenly drop words and manufacture others in their places out of mere caprice or superstition, and a few years' separation suffices to produce a marked dialectic difference; though it is everywhere true that the basic radicals of each stock and the main outlines of its grammatical forms reveal a surprising tenacity in the midst of these surface changes. Vocabularies collected by the earliest navigators are easily recognized from existing tongues, and the widest wanderings of vagrant bands can be traced by the continued relationship of their dialects to the parent stem.

In their copious forms and facility of reproduction they remind one of those anomalous animals, in whom, when a limb is lopped, it rapidly grows again, or even if cut in pieces each part will enter a separate life quite unconcerned about his fellows. But as the naturalist is far from regarding this superabundant vitality as a characteristic of a higher type, so the philologist justly assigns these tongues a low position in the linguistic scale. Fidelity to form, here as everywhere, is the test of excellence.

At the outset, we divine there can be nothing very subtle in the mythologies of nations with such languages. Much there must be that will be obscure, much that is vague, an exhausting variety in repetition, and a strong tendency to lose the idea in the symbol.

What definiteness of outline might be preserved must depend on the care with which the old stories of the gods were passed from one person and one generation to another. The fundamental myths of a race have a surprising tenacity of life. How many centuries had elapsed between the period the Germanic hordes separated from the Argans of Central Asia, and when Tacitus listened to their wild songs on the banks of the Rhine? Yet we know that through those unnumbered ages of barbarism and aimless roving, these songs, "their only sort of history or annals," says the historian, had preserved intact the story of Mannus, the Sanscrit Manu, and his three sons, and of the great god Tuisco, the Indian Dyu.

So much the more do all means invented by the red race to record and transmit thought merit our careful attention. Few and feeble they seem to us, mainly shifts to aid the memory. Of some such, perhaps, not a single tribe was destitute. The tattoo marks on the warrior's breast, his string of grisly scalps, the bear's claws around his neck, were not only trophies of his prowess, but records of his exploits, and to the contemplative mind contain the rudiments of the beneficent art of letters. Did he draw in rude outline on his skin tent figures of men transfixed with arrows as many as he had slain enemies, his education was rapidly advancing. He had mastered the elements of *picture writing*, beyond which hardly the wisest of his race progressed. Figures of the natural objects connected by symbols having fixed meanings make up the whole of this art. The relative frequency of the latter marks its advancement from a merely figurative to an ideographic notation.

On what principle of mental association a given sign was adopted to express a certain idea, why, for instance, on the Chipeway scrolls a circle means *spirits*, and a horned snake *life*, it is often hard to guess. The difficulty grows when we find that to the initiated the same sign calls up quite different ideas, as the subject of the writer varies from war to love, or from the chase to religion. The connection is generally beyond the power of divination, and the key to ideographic writing once lost can never be recovered.

The number of such arbitrary characters in the Chipeway notation is said to be over two hundred; but if the distinction between a figure and a symbol were rigidly applied, it would be much reduced. This kind of writing, if it deserves the name, was common throughout the continent, and many specimens of it, scratched on the plane surfaces of stones, have been preserved to the present day. Such is the once celebrated inscription on Dighton Rock, Massachusetts, long supposed to be a record of the Northmen of Vinland; such are those that mark the faces of the cliffs which overhang the waters of the Orinoco, and those that in Oregon, Peru and La Plata have been the subject of much curious speculation. They are alike the mute epitaphs of vanished generations.[3]

I would it could be said that in favorable contrast to our ignorance of these inscriptions is our comprehension of the highly wrought pictography of the Nahuas or Aztecs.[4] No nation ever reduced it more to a system. It was in constant use in the daily transactions of life. They manufactured for writing purposes a thick, coarse paper from the leaves of the agave plant by a process of maceration and pressure.

An Aztec book closely resembles one of our quarto volumes. It is made of a single sheet, twelve to fifteen inches wide, and often sixty or seventy feet long, and is not rolled, but folded either in squares or zigzags in such a manner that on opening it there are two pages exposed to view. Thin wooden boards are fastened to each of the outer leaves, so that the whole presents as neat an appearance, remarks Peter Martyr, as if it had come from the shop of a skilful bookbinder. They also covered buildings, tapestries and scrolls of parchment with these devices, and for trifling transactions were familiar with the use of *slates* of soft stone from which the figures could readily be erased with water. What is still more astonishing, there is reason to believe, in some instances, their figures were not painted, but actually *printed* with movable blocks of wood on which the symbols were carved in relief, though this was probably confined to those intended for ornament only.

In these records we discern something higher than a mere symbolic notation. They contain the germ of a phonetic alphabet, and represent sounds of spoken language. The symbol is often not connected with the *idea* but with the *word*. The mode in which this is done corresponds precisely to that of the rebus. It is a simple method, readily suggesting itself. In the middle ages it was much in vogue in Europe for the same purpose for which it

[3] The classical work on the subject is Garrick Mallery, *Picture Writing of the American Indians* (Washington, 1893).

[4] The Aztecs and many other tribes of Mexico spoke the Nahuatl language, and hence are called collectively *Nahuas*.

was chiefly employed in Mexico at the same time—the writing of
proper names. For example, the English family Bolton was
known in heraldry by a *tun* transfixed by a *bolt*. Precisely so the
Mexican emperor Ixcoatl is mentioned in the Aztec manuscripts
under the figure of a serpent *coatl*, pierced by obsidian knives
ixtli; and Moquauhzoma by a mouse-trap *montli*, an eagle
quauhtli, a lancet *zo*, and a hand *maitl*.

As a syllable could be expressed by any object whose name
commenced with it, as few words can be given the form of a
rebus without some change, as the figures sometimes represent
their full phonetic value, sometimes only that of their initial
sound, and as universally the attention of the artist was directed
less to the sound than to the idea, the didactic painting of the
Mexicans, whatever it might have been to them, is a sealed book
to us, and must remain so in great part. Moreover, in many instances it is undetermined whether it should be read from the
first to the last page, or *vice versa*, whether from right to left or
from left to right, from bottom to top or from top to bottom,
around the edges of the page toward the centre, or each line in
the opposite direction from the preceding one. There are good
authorities for all these methods, and they may all be correct, for
there is no evidence that any fixed rule had been laid down in this
respect.

Immense masses of such documents were stored in the archives
of ancient Mexico. The historian Torquemada asserts that five
cities alone yielded to the Spanish governor on one requisition no
less than sixteen thousand volumes or scrolls! Every leaf was
destroyed. Indeed, so thorough and wholesale was the destruction
of these memorials now so precious in our eyes that very few
remain to whet the wits of antiquaries.

What there are, however, have been diligently collected and
published by the interest of learned societies and the generosity
of individuals, so that the student has a reasonable apparatus at
hand for his attention.

Beyond all others the Mayas, resident on the peninsula of
Yucatan and in the adjacent parts of Central America, seem to

have approached nearest to a definite graphic system. Several of their books, written before the Europeans invaded their country, have been preserved, and innumerable inscriptions on the stone facades of walls, on their pottery, and on wooden beams, remain to attest the uniformity of their method throughout nearly the whole area occupied by their many affiliated tribes. This native literature has been searchingly analyzed by Förstemann, Seler, Schellhas, Cyrus Thomas and other scholars, and the results though far from exhaustive are so complete that the general tenor and purpose of most of such writings can be ascertained. We do not find a developed phonetic system and yet one more than pictographic. The figures are combinations of symbols, ideograms and phonetic equivalents, the last mentioned being in sufficiently large proportion to render some knowledge of the Maya language necessary to an interpretation of the records.

In South America, also, there is said to have been a nation who cultivated the art of picture writing, the Panos, on the river Ucayale. A missionary, Narcisso Gilbar by name, once penetrated, with great toil, to one of their villages. As he approached he beheld a venerable man seated under the shade of a palm tree, with a great book open before him from which he was reading to an attentive circle of auditors the wars and wanderings of their forefathers. With difficulty the priest got a sight of the precious volume, and found it covered with figures and signs in marvelous symmetry and order. No wonder such a romantic scene left a deep impression on his mind.

The Peruvians adopted a totally different and unique system of records, that by means of the *quipu*. This was a base cord, the thickness of the finger, of any required length, to which were attached numerous small strings of different colors, lengths, and textures, variously knotted and twisted one with another. Each of these peculiarities represented a certain number, a quality, quantity, or other idea, but *what*, not the most fluent *quipu* reader could tell unless he was acquainted with the general topic treated of. Therefore, whenever news was sent in this manner a person accompanied the bearer to serve as verbal commentator, and to prevent confusion the *quipus* relating to the various departments of knowledge were placed in separate storehouses one for war, another for taxes, a third for history, and so forth.

On what principle of mnemotechnics the ideas were connected with the knots and colors we are very much in the dark; it has even been doubted whether they had any application beyond the art of numeration.[5] Each combination had, however, a fixed ideographic value in a certain branch of knowledge, and thus the *quipu* differed essentially from the Catholic rosary, the Jewish phylactery, or the knotted strings of the natives of North America and Siberia, to all of which it has at times been compared.

The *wampum* used by the tribes of the north Atlantic coast was, in many respects, analogous to the quipu. In early times it was composed chiefly of bits of wood or shell of equal size, but different colors. These were hung on strings which were woven into belts and bands, the hues, shapes, sizes, and combinations of the strings hinting their general significance. Thus the lighter shades were invariably harbingers of peaceful or pleasant tidings, while the darker portended war and danger. The general substitution of beads in place of wood, and the custom of embroidering figures in the belts were, probably, introduced by European influence.

Besides these, various simpler mnemonic aids were employed, such as parcels of reeds of different lengths, notched sticks, knots in cords, strings of pebbles or fruit-stones, circular pieces of wood, small wheels or slabs pierced with different figures which the English liken to "cony holes," and at a victory, a treaty, or the founding of a village, sometimes a pillar or heap of stones was erected equalling in number the persons present at the occasion, or the count of the fallen.

This exhausts the list. All other methods of writing, the hieroglyphs of the Micmacs of Acadia, the syllabic alphabet of the Cherokees, the pretended traces of Greek, Hebrew, and Celtiberic letters which have from time to time been brought to the

[5] An early author on Peru states that the most recondite theories of the native religious philosophy were recorded by *quipus*.

notice of the public, have been without exception the products of foreign civilization or simply frauds. Not a single coin, inscription, or memorial of any kind whatever, has been found on the American continent showing the employment, either generally or locally, of any other means of writing than those specified.

Poor as these substitutes for a developed phonetic system seem to us, they were of great value to the uncultivated man. In his legends their introduction is usually ascribed to some heaven-sent benefactor, the antique characters were jealously adhered to, and the pictured scroll of bark, the quipu ball, the belt of wampum, were treasured with provident care, and their import minutely expounded to the most intelligent of the rising generation. In all communities beyond the stage of barbarism a class of persons was set apart for this duty and no other. Thus, for example, in ancient Peru, one college of priests styled *amauta*, learned, had exclusive charge over the quipus containing the mythological and historical traditions; a second, the *haravecs*, singers, devoted themselves to those referring to the national ballads and dramas; while a third occupied their time solely with those pertaining to civil affairs.

Such custodians preserved and prepared the archives, learned by heart with their aid what their fathers knew, and in some countries, as, for instance, among the Panos mentioned above, and the Quichés of Guatemala, repeated portions of them at times to the assembled populace. It has even been averred by one of their converted chiefs, long a missionary to his fellows, that the Chipeways of Lake Superior have a college composed of ten "of the wisest and most venerable of their nation," who have in charge the pictured records containing the ancient history of their tribe. These are kept in an underground chamber, and are disinterred every fifteen years by the assembled guardians, that they may be repaired, and their contents explained to new members of the society.[6]

In spite of these precautions, the end seems to have been very imperfectly attained. The most distinguished characters, the

---

[6] George Copway, *Traditional History of the Ojibway Nation*, p. 130 (London, 1850). Mr. Horatio Hale tells me that the Iroquois still preserve a similar institution to keep up the interpretation of their wampum belts.

weightiest events in national history faded into oblivion after a few generations. The time and circumstances of the formation of the league of the Five Nations, the dispersion of the mound builders of the Ohio valley in the fifteenth century, the chronicles of Peru or Mexico beyond a century or two anterior to the conquest, the genealogies of their ruling families, are preserved in such a vague and contradictory manner that they have slight value as history.

Their mythology fared somewhat better, for not only was it kept fresh in the memory by frequent repetition; but being itself founded in nature, it was constantly nourished by the truths which gave it birth. Nevertheless, we may profit by the warning to remember that their myths are myths only, and not the reflections of history or heroes.

Rising from these details to a general comparison of the symbolic and phonetic systems in their reactions on the mind, the most obvious are their contrasted effects on the faculty of memory. Letters represent elementary sounds, which are few in any language, while symbols stand for ideas, and they are numerically infinite. The transmission of knowledge by means of the latter is consequently attended with most disproportionate labor. It is almost as if we could quote nothing from an author unless we could recollect his exact words. We have a right to look for excellent memories where such a mode is in vogue, and in the present instance we are not disappointed. "These savages," exclaims La Hontan, "have the happiest memories in the world!" It was etiquette at their councils for each speaker to repeat verbatim all his predecessors had said, and the whites were often astonished and confused at the verbal fidelity with which the natives recalled the transactions of long past treaties.

Their songs were inexhaustible. An instance is on record where an Indian sang two hundred on various subjects.[7] Such a fact

---

[7] Morse, *Report on the Indian Tribes*, App. p. 352. Similar instances have been reported by Dr. Washington Matthews, Mr. Frank H. Cushing and other close observers of the modern Indian.

reminds us of a beautiful expression of the elder Humboldt: "Man," he says, "regarded as an animal, belongs to one of the singing species; but his notes are always associated with ideas." The youth who were educated at the public schools of ancient Mexico—for that realm, so far from neglecting the cause of popular education, established houses for gratuitous instruction, and to a certain extent made the attendance upon them obligatory—learned by rote long orations, poems and prayers with a facility astonishing to the conquerors, and surpassing anything they were accustomed to see in the universities of Old Spain.

A phonetic system actually weakens the retentive powers of the mind by offering a more facile plan for preserving thought. "*Ce que je mets sur papier, je remets de ma mémoire*" is an expression of old Montaigne which he could never have used had he employed ideographic characters.

Memory, however, is of far less importance than a free activity of thought, untrammelled by forms or precedents, and ever alert to novel combinations of ideas. Give a race this, and it will guide it to civilization as surely as the needle directs the ship to its haven. It is here that ideographic writing reveals its fatal inferiority. It is forever specifying, materializing, dealing in minutiæ. In the Egyptian symbolic alphabet there is a figure for a virgin, another for a married woman, for a widow without offspring, for a widow with one child, two children, and I know not in how many other circumstances, but for *woman* there is no sign. It must be so in the nature of things, for the symbol represents the object as it appears or is fancied to appear, and not as it is *thought*. Furthermore, the constant learning by heart infallibly leads to heedless repetition and mental servility.

A symbol when understood is independent of sound, and is as universally current as an Arabic numeral. But this divorce of spoken and written language is of questionable advantage. It at once destroys all permanent improvement in a tongue through elegance of style, sonorous periods, or delicacy of expression, and the life of the language itself is weakened when its forms are left to fluctuate uncontrolled. Written poetry, grammar, rhetoric, all are impossible to the student who draws his knowledge from such a source.

Finally, it has been justly observed by the younger Humboldt that the painful fidelity to the antique figures transmitted from barbarous to polished generations is injurious to the æsthetic sense, and dulls the mind to the beautiful in art and nature.

The transmission of thought by figures and symbols would, on the whole, therefore, foster those narrow and material tendencies which the genius of incorporative languages would seem calculated to produce. Its one redeeming trait of strengthening the memory will serve to explain the strange tenacity with which certain myths have been preserved through widely dispersed families, as we shall hereafter see.

Besides this of language there are two traits in the history of the red man without parallel in that of any other variety of our species which has achieved any notable progress in civilization.

The one is his *isolation*. Cut off time out of mind from the rest of the world, he never underwent those crossings of blood and culture which so modified and on the whole promoted the growth of the old world nationalities. In his own way he worked out his own destiny, and what he won was his with a more than ordinary right of ownership. For all those old dreams of the advent of the Ten Lost Tribes, of Buddhist priests, of Welsh princes, or of Phenician merchants on American soil, and there exerting a permanent influence, have been consigned to the dust-bin by every unbiased student, and when we see learned men essaying to resuscitate them, we regretfully look upon it in the light of a scientific anachronism.[8] The most competent observers are agreed that American art bears the indisputable stamp of its indigenous growth. Those analogies and identities which have been brought forward to prove its Asiatic or European or Poly-

---

[8] These words, written thirty years ago, have not been in the least invalidated by subsequent research. There are still a few writers who, misconstruing the meaning of analogies of culture, continue to produce them as evidence of the foreign origin of native American civilization; but their number is yearly diminishing.

nesian origin, whether in myth, folk-lore or technical details, belong wholly and only to the uniform development of human culture under similar conditions. This is their true anthropological interpretation, and we need no other.

The second trait is the entire absence of the herdsman's life with its softening associations. Throughout the continent there is not a single authentic instance of a pastoral tribe, not one of an animal raised for its milk, nor for the transportation of persons, and very few for their flesh.[9] It was essentially a hunting race. The most civilized nations looked to the chase for their chief supply of meat, and the courts of Cuzco and Mexico enacted stringent game and forest laws, and at certain periods the whole population turned out for a general crusade against the denizens of the forest. In the most densely settled districts the conquerors found vast stretches of primitive woods.

If we consider the life of a hunter, pitting his skill and strength against the marvelous instincts and quick perceptions of the brute, training his senses to preternatural acuteness, but blunting his more tender feelings, his sole aim to shed blood and take life, dependent on luck for his food, exposed to deprivations, storms and long wanderings, his chief diet flesh, we may more readily comprehend that conspicuous disregard of human suffering, those sanguinary rites, that vindictive spirit, that inappeasable restlessness, which we so often find in the chronicles of ancient America. The old English law with reason objected to accepting a butcher as a juror on a trial for life; here is a whole race of butchers.

The one mollifying element was agriculture. On the altar of Mixcoatl, god of hunting, the Aztec priest tore the heart from the human victim and smeared with the spouting blood the snake that coiled its length around the idol; flowers and fruits, yellow

[9] The lamas in Peru were domesticated in considerable numbers, chiefly for the fleece. Some similar animal may have been tamed by the ancient inhabitants of the Rio Salado, and Gomara asserts that a tribe near Cape Hatteras kept flocks of deer. Dogs were occasionally trained to draw loads, but not as pack animals.

ears of maize and clusters of rich bananas decked the shrine of
Centeotl, beneficent patroness of agriculture, and bloodless offerings alone were her appropriate dues.

This shows how clear, even to the native mind, was the contrast between these two modes of subsistence. By substituting a
sedentary for a wandering life, by supplying a fixed dependence
for an uncertain contingency, and by admonishing man that in
preservation, not in destruction, lies his most remunerative sphere
of activity, we can hardly estimate too highly the wide distribution of the *zea mays*. This was the only general cereal, and it was
found in cultivation from the southern extremity of Chili to the
fiftieth parallel of north latitude, beyond which limits the low
temperature renders it an uncertain crop. In their legends it is
represented as the gift of the Great Spirit (Chipeways), brought
from the terrestrial Paradise by the sacred animals (Quichés),
and symbolically the mother of the race (Nahuas), and the
material from which was moulded the first of men (Quichés).[10]

As the races, so the great families of man who speak dialects of
the same tongue are, in a sense, individuals, bearing each its own
physiognomy. When the whites first heard the uncouth gutturals
of the Indians, they frequently proclaimed that hundreds of radically diverse languages, invented, it was piously suggested, by the
devil for the annoyance of missionaries, prevailed over the continent. Earnest students of such matters—Gallatin, Turner, Buschmann, Adam—have, however, demonstrated that three-fourths of
the area of America, at its discovery, was controlled by tribes
using dialects traceable to ten or a dozen primitive stems. The
names of these, their geographical position in the sixteenth century, and, so far as it is safe to do so, their individual character, I
shall briefly mention.

Fringing the shores of the Northern Ocean from Mount St.
Elias on the West to the Gulf of St. Lawrence on the east, rarely

---

[10] Dr. J. W. Harshberger, in his *Maize: a Botanical and Economic Study*
(1893), enters at considerable length into the historical question of its origin
and early distribution in America.

seen a hundred miles from the coast, were the Eskimos.[11] They occupy the intermediate geographical position between the races of the Old and New Worlds, and in physical appearance and mental traits have been in parts influenced by the former, but in language betray their near kinship to the latter. An amphibious race, born fishermen, in their buoyant skin kayaks they brave fearlessly the tempests, make long voyages, and merit the sobriquet bestowed upon them by Von Baer, "the Phenicians of the north." Contrary to what one might suppose, they are, amid their snows, a contented, light-hearted people, knowing no longing for a sunnier clime, given to song, music and merry tales. They are cunning handicraftsmen to a degree, but withal wholly ingulfed in a sensuous existence. The desperate struggle for life engrosses them, and their mythology is comparatively barren.

South of them, extending in a broad band across the continent from Hudson's Bay to the Pacific, and almost to the Great Lakes below, is the Athapascan stock. Its affiliated tribes rove far north to the mouth of the Mackenzie River, and wandering still more widely in an opposite direction along both declivities of the Rocky Mountains, people portions of the coast of Oregon south of the mouth of the Columbia, and spreading over the plains of New Mexico under the names of Apaches, Navajos, and Lipans, almost reached the tropics at the delta of the Rio Grande del Norte, and on the shores of the Gulf of California.

No wonder they deserted their fatherland and forgot it altogether, for it is a very *terra damnata*, whose wretched inhabitants are cut off alike from the harvest of the sea and the harvest of the soil. The profitable culture of maize does not extend beyond the fiftieth parallel of latitude, and less than seven degrees farther

---

[11] The name Eskimo is from the Algonkin word *Eskimantick*, eaters of raw flesh. There is reason to believe that at one time they possessed the Atlantic coast considerably to the south. The Northmen, in the year 1000, found the natives of Vinland, possibly near Cape Cod, of the same race as they were familiar with in Labrador. They call them contemptuously *Skralingar*, chips, and describe them as numerous and short of stature. It is curious that the traditions of the Tuscaroras, who placed their arrival on the Virginian coast about 1300, spoke of the race they found there (called Tacci or Dogi) as eaters of raw flesh and ignorant of maize.

north the mean annual temperature everywhere east of the mountains sinks below the freezing point.[12] Agriculture is impossible, and the only chance for life lies in the uncertain fortunes of the chase and the penurious gifts of an arctic flora.

The denizens of these wilds are abject, slovenly, hopelessly savage, "at the bottom of the scale of humanity in North America," says Dr. Richardson; and their relatives who have wandered to the more genial climes of the south are as savage as they, as perversely hostile to a sedentary life, as gross and narrow in their moral notions. This wide-spread stock, scattered over forty-five degrees of latitude, covering thousands of square leagues, reaching from the Arctic Ocean to the confines of the ancient empire of the Montezumas, presents in all its subdivisions the same mental physiognomy and linguistic peculiarities.[13]

Best known to us of all the Indians are the Algonkins and Iroquois, who, at the time of the discovery, were the sole possessors of the region now embraced by Canada and the eastern United States north of the thirty-fifth parallel. The latter, under the names of the Five Nations, Hurons, Tuscaroras, Susquehannocks, Nottoways and others, occupied much of the soil from the St. Lawrence and Lake Ontario to the Roanoke, and the Cherokees, whose homes were in the secluded vales of East Tennessee, appear to have been one of their early offshoots.[14] They were a race of warriors, courageous, cruel, unimaginative, but of rare political sagacity. They are more like ancient Romans than Indians, and are leading figures in the colonial wars.

The Algonkins surrounded them on every side, occupying the rest of the region mentioned and running westward to the base of

[12] Richardson, *Arctic Expedition*, p. 374.

[13] The late Professor W. W. Turner of Washington, and Professor Buschmann of Berlin, are the two scholars who have traced the boundaries of this widely dispersed family. The name is drawn from Lake Athapasca in British America. There is some affinity between the Otomi of Mexico and the Athapascan dialects. They are also known as the Déné or Tinné.

[14] The Cherokee tongue has a limited number of words in common with the Iroquois, and its structural similarity is close. Their name is properly Atsálagi, and is that by which they call a person of their own people.

the Rocky Mountains, where one of their famous bands, the Blackfeet, still hunts over the valley of the Saskatchewan. They were more genial than the Iroquois, of milder manners and more vivid fancy, and were regarded by these with a curious mixture of respect and contempt. Some writer has connected this difference with their preference for the open prairie country in contrast to the endless and sombre forests where were the homes of the Iroquois.[15]

Their history abounds in great men, whose ambitious plans were foiled by the levity of their allies and their want of persistence. They it was, who under King Philip fought the Puritan fathers; who at the instigation of Pontiac doomed to death every white trespasser on their soil; who led by Tecumseh and Black Hawk gathered the clans of the forest and mountain for the last pitched battle of races in the Mississippi valley. To them belonged the mild mannered Lenni Lenape, who little foreboded the hand of iron that grasped their own so softly under the elm tree of Shackamaxon, to them the restless Shawnee, the gypsy of the wilderness, the Chipeways of Lake Superior, and also to them the Indian girl Pocahontas, who in the legend averted from the head of the white man the blow which, rebounding, swept away her father and all his tribe.

Between their southernmost outposts and the Gulf Coast were a number of clans speaking dialects of the Chahta-Muskoki tongue, including the Choctaws, Chicasaws, Upper and Lower Creeks and the Seminoles. Their common legend stated that long ago they entered this district from the west, and destroyed or allied themselves with its earlier occupants. Among these were the Uchees and the Timucuas, the latter possessing the greater

---

15 The term Algonkin may be a corruption of *agomcegwin*, people of the other shore. Algic, often used synonymously, is an adjective manufactured by Mr. Schoolcraft "from the words Alleghany and Atlantic" (*Algic Researches*, ii. p. 12). There is no occasion to accept it, as there is no objection to employing Algonkin both as substantive and adjective. Iroquois is a French compound of the native word *hiro*, I have said, and *kouè*, an interjection of assent or applause, terms constantly heard in their councils.

part of the peninsula of Florida when it was first explored by the Spanish and French colonists in the sixteenth century.[16] The Chahta-Muskoki dialects stretched from the Savannah and Tennessee Rivers to the Gulf Coast, and from the Mississippi to the Atlantic seaboard; but no trace of that tongue or of any other on the northern mainland existed on the Bahamas or the Antilles; nor, so far as is now known, did any linguistic stock of the West Indian Archipelago or South American continent locate a colony in Florida or the Gulf States.

North of the Arkansas River on the right bank of the Mississippi, quite to its source, stretching over to Lake Michigan at Green Bay, and up the valley of the Missouri west to the mountains, resided the Dakotas, an erratic folk, averse to agriculture, but daring hunters and bold warriors, tall and strong of body.[17] Their religious notions have been carefully studied, and as they are remarkably primitive and transparent, they will often be referred to. The Sioux and the Winnebagos are well known branches of this family.

Some distant fragments of it, such as the Tuteloes of Virginia and the Catawbas of Carolina, were found east of the Alleghanies near the seaboard, and the Biloxis on the Gulf Coast in Louisiana.[18]

We have seen that Dr. Richardson assigned to a portion of the Athapascas the lowest place among North American tribes; but there are some in New Mexico who might contest the sad distinction, the Root Diggers, Comanches and others, members of the Snake or Shoshonee family, scattered extensively northwest of Mexico. It has been said of a part of these that they are "nearer the brutes than probably any other portion of the human race on

[16] By a strange chance the language of the Timucuas has been preserved, though probably the last soul that could speak it died more than a century ago. Their high artistic capacity, as revealed in the collections of Clarence Moore and Frank H. Cushing, lend to them especial interest.

[17] Dakota, a native word, means friends or allies. By the Bureau of American Ethnology the stock is called the "Siouan."

[18] On these consult the excellent monograph of James Mooney, *The Siouan Tribes of the East* (Washington, 1894).

the face of the globe."[19] Their habits in some respects are more brutish than those of any brute, for there is no limit to man's moral descent or ascent, and the observer might well be excused for doubting whether such a stock ever had a history in the past, or the possibility of one in the future. Yet these debased creatures speak a related dialect, and partake in some measure of the same blood as the famous Aztec race, who founded the empire of Anahuac, and raised architectural monuments rivalling the most famous structures of the ancient world.[20]

This great family, the "Uto-Aztecan,"[21] whose language has been traced from Nicaragua to the Columbia River, and whose bold intellects and enterprising character colored much of the civilization in this wide area, seems to have journeyed southward at some remote epoch from a centre between the Great Lakes and the Rocky Mountains. They peopled the Sierras of Sonora and controlled the land between the Pacific and the Gulf of Mexico. One of their small bands, the Toltecs, became invested in later legend with the halo of heroes and magicians, and were mythically represented as the founders of that civilization which it is probable they largely borrowed in germ from tribes in the south of Mexico. Such as it was, they readily assimilated and

[19] *Report of the Commissioner of Indian Affairs,* 1854, p. 209. Professor R. Virchow assigns to one of their skulls the very lowest position of any he had examined.

[20] According to Professor Buschmann Aztec is probably from *istae*, white, and Nahuatlacatl signifies those who speak the language *Nahuatl*, clear sounding, sonorous. The Abbé Brasseur (de Bourbourg), on the other hand, derives the latter from the Quiché *nawal*, intelligent, and adds the amazing information that this is identical with the English *know all!!* The Shoshonees when first known dwelt as far north as the headwaters of the Missouri, and in the country now occupied by the Black Feet. Their language, which includes that of the Comanche, Wihinasht, Utah, and kindred bands, was first shown to have many and marked affinities with that of the Aztecs by Professor Buschmann in his great work, *Ueber die Spüren der Aztekischen Sprache im nördlichen Mexico und höheren Amerikanischen Norden*, p. 648 (Berlin, 1854).

[21] Such is the general name I have proposed for it in my *American Race*, p. 118 (Philadelphia, 1891).

increased it, and their distant colonies in Nicaragua and Costa Rica carried it with them to these remote points.

Of an older and higher civilization than the Nahuas were the Mayan tribes. At the discovery, their contiguous bands occupied all the soil of Yucatan and most of that of Guatemala, Chiapas, Tabasco and Western Honduras. An outlying colony dwelt in the valley of the Rio Panuco north of Vera Cruz. They were the builders of the famous ruins of Palenque, Copan, Uxmal and Chichen Itza, as well as of hundreds less known but not less majestic cities, now hidden in the shades of the tropical forests.

Their language is radically distinct from that of the Aztecs, but their calendar and a portion of their mythology are common property. They seem an ancient race of mild manners and considerable polish. Their own annals, preserved by means of their calendars and graphic methods, carry their history back nearly to the beginning of the Christian era.[22]

No American nation offers a more promising field for study. Their stone temples still bear testimony to their uncommon skill in the arts. A trustworthy tradition dates the close of the golden age of Yucatan a century anterior to its discovery by Europeans. Previously it had been one kingdom, under one ruler, and prolonged peace had fostered the growth of the fine arts; but when their capital Mayapan fell, internal dissensions ruined most of their cities.

Very slight connection has been shown between the civilization of North and South America, and that only near the Isthmus of Panama. In the latter continent it was confined to two totally foreign tribes, the Muyscas, whose empire, called that of the Zacs, was in the neighborhood of Bogotá, and the Peruvians, who were divided into two primary divisions, the one the Quichuas, including the Incas and Aymaras, possessing the Andean region, and the Yuncas of the coast. The former were the dominant tribe and extended their language and race along the highlands of the Cordilleras from the Equator to the thirtieth degree of south latitude. Lake Titicaca seems to have been the cradle of their

22 *The Maya Chronicles*, edited by D. G. Brinton (Philadelphia, 1882).

civilization, offering another example how inland seas and well-watered plains favor the change from a hunting to an agricultural life.

These four nations, the Aztecs, the Mayas, the Muyscas and the Peruvians, developed spontaneously and independently under the laws of human progress what civilization was found among the red race. They owed nothing to Asiatic or European teachers. The Incas it was long supposed spoke a language of their own, and this has been thought evidence of foreign extraction; but Wilhelm von Humboldt has shown conclusively that it was but a dialect of the common tongue of their country.[23]

When Columbus first touched the island of Cuba, he was regaled with horrible stories of one-eyed monsters who dwelt on the other islands, but plundered indiscriminately on every hand. These turned out to be the notorious Caribs, whose other name *Cannibals*, has descended as a common noun to our language, expressive of one of their inhuman practices. These warlike robbers had extended their plundering voyages to Cuba and Haiti and permanently occupied some of the Lesser Antilles, but pointed for their home to the mainland of South America. This they possessed along the shore west of the mouth of the Orinoco nearly to the Cordilleras. Their original home was far to the South, and the most primitive dialects of their tongue are found to-day surviving in the highlands near the sources of the River Plate. They won renown as bold fighters, daring navigators and skilled carftsmen; but that they ever formed permanent settlements in any part of the northern continent is now not credited by careful students.[24]

[23] His opinion was founded on an analysis of fifteen words of the secret language of the Incas preserved in the Royal Commentaries of Garcilasso de la Vega. On examination, they all proved to be modified forms from the *lengua general*. The Quichuas of Peru must not be confounded with the Quichés, a Mayan tribe of Guatemala. *Quiché* is the name of a place, and means "many trees"; the derivation of Quichua is unknown. Muyscas means "men." This nation also called themselves Chibchas.

[24] The distribution of the Caribs has been especially studied by von den Steinen (*Unter den Naturvölkern Zentral-Brasiliens*, Berlin, 1894). He gives the meaning of "caraibe" as stranger, foreigner, "not like us."

Except the islands seized by these marauders the whole of the West Indian Archipelago at the arrival of Columbus was peopled by a branch of the Arawack stock.[25] They had at some remote time migrated from the mainland, the coast of which they then occupied between the mouths of the Orinoco and the Amazon. They have abundant affiliations in the southern continent, and there are reasons to believe that their primitive home was in the Bolivian highlands, where we still meet representatives of their family.

In the immense territory of the Amazon basin were numerous tribes not yet clearly distinguished; but the most prominent in history are the members of the Tupi stock. They dwelt on the Atlantic coast from the mouth of the Amazon to the Plate River and along the shore and tributaries of the former almost to the great Cordillera of the west. Their tongue has a comparatively rich literature and is still known as the "general language," *lingoa geral*, of Brazil. Like their neighbors, the Arawacks, they had a moderately high development, carrying on some agriculture, building permanent villages and manufacturing excellent boats and graceful pottery.

The immense forest-covered tract in the northern portion of the Argentine Republic called the Grand Chaco, the Great Hunting Ground, was peopled by roving tribes of still undetermined affinities; while south of it the extensive grassy plains known as the Pampas were controlled by sparse population affined to the Araucanians of Chili, a warlike, freedom-loving race, unconquered for centuries by the white invaders. The inhospitable tracts of Patagonia and the Land of Fire were the abode of isolated groups, many of them in the lowest stages of culture and the utmost apparent wretchedness.

There are many small tribes who seem to have no linguistic affinities with others, especially on the Pacific coast. The lack of inland water communication, the difficult nature of the soil, and

---

[25] The evidence for this will be found in my article, *The Arawack Language of Guiana in its Linguistic and Ethnological Relations*, in the Transactions of the American Philosophical Society, 1871.

perhaps the greater antiquity of the population there, seem to have isolated and split up beyond recognition the indigenous families on that shore of the continent; while the great river systems and broad plains of the Atlantic slope facilitated migration and intercommunication, and thus preserved national distinctions over thousands of square leagues.[26]

These natural features of the continent, compared with the actual distribution of languages, offer our only guides in forming an opinion as to the migrations of these various families in ancient times. Their traditions, take even the most cultivated, are confused, contradictory, and in great part manifestly fabulous. To construct from them by means of daring combinations and forced interpretations a connected account of the race during the centuries preceding Columbus were with the aid of a vivid fancy an easy matter, but would be quite unworthy the name of history. The most that can be said with certainty is that the general course of migrations in both Americas was from the high latitudes toward the tropics, and from the great western chain of mountains toward the east.

No reasonable doubt exists but that the Athapascas, Algonkins, Iroquois, Chahta-Muskokis and Nahuas all migrated from the north or west to the regions they occupied. In South America, curiously enough, the direction is largely reversed. The Caribs, the Arawacks and the Tupis, and perhaps we should add the Aymaras and the Quichuas (though their relationship is not wholly sure), according to both linguistic and legendary testimony, wandered forth from the steppes and valleys at the head waters of the Rio de la Plata toward the Gulf of Mexico, where they came face to face with the other wave of migration surging down from high northern latitudes. For the banks of the river Paraguay and the steppes of the Bolivian Cordilleras are unquestionably the earliest traditional homes of all these stocks.

[26] The reader who desires a closer acquaintance with the linguistic stocks and various aboriginal tribes is referred to my work, *The American Race; a Linguistic Classification and Ethnographic Description of the Native Tribes of North and South America* (New York, 1891), p. 392.

These movements took place not in large bodies under the stimulus of a settled purpose, but step by step, family by family, as the older hunting grounds became too thickly peopled. This fact hints unmistakably at the gray antiquity of the race. It were idle even to guess how great this must be, but it is possible to set limits to it in both directions.

On the one hand, the laws of the evolution of the higher vertebrates offer no support to the idea that the species Man was developed on the American continent. Its living and fossil fauna are alike devoid of high apes, of tailless monkeys, or those with thirty-two teeth; in the absence of which links we must accept man as an immigrant, not a native in the new world. Nor can we place his advent extremely remote. The persistent examination of the glacial moraines which date back to the close of the Ice Age, of the Equus beds west of the Mississippi and the megalonyx layers in the caves of the Alleghanies, of the undisturbed, auriferous gravels of the Pacific, and the Trenton and similar ancient gravels of the Atlantic slope, has resulted in seriously weakening the numerous alleged evidences of the presence of man at the dates of their deposit. No so-called "palæolithic" art, none older than or different from that of the modern red Indian, as we know him through the descriptions of the early travelers, has been established by evidence so clear as to be beyond grave doubt; and the same may be said of the similar supposed discoveries in other portions of the continent.[27]

The cranial forms of the American aborigines have by some been supposed to present anomalies distinguishing their race from all others, and even its chief families from one another. This, too, falls to the ground before a rigid analysis. The last

[27] This appears at the present time (1896) to be the result of the investigations which for several years have been carried on by Mr. Thomas Wilson, Prof. F. W. Wright, C. C. Abbott and F. W. Putnam on the one side, and W. J. McGee, W. H. Holmes and Gerard Fowke on the other; to mention only a few of those interested in them. As for the South American evidences, advanced by F. Ameghino, Burmeister, Lovisato and others, they are too undeterminate to be convincing. Any day, however, unquestionable evidence of glacial or pre-glacial man in America may be exhumed. There is no reason why he should not have been on this continent that long ago.

word of craniology, which at one time promised to revolutionize
ethnology and even history, is that no one form of the skull is
peculiar to the natives of the New World; that in the same linguistic family one glides into another by imperceptible degrees;
and that there is as much diversity, and the same diversity, among
them in this respect as among the races of the Old Continent.[28]
Peculiarities of structure, though they may pass as general truths,
offer no firm foundation whereon to construct a scientific ethnography. Anatomy shows nothing unique in the Indian, nothing
demanding for its development an antiquity beyond that of other
races, still less an original diversity of species.

On the other hand, the remains of primeval art and the impress
he made upon nature bespeak for man a residence in the New
World coeval with the most distant events of history. By remains
of art I do not so much refer to those desolate palaces which
crumble forgotten in the gloom of tropical woods, nor even the
enormous earthworks of the Mississippi valley covered with the
mould of generations of forest trees, but rather to the humbler
and less deceptive relics of his kitchens and his haunts.

On the Atlantic coast one often sees the refuse of Indian villages, where generation after generation have passed their summers in fishing, and left the bones, shells and charcoal as their
only epitaph. How many such summers would it require for one
or two hundred people thus gradually to accumulate a mound of
offal eight or ten feet high and a hundred yards across, as is
common enough? How many generations to heap up that at the
mouth of the Altamaha River, examined and pronounced exclusively of this origin by Sir Charles Lyell,[29] which is about this
height, and covers ten acres of ground?

Those who, like myself, have tramped over many a ploughed

[28] These conclusions, based at the time they were written (1867) on
studies of the Morton collections of skulls in Philadelphia, confirmed by
J. Aitken Meigs (*Catalogue of Human Crania*), are substantially those
reached by Prof. Virchow in his *Crania Ethnica Americana* (Berlin, 1892);
whose conclusions should be checked by the observations of Prof. G. Sergi,
in his *Le Varieta Umane*, 1895.

[29] *Second Visit to the United States*, i, p. 252.

field in search of arrow-heads, must have sometimes been amazed at the numbers which are sown over the face of our country, betokening a most prolonged possession of the soil by their makers. For a hunting population is always sparse, and the collector finds only those arrow-heads which lie upon the surface. Even a certain degree of civilization is most ancient; for the evidences are abundant that the mines of California and Lake Superior were worked by tribes using metals at a very remote epoch.

Still more forcibly does nature herself bear witness to this antiquity of possession. Botanists declare that a very lengthy course of cultivation is required so to alter the form of a plant that it can no longer be identified with the wild species; and still more protracted must be the artificial propagation for it to lose its power of independent life, and to rely wholly on man to preserve it from extinction. Now this is precisely the condition of the maize, tobacco, cotton, quinoa and mandioca plants, and of that species of palm called by botanists the *Gulielma speciosa;* all have been cultivated from immemorial time by the aborigines of America, and, except cotton, by no other race; few of them can be positively identified with any known wild species; several are sure to perish unless fostered by human care.

What numberless ages does this suggest? How many centuries elapsed ere man thought of cultivating Indian corn? How many more ere it had spread over nearly a hundred degrees of latitude, and lost all semblance to its original form? Who has the temerity to answer these questions? The judicious thinker will perceive in them satisfactory reasons for dropping once for all the vexed inquiry, "how America was peopled," and will smile at its imaginary solutions, whether they suggest Jews, Japanese, or, as some say, Egyptians.

While these and other considerations testify forcibly to that isolation I have already mentioned, they are almost equally positive for an extensive intercourse in very distant ages between the great families of the race, and for a prevalent unity of mental type, or perhaps they hint at a still visible oneness of descent. In their stage of culture, the maize, cotton and tobacco could hardly have spread so widely by commerce alone; although the activity of primitive barter must be placed very high. There must have been also wide wanderings, distant colonization by war or in peace, carrying the arts of a tribe bodily into remote realms.

We cannot overlook the unity of the physical type throughout the continent. The American race is physically more homogeneous than any other on the globe. There is no mistaking a group of American Indians, whether they come from Chili or from Canada, from the shores of Hudson Bay or the banks of the Amazon. And this superficial resemblance is a correct indication of what a close anatomical study confirms.

Then there are verbal similarities running through wide families of languages which, in the words of Professor Buschmann, are calculated "to fill us with bewildering amazement," some of which will hereafter be pointed out; and lastly, passing to the psychological constitution of the race, we may quote the words of a sharp-sighted naturalist, whose monograph on one of its tribes is unsurpassed for profound reflections: "Not only do all the primitive inhabitants of America stand on one scale of related culture, but that mental condition of all in which humanity chiefly mirrors itself, to wit, their religious and moral consciousness, this source of all other inner and outer conditions, is one with all, however diverse the natural influences under which they live."

Penetrated with the truth of these views, all artificial divisions into tropical or temperate, civilized or barbarous, will in the present work, so far as possible, be avoided, and the race will be studied as a unit, its religion as the development of ideas common to all its members, and its myths as the garb thrown around these ideas by imaginations more or less fertile, but seeking everywhere to embody the same notions.

In the pursuance of this study we shall discover similarities in the mythical concepts of the red race as striking as are its peculiar physical features, and not unfrequently not less singular analogies with the tropes and tales, the rituals and symbols, in which many a nation of the old world or of the distant islands of the east, chose as the appropriate forms under which to express their notions of the gods and their doings.

The explanation of such parallels has exercised the minds of students of mythology and folk-lore. There are those who would see in them sufficient evidence of former contact and transference, while another school believes that unless there is precise proof of connection in the tale itself or from other sources, it is more likely that the true explanation lies in the oneness of the human mind, the narrow limits in which it works in primitive conditions, and the almost fatal certainty with which it will seek the same concrete forms under which to convey a given abstract idea.

We may indeed assume that a myth has been diffused from one source when it is found with marked peculiarities in nations in geographical contact; when the proper names it contains are the same in different versions, or obviously merely translations the one from the other; where the features of one landscape and culture are retained in another and different horizon; or where a tribe preserved the memory of the importation of the tale or ritual from a foreign centre.

Thus, as Dr. Boas and Father Morice have pointed out, the tribes of the northwest coast as well as the Athabascan bands far inland, drew largely from some common source of mythological conception; we know as a fact that the Eskimos and the Algonkins of Labrador "swapped stories" until the legendary lore of the one nation colored that of the other; the same has been shown by Von den Steinen and Ehrenreich of the tales of the Arawacks, Tupis and Caribs of South America; and the evidence is incontrovertible that the peculiar divinatory calendar of Mexico and Central America with its mass of associated rite and myth was in use among tribes belonging to seven different linguistic stocks.

These and similar examples testify amply to the transference of myths; but when writers would bring into prominence the mere external similarities of narratives, no matter how minute these may seem, and on these alone insist that there was an early historic connection between Yucatan and New Zealand, or between tribes of Hudson Bay and Syria, or of Mexico and ancient Egypt, or those of the shores of the Amazon and the Siberian Lena—as has repeatedly been set forth and is still advocated by some—then the student of myths who follows the precepts of a sound anthropology will prefer the interpretation which in such recognizes merely psychological parallels, proofs of the unity of the soul of man, obliged or inclined to follow the same paths when setting forth on that quest which has for its goal the invisible world and the home of the gods.

BIBLIOGRAPHICAL NOTE

As the subject of American mythology is an unfamiliar one to most readers, and as in its discussion everything depends on a careful selection of authorities, it is well at the outset to review briefly what has already been written upon it, and to assign the relative amount of weight that in the following pages will be given to the works most frequently quoted. The conclusions I have arrived at are at times different from those who have previously touched upon the topic, so such a step seems doubly advisable.

The first who undertook a philosophical survey of American religions was Dr. Samuel Farmer Jarvis, in 1819 (*A Discourse on the Religion of the Indian Tribes of North America*, Collections of the New York Historical Society, vol. iii., New York, 1821). He confined himself to the tribes north of Mexico, a difficult portion of the field, and at that time not very well known. The notion of a state of primitive civilization prevented Dr. Jarvis from forming any correct estimate of the native religions, as it led him to look upon them as deteriorations from purer faiths instead of developments. Thus he speaks of them as having "departed less than among any other nation from the form of primeval truth," and also mentions their "wonderful uniformity" (pp. 219, 221).

The well-known American ethnologist, Mr. E. G. Squier, also published a work on the subject, of wider scope than its title indicated (*The Serpent Symbol in America*, New York, 1851). Though written in a much more liberal spirit than the preceding, it is in the interests of one school of mythology, and it the rather shallow physical one, so fashionable in Europe half a century ago. Thus, with a sweeping generalization, he says, "The religions or superstitions of the American nations, however different they may appear to the superficial glance, are rudimentally the same, and are only modifications of that primitive system which under its physical aspect has been denominated Sun or Fire worship" (p. 111). With this he combines the doctrine, that the chief topic of mythology is the adoration of the generative power; and to rescue such views from their materializing tendencies, imagines to counterbalance them a clear universal monotheism. "We claim to have shown," he says (p. 154), "that the grand conception of a Supreme Unity and the doctrine of the reciprocal principles existed in America in a well-defined and clearly recognized form"; and elsewhere that "the monotheistic idea stands out clearly in *all* the religions of America" (p. 151).

These are views which to-day probably have no defenders; certainly not among those who have made a study of the scientific analysis of primitive religions.

The important work on the Indians edited by Mr. Henry R. Schoolcraft (*History, Condition and Prospects of the Indian Tribes of the United States,* Washington, 1851–59) derives its chief or perhaps only value from the reports of original observers which it contains. The general views of aboriginal history and religion expressed by its editor are shallow and untrustworthy.

A German professor, Dr. J. G. Müller, about forty years ago, wrote quite a voluminous work on American primitive religions (*Geschichte der Amerikanischen Ur-religionen,* p. 707: Basel, 1855). His theory is that "at the south a worship of nature with the adoration of the sun as its centre, at the north a fear of spirits combined with fetichism, made up the two fundamental divisions of the religion of the red race" (pp. 89, 90). This imaginary antithesis he traces out between the Algonkian and Appalachian tribes, and between the "Toltecs" of Guatemala and the Aztecs of Mexico. His quotations are nearly all at second hand, and so little does he criticize his facts as to confuse the Vaudoux worship of the Negroes with that of Votan in Chiapa. While an industrious compilation, his volume must be used with constant caution.

Very much better was the Anthropology of the late Dr. Theodore Waitz (*Anthropologie der Naturvoelker:* Leipzig, 1862–66). No more comprehensive, sound and critical work on the indigenes of America as a whole has since been written. But on their religions the author is unfortunately defective, being led astray by the hasty and groundless generalizations of others. His great anxiety, moreover, to subject all moral sciences to a realistic philosophy, was peculiarly fatal to any correct appreciation of religious growth, and here, therefore, his views are neither new nor tenable.

It is unfortunate that we cannot praise the work in this department of the indefatigable and meritorious Abbé E. C. Brasseur (de Bourbourg). His fixed idea was to explain American mythology after the example of Euhemerus, of Thessaly, as the apotheosis of history. This theory, which has been repeatedly applied to other mythologies with invariable failure, is now disowned by every distinguished student of European and Oriental antiquity; and to seek to introduce it into American religions is simply to render them still more obscure and unattractive, and to deprive them of the only general interest they now have, that of illustrating the gradual development of the religious ideas of humanity.

But while thus regretting the use he has made of them, all interested in American antiquity cannot too much thank this indefatigable explorer for the priceless materials he unearthed in the neglected libraries of Spain and Central America, and laid before the public. For the present purpose the most significant of these is the sacred national book of the Quichés, a tribe of Guatemala. This contains their legends, written in the original tongue, and transcribed by Father Francisco Ximenes about 1725. The manuscripts of this missionary were used early in the present century, by Don Felix Cabrera, but were supposed to be entirely lost even by the Abbé Brasseur himself in 1850 (*Lettre à M. le Duc de Valmy*, Mexique, Oct. 15, 1850). Made aware of their importance by the expressions of regret used in the Abbé's letters, Dr. C. Scherzer, in 1854, was fortunate enough to discover them in the library of the University of San Carlos in the City of Guatemala. The legends were in Quiché with a Spanish translation and scholia. The Spanish was copied by Dr. Scherzer and published in Vienna, in 1856, under the title *Las Historias del Origen de los Indios de Guatemala, por el R. P. F. Francisco Ximenes*. In 1855 the Abbé Brasseur took a copy of the original which he brought out at Paris in 1861, with a translation of his own, under the title *Vuh Popol: Le Livre Sacré des Quichés et les Mythes de l'Antiquité Américaine*. Internal evidence proves that these legends were written down by a converted native some time in the seventeenth century. They carry the national history back about two centuries, beyond which all is professedly mythical. Although both translations are colored by the peculiar views of their makers, and lacking in accuracy, this is one of the most valuable works on American mythology extant.

Another authority of inestimable value was placed within the reach of scholars some years ago. This is the reprint of the *Relations de la Nouvelle France*, containing the annual reports of the Jesuit missionaries among the Iroquois and Algonkins from and after 1611.

The annual reports of the Bureau of Ethnology at Washington, which began to appear in 1881, contain a mass of material indispensable to the student of the myths of the Indians dwelling within the

area of the United States. Though the contributions contained vary
in merit with the faculties and opportunities of the observer for investigations of this nature, they all have solid value. Especially those
by the late Rev. James Owen Dorsey may be mentioned as models of
their kind.

Canadian legends and tales have been diligently and accurately
edited by the Abbé Petitot (*Traditions Indiennes du Canada*, 1888,
etc.); those on the northwest coast by Dr. Franz Boas; and at an
earlier date those of the vanishing Californian tribes by Mr. Stephen
Powers (*Indian Tribes of California*, 1877).

On the mythology of Mexico and Central America, the comprehensive work of H. H. Bancroft (*The Native Races of the Pacific States*,
1875) is important for its encyclopædic survey of the literature of the
subject, but does not attempt a serious analysis of the religious concepts of the tribes. For this we must turn to the numerous essays of
Professor Eduard Seler, of Berlin; of Dr. P. Schellhas; and of Alfredo
Chavero in Mexico.

Our understanding of Peruvian mythology has been greatly fur-
thered by the collations and linguistic analyses of von Tschudi and
Dr. Middendorf; while the great stems of eastern South America, the
Caribs, the Tupi-Guaranis and the Arawacks, have been fruitfully
examined by Barbosa Rodriguez, von den Steinen, Paul Ehrenreich,
Lafone Quevedo and others.

Singularly few attempts have been made toward the philosophical
analysis of American religions, either in the whole or of any one tribe.
Nearly all writers have confined themselves to collecting tales, or else
have contented themselves with such superficialities as "sun worship,"
"snake worship," etc. Major J. W. Powell's *Mythology of the North
American Indians* (1881) aims at something broader, but is too brief
to be satisfactory. Dr. Albert Reville's *Origin and Growth of Religion
as Illustrated by the Native Religions of Mexico and Peru* (Hibbart
lectures, 1884), reveals but a second-hand acquaintance with those
religions, and none whatever with the languages in which they were
couched. The Abbé Petitot's *Accord des Mythologies* (Paris, 1890),
based on American religions, measures all by a merely dogmatic
standard.

A mass of new material has been provided within the last score of
years for the study of American mythology. Much of it offers the
expression of religious thought genuinely aboriginal in character; but
much is also obviously modified by contact with the whites and by
the infiltration of ideas belonging to their intellectual horizon.

CHAPTER II

THE IDEA OF GOD

An intuition common to the species.—Words expressing it in American languages derived either from ideas of above in space, or of life manifested by breath.—Examples.—No conscious monotheism, and but little idea of immateriality discoverable.—Still less any moral dualism of deities, the Great Good Spirit and the Great Bad Spirit being alike terms and notions of foreign importation.

If we accept the definition that mythology is the idea of God expressed in symbol, figure and narrative, and always struggling toward a clearer utterance, it is well not only to trace this idea in its very earliest embodiment in language, but also, for the sake of comparison, to ask what is its latest and most approved expression. The reply to this is given us by Immanuel Kant. He has shown that our reason, dwelling on the facts of experience, constantly seeks the principles which connect them together, and only rests satisfied in the conviction that there is a highest and first principle which reconciles all their discrepancies and binds them into one. This he calls the Ideal of Reason. It must be true, for it is evolved from the laws of reason, our only test of truth.

Furthermore, the sense of personality and the voice of conscience, analyzed to their sources, can only be explained by the assumption of an infinite personality and an absolute standard of right. Or, if to some all this appears but wire-drawn metaphysical subtlety, they are welcome to the definition of the realist, that the idea of God is the sum of those intelligent activities which the individual, reasoning from the analogy of his own actions, imagines to be behind and to bring about natural phenomena. If either of these be correct, it were hard to conceive how any tribe or even any sane man could be without some notion of divinity.

Certainly in America no instance of its absence has been discovered. Obscure, grotesque, unworthy it often was, but everywhere man was oppressed with a *sensus numinis*, a feeling that invisible, powerful agencies were at work around him, who, as they willed, could help or hurt him. In every heart was an altar to the Unknown God.

Not that it was customary to attach any idea of unity to these unseen powers. The supposition that in ancient times and in very unenlightened conditions, before mythology had grown, a monotheism prevailed, which afterwards at various times was revived by reformers, is a belief that should have passed away when the delights of savage life and the praises of a state of nature ceased to be the themes of the philosophers. We are speaking of a people little capable of abstraction. The exhibitions of force in nature seemed to them the manifestations of that mysterious power felt by their self-consciousness; to combine these various manifestations and recognize them as the operations of one personality, was a step not easily taken. Yet He is not far from every one of us. "Whenever man thinks clearly, or feels deeply, he conceives God as self-conscious unity," says Carriere with admirable insight; and elsewhere, "we have monotheism, not in contrast to polytheism, not clear to the thought, but in living intuition in the religious sentiment."

Thus it was among the Indians. Therefore a word is usually found in their languages analogous to none in any European tongue, a word comprehending all manifestations of the unseen world, yet conveying no sense of personal unity. It has been rendered spirit, demon, God, devil, mystery, magic, but commonly and rather absurdly by the English and French, "medicine." In the Algonkin dialects this word is *manito* and *oki*, in Iroquois *otkon*, in the Hidatsa *hopa;* the Dakota has *wakan*, the Aztec *teotl*, the Quichua *huaca*, and the Maya *ku*.

They all express in its most general form the idea of the supernatural. And as in this word, supernatural, we see a transfer of a conception of place, and that it literally means that which is *above* the natural world, so in such as we can analyze of these vague and primitive terms the same trope appears discoverable. *Wakan* as an adverb means *above*, *oki* is but another orthography for *oghee*, and *otkon* seems allied to *hetken*, both of which have the same signification.

The transfer is no mere figure of speech, but has its origin in the very texture of the human mind. The heavens, the upper regions, are in every religion the supposed abode of the divine. What is higher is always the stronger and the nobler; a *superior* is one who is better than we are, and therefore a chieftain in Algonkin in called *oghee-ma*, the higher one.

There is, moreover, a naif and spontaneous instinct which leads man in his ecstasies of joy, and in his paroxysms of fear or pain, to lift his hands and eyes to the overhanging firmament. There the sun and bright stars sojourn, emblems of glory and stability. Its azure vault has a mysterious attraction which invites the eye to gaze longer and longer into its infinite depths. Its deep color brings thoughts of serenity, peace, sunshine and warmth. Even the rudest hunting tribes felt these sentiments, and as a metaphor in their speeches, and as a paint expressive of friendly design, blue was in wide use among them.

So it came to pass that the idea of God was linked to the heavens long ere man asked himself, are the heavens material and God spiritual, is He one, or is He many? Numerous languages bear trace of this. The Latin Deus, the Greek Zeus, the Sanscrit Dyaus, the Chinese Tien, all originally refer to the sky above, and our own word heaven is often employed synonymously with God.

There is at first no personification in these expressions. They embrace all unseen agencies, they are void of personality, and yet to the illogical primitive man there is nothing contradictory in making them the object of his prayers. The Mayas had legions of

Gods; "*ku*," says their historian, "does not signify any particular god; yet their prayers are sometimes addressed to *kue*," which is the same word in the vocative case.

As the Latins called their united divinities *Superi*, those above, so Captain John Smith found that the Powhatans of Virginia employed the word *oki*, above, in the same sense, and it even had passed into a definite personification among them in the shape of an "idol of wood evil-favoredly carved." In purer dialects of the Algonkin it is always indefinite, as in the terms *nipoon oki*, spirit of summer, *pipoon oki*, spirit of winter. Perhaps the word was introduced into Iroquois by the Hurons, neighbors and associates of the Algonkins. The Hurons applied it to that demoniac power "who rules the seasons of the year, who holds the winds and the waves in leash, who can give fortune to their undertakings, and relieve all their wants."

In another and far distant branch of the Iroquois, the Nottoways of southern Virginia, it reappears under the curious form *quaker*, doubtless a corruption of the Powhatan *qui-oki*, lesser gods.[1] The proper Iroquois name of him to whom they prayed was *garonhia*, which again turns out on examination to be their common word for *sky*, and again in all probability from the verbal root *gar*, to be above. The Californian tribes spoke of their chief deity as "The Old Man above," reminding us of "Der Alte im Himmel" of Mephistopheles; and the Creek term for their Jove is "He who lives in the sky." In the legends of the Aztecs and Quichés such phrases as "Heart of the Sky," "Lord of the Sky," "Prince of the Azure Planisphere," "He above all," are of frequent occurrence; and by a still bolder metaphor, the Araucanians, according to Molina, entitled their greatest god "The Soul of the Sky."

This last expression leads to another train of thought. As the philosopher, pondering on the workings of self-consciousness, recognizes that various pathways lead up to God, so the primitive

---

[1] This word is found in Gallatin's vocabularies (*Transactions of the Am. Antiq. Soc.*, vol. ii.), and may have partially induced that distinguished ethnologist to ascribe, as he does in more than one place, whatever notions the eastern tribes had of a Supreme Being to the teachings of the Quakers.

man, in forming his language, sometimes trod one, sometimes another. Whatever else skeptics have questioned, no one has yet presumed to doubt that if a God and a soul exist at all, they are of like essence.

This firm belief has left its impress on language in the names devised to express the supernal, the spiritual world. If we seek hints from idioms more familiar to us than the tongues of the Indians, and take for example this word *spiritual*, we find it is from the Latin *spirare*, to blow, to breathe. If in Latin again we look for the derivation of *animus*, the mind, *anima*, the soul, they point to the Greek *anemos*, wind, and *aémi*, to blow. In Greek the words for soul or spirit, *psuche, pneuma, thumos,* all are directly from verbal roots expressing the motion of the wind or the breath. The Hebrew word *ruah* is translated in the Old Testament sometimes by wind, sometimes by spirit, sometimes by breath. The Egyptian *kneph* is another example.

Etymologically, in fact, ghosts and gusts, breaths and breezes, the Great Spirit and the Great Wind, are one and the same. It is easy to guess the reason of this. The soul is the life, the life is the breath. Invisible, imponderable, quickening with vigorous motion, slackening in rest and sleep, passing quite away in death, it is the most obvious sign of life. All nations grasped the analogy and identified the one with the other. But the breath is nothing but wind. How easy, therefore, to look upon the wind that moves up and down and to and fro upon the earth, that carries the clouds, itself unseen, that calls forth the terrible tempests and the various seasons, as the breath, the spirit of God, as God himself? So in the Mosaic record of creation, it is said "a mighty wind" passed over the formless sea and brought forth the world, and when the Almighty gave to the clay a living soul, he is said to have breathed into it "the wind of lives."

Armed with these analogies, we turn to the primitive tongues of America, and find them there as distinct as in the Old World. In Dakota *niya* is literally breath, figuratively life; Elliott in his translation of the Bible into the Massachusetts tongue renders soul by *nashanonk*, a breathing; in Netela *piuts* is life, breath, and soul; *silla*, in Eskimo, means air, it means wind, but it is also the word that conveys the highest idea of the world as a whole, and the reasoning faculty. The supreme existence they call *Sillam Innua*, Owner of the Air, or of the All; or *Sillam Nelega*, Lord of the Air or Wind. In the Yakama tongue of Oregon *wkrisha* signifies there is wind, *wkrishwit* life; with the Aztecs, *ehecatt* expressed both air, life, and the soul, and personified in their myths it was said to have been born of the breath of Tezcatlipoca, their highest divinity, who is himself often called Yoalli ehecatl, the Wind of Night.

The descent is, indeed, almost perceptible which leads to the personification of the wind as God, which merges this manifestation of life and power in one with its unseen, unknown cause. Thus it was a worthy epithet which the Creeks applied to their supreme invincible ruler, when they addressed him as ESAUGETUH EMISSEE, Master of Breath, and doubtless it was at first but a title of equivalent purport which the Cherokees, their neighbors, were wont to employ, OONAWLEH UNGGI, Eldest of Winds, but rapidly leading to a complete identification of the divine with the natural phenomena of meteorology. This seems to have taken place in the same group of nations, for the original Choctaw word for Deity was HUSHTOLI, the Storm Wind.

The idea, indeed, was constantly being lost in the symbol. In the legends of the Quichés, the mysterious creative power is HURAKAN, a name of no appropriateness in their language, one which was perhaps brought them from the Antilles, which finds its meaning in the ancient tongue of Haiti, and which, under the forms of *hurricane, ouragan, orkan,* was adopted into European marine languages as the native name of the terrible tornado of the Carribean Sea.

Mixcohuatl, the Cloud Serpent, chief divinity of several tribes in ancient Mexico, is to this day the correct term in their language for the tropical whirlwind, and the natives of Panama worshipped the same phenomenon under the name Tuyra. To kiss the air was in Peru the commonest and simplest sign of adoration to the collective divinities.

Many writers on mythology have commented on the prominence so frequently given to the winds. None has traced it to its
true source. The facts of meteorology have been thought all
sufficient for a solution. As if man ever did or ever could draw
the idea of God from nature! In the identity of wind with breath,
of breath with life, of life with soul, of soul with God, lies the far
deeper and far truer reason, whose insensible development I have
here traced, in outline, indeed, but confirmed by the evidence of
language itself.

Let none of these expressions, however, be construed to prove
the distinct recognition of one Supreme Being. Of monotheism
either as displayed in the one personal definite God of the Semitic
races, or in the pantheistic sense of the Brahmins, there was not a
single instance on the American continent. The missionaries
found no word in any of their languages fit to interpret *Deus*,
God.

How could they expect it? The associations we attach to that
name are the accumulated fruits of nigh two thousand years of
Christianity. The phrases Good Spirit, Great Spirit, and similar
ones, have occasioned endless discrepancies in the minds of
travelers. In most instances they are entirely of modern origin,
coined at the suggestion of missionaries, applied to the white
man's God. Very rarely do they bring any conception of personality to the native mind, very rarely do they signify any object of
worship, perhaps never did in the olden times.

The Jesuit Relations state positively that there was no one
immaterial god recognized by the Algonkin tribes, and that the
title, the Great Manito, was introduced first by themselves in its
personal sense. The supreme Iroquois Deity Neo or Hawaneu,
triumphantly adduced by many writers to show the monotheism
underlying the native creeds, and upon whose name Mr. Schoolcraft has built some philological reveries, turns out on closer
scrutiny to be the result of Christian instruction, and the words
themselves to be corruptions of the French *Dieu* and *le bon Dieu!*

Innumerable mysterious forces are in activity around the child
of nature; he feels within him something that tells him they are

not of his kind, and yet not altogether different from him; he sums them up in one word drawn from sensuous experience. Does he wish to express still more forcibly this sentiment, he doubles the word, or prefixes an adjective, or adds an affix, as the genius of his language may dictate. But it still remains to him but an unapplied abstraction, a mere category of thought, a frame for the All. It is never the object of veneration or sacrifice, no myth brings it down to his comprehension, it is not installed in his temples.

Man cannot escape the belief that behind all form is one essence; but the moment he would seize and define it, it eludes his grasp, and by a sorcery more sadly ludicrous than that which blinded Titania, he worships not the Infinite he thinks, but a base idol of his own making. As in the Zend Avesta behind the eternal struggle of Ormuzd and Ahriman looms up the undisturbed and infinite Zeruana Akerana; as in the pages of the Greek poets we here and there catch glimpses of a Zeus who is not he throned on Olympus, nor he who takes part in the wrangles of the gods, but stands far off and alone, one yet all "who was, who is, who will be"; so the belief in an Unseen Spirit, who asks neither supplication nor sacrifice, who, as the natives of Texas told Joutel in 1684, "does not concern himself about things here below," who has no name to call him by, and is never a figure in mythology, was doubtless occasionally present to their minds.

It was present not more but far less distinctly and often not at all in the more savage tribes, and no assertion can be more contrary to the laws of religious progress than that which pretends that a purer and more monotheistic religion exists among nations devoid of mythology. There are only two instances on the American continent where the worship of an immaterial God was definitely instituted, and these as the highest conquests of American natural religions deserve especial mention.

They occurred, as we might expect, in the two most civilized nations, the Quichuas of Peru, and the Nahuas of Tezcuco. It is related that about the year 1440, at a grand religious council held at the consecration of the newly-built temple of the Sun at Cuzco, the Inca Yupanqui rose before the assembled multitude, and spoke somewhat as follows:

"Many say that the Sun is the Maker of all things. But he who makes should abide by what he has made. Now many things happen when the Sun is absent; therefore he cannot be the universal creator. And that he is alive at all is doubtful, for his trips do not tire him. Were he a living thing, he would grow weary like ourselves; were he free, he would visit other parts of the heavens. He is like a tethered beast who makes a daily round under the eye of a master; he is like an arrow, which must go whither it is sent, not whither it wishes. I tell you that he, our Father and Master the Sun, must have a lord and master more powerful than himself, who constrains him to his daily circuit without pause or rest."

To express this greatest of all existences, a name was proclaimed, based upon that of the highest divinities known to the ancient Inca race, Illatici Viracocha Pachacamac, literally, "the thunder vase, the foam of the sea, animating the world,"—mysterious and symbolic names drawn from the deepest religious instincts of the soul, whose hidden meanings will be unravelled hereafter. A temple was constructed in a vale by the sea near Callao, wherein his worship was to be conducted without images or human sacrifices. The Inca was ahead of his age, however, and when the Spaniards visited the temple of Pachacamac in 1525, they found not only the walls adorned with hideous paintings, but an ugly idol of wood representing a man of colossal proportions set up therein, and receiving the prayers of the votaries.

No better success attended the attempt of Nezahuatl, lord of Tezcuco, which took place about the same time. He had long prayed to the gods of his forefathers for a son to inherit his kingdom, and the altars had smoked vainly with the blood of slaughtered victims. At length, in indignation and despair, the prince exclaimed, "Verily, these gods that I am adoring, what are they but idols of stone without speech or feeling? They could not have made the beauty of the heaven, the sun, the moon, and the stars which adorn it, and which light the earth, with its countless streams, its fountains and waters, its trees and plants, and its various inhabitants. There must be some god, invisible and unknown, who is the universal creator. He alone can console me in my affliction and take away my sorrow."

Strengthened in this conviction by a timely fulfilment of his heart's desire, he erected a temple nine stories high to represent the nine heavens, which he dedicated "to the Unknown God, the Cause of Causes." This temple, he ordained, should never be polluted by blood, nor should any graven image ever be set up within its precincts.

In neither case, be it observed, was any attempt made to substitute another and purer religion for the popular one. The Inca continued to receive the homage of his subjects as a brother of the sun, and the regular services to that luminary were never interrupted. Nor did the prince of Tezcuco afterwards neglect the honors due his national gods, nor even refrain himself from plunging the knife into the breasts of captives on the altar of the god of war. They were but expressions of that monotheism which is ever present, "not in contrast to polytheism, but in living intuition in the religious sentiments."

If this subtle but true distinction be rightly understood, it will excite no surprise to find such epithets as "endless," "omnipotent," "invisible," "adorable," such appellations as "the Maker and Moulder of All," "the Mother and Father of Life," "the One God complete in perfection and unity," "the Creator of all that is," "the Soul of the World," in use and of undoubted indigenous origin not only among the civilized Aztecs, but even among the Haitians, the Araucanians, the Lenni Lenape, and others. It will not seem contradictory to hear of them in a purely polytheistic worship; we shall be far from regarding them as familiar to the popular mind, and we shall never be led so far astray as to adduce them in evidence of a monotheism in either technical sense of that word.

In point of fact they were not applied to any particular god even in the most enlightened nations, but were terms of laudation and magniloquence used by the priests and devotees of every several god to do him honor. They prove something in regard to a consciousness of divinity hedging us about, but nothing at all in favor of a recognition of one God; they exemplify how profound is the conviction of a highest and first principle, but they do not offer the least reason to surmise that this was a living reality in doctrine or practice.

The confusion of these distinct ideas has led to much misconception of the native creeds. But another and more fatal error was that which distorted them into a dualistic form, ranging on one hand the good spirit with his legions of angels, on the other the evil one with his swarms of fiends, representing the world as the scene of their unending conflict, man as the unlucky football who gets all the blows.

This notion, which has its historical origin among the Parsees of ancient Iran, is unknown to savage nations. "The Hidatsa," says Dr. Matthews, "believe neither in a hell nor a devil." "The idea of the Devil," justly observes Jacob Grimm, "is foreign to all primitive religions." Yet Professor Mueller, in his voluminous work on those of America, after approvingly quoting this saying, complacently proceeds to classify the deities as good or bad spirits!

This view, which has obtained without question in earlier works on the native religions of America, has arisen partly from habits of thought difficult to break, partly from mistranslations of native words, partly from the foolish axiom of the early missionaries, "The gods of the gentiles are devils." Yet their own writings furnish conclusive proof that no such distinction existed out of their own fancies. The same word (*otkon*) which Father Bruyas employs to translate into Iroquois the term "devil," in the passage "the Devil took upon himself the figure of a serpent," he is obliged to use for "spirit" in the phrase, "at the resurrection we shall be spirits," which is a rather amusing illustration how impossible it was by any native word to convey the idea of the spirit of evil.

When, in 1570, Father Rogel commenced his labors among the tribes near the Savannah River, he told them that the deity they adored was a demon who loved all evil things, and they must hate him; whereupon his auditors replied, that so far from this being the case, whom he called a wicked being was the power that sent them all good things, and indignantly left the missionary to preach to the winds.

A passage often quoted in support of this mistaken view is one in Winslow's "Good News from New England," written in 1622. The author says that the Indians worship a good power called Kiehtan, and another "who, as farre as wee can conceive, is the Devill," named Hobbamock, or Hobbamoqui. The former of these names is merely the word "great," in their dialect of Algonkin, with a final *n*, and is probably an abbreviation of Kittanitowit, the great manito, a vague term mentioned by Roger Williams and other early writers, manufactured probably by them and not the appellation of any personified deity. The latter, so far from corresponding to the power of evil, was, according to Winslow's own statement, the kindly god who cured diseases, aided them in the chase, and appeared to them in dreams as their protector. Therefore, with great justice, Dr. Jarvis has explained it to mean "the *oke* or tutelary deity which each Indian worships," as the word itself signifies.

So in many instances it turns out that what has been reported to be the evil divinity of a nation, to whom they pray to the neglect of a better one, is in reality the highest power they recognize. Thus Juripari, worshipped by certain tribes of Brazil, and said to be their wicked spirit, is in fact the name in their language for supernatural in general; and Aka-kanet, sometimes mentioned as the father of evil in the mythology of the Araucanians, is the benign power appealed to by their priests, who is throned in the Pleiades, who sends fruits and flowers to the earth, and is addressed as "grandfather."[2] The Çupay of the Peruvians

---

[2] Mueller, *Amer. Urreligionen*, pp. 265, 272, 274. Well may he remark: "The dualism is not very striking among these tribes"; as a few pages previous he says of the Caribs, "The dualism of gods is anything but rigidly

never was, as Prescott would have us believe, "the shadowy embodiment of evil," but simply and solely their god of the dead, the Pluto of their pantheon, corresponding to the Mictla of the Mexicans.

The evidence on the point is indeed conclusive. The Jesuit missionaries very rarely distinguish between good and evil deities when speaking of the religion of the northern tribes; and the Moravian Brethren among the Algonkins and Iroquois place on record their unanimous testimony that "the idea of a devil, a prince of darkness, they first received in later times through the Europeans." So the Cherokees, remarks an intelligent observer, "know nothing of the Evil One and his domains, except what they have learned from white men."

The term Great Spirit conveys, for instance, to the Chipeway just as much the idea of a bad as of a good spirit; he is unaware of any distinction until it is explained to him. "I have never been able to discover from the Dakotas themselves," remarks the Rev. G. H. Pond, who had lived among them as a missionary for eighteen years, "the least degree of evidence that they divide the gods into classes of good and evil, and am persuaded that those persons who represent them as doing so, do it inconsiderately, and because it is so natural to subscribe to a long-cherished popular opinion."

Very soon after coming in contact with the whites, the Indians caught the notion of a bad and good spirit, pitted one against the other in eternal warfare, and engrafted it on their ancient traditions. Writers anxious to discover Jewish or Christian analogies, forcibly construed myths to suit their pet theories, and for indolent observers it was convenient to catalogue their gods in antithetical classes. In Mexican and Peruvian mythology this is so plainly false that historians no longer insist upon it, but as a popular error it still holds its ground with reference to the more barbarous and less known tribes.

---

observed. The good gods do more evil than good. Fear is the ruling religious sentiment." To such a lame conclusion do these venerable prepossessions lead. "*Grau ist alle Theorie.*"

Perhaps no myth has been so often quoted in its confirmation as that of the ancient Iroquois, which narrates the conflict between the first two brothers of our race. It is of undoubted native origin and venerable antiquity. The version given by the Tuscarora chief Cusic in 1825, relates that in the beginning of things there were two brothers, Enigorio and Enigohahetgea, names literally meaning the Good Mind and the Bad Mind. The former went about the world furnishing it with gentle streams, fertile plains and plenteous fruits, while the latter maliciously followed him, creating rapids, thorns, and deserts. At length the Good Mind turned upon his brother in anger, and crushed him into the earth. He sank out of sight in its depths, but not to perish, for in the dark realms of the underworld he still lives, receiving the souls of the dead and being the author of all evil.

Now when we compare this with the version of the same legend given by Father Brebeuf, missionary to the Hurons in 1636, we find its whole complexion altered; the moral dualism vanishes; the names Good Mind and Bad Mind do not appear; it is the struggle of Ioskeha, the White one, with his brother Tawiscara, the Dark one, and we at once perceive that Christian influence in the course of two centuries had given the tale a meaning foreign to its original intent.

So it is with the story the Algonkins tell of their hero Manibozho, who, in the opinion of a well-known writer, "is always placed in antagonism to a great serpent, a spirit of evil." It is to the effect that after conquering many animals, this famous magician tried his arts on the prince of serpents. After a prolonged struggle, which brought on the general deluge and the destruction of the world, he won the victory.

The first authority we have for this narrative is even later than Cusic; it is Mr. Schoolcraft in our own day; the legendary cause of the deluge as related by Father Le Jeune, in 1634, is quite dissimilar, and makes no mention of a serpent; and, as we shall hereafter see, neither among the Algonkins nor any other Indians, was the serpent usually a type of evil, but quite the reverse.

The comparatively late introduction of such views into the

native legends finds a remarkable proof in the myths of the Quichés, which were committed to writing in the seventeenth century. They narrate the struggles between the rulers of the upper and the nether world, the descent of the former into Xibalba, the Realm of Phantoms, and their victory over its lords, One Death and Seven Deaths. The writer adds of the latter, who clearly represent to his mind the Evil One and his adjutants, "in the old times they did not have much power; they were but annoyers and opposers of men, and, in truth, they were not regarded as gods. But when they appeared it was terrible. They were of evil, they were owls, fomenting trouble and discord."

In this passage, which, be it said, seems to have impressed the translators very differently, the writer appears to compare the great power assigned by the Christian religion to Satan and his allies, with the very much less potency attributed to their analogues in heathendom, the rulers of the world of the dead.

A little reflection will convince the most incredulous that any such dualism as has been fancied to exist in the native religions, could not have been of indigenous growth. The gods of the primitive man are beings of thoroughly human physiognomy, painted with colors furnished by intercourse with his fellows. These are his enemies or his friends, as he conciliates or insults them. No mere man, least of all a savage, is kind and benevolent in spite of neglect and injury, nor is any man causelessly and ceaselessly malicious. Personal, family, or national feuds render some more inimical than others, but always from a desire to guard their own interests, never out of a delight in evil for its own sake.

Thus the cruel gods of death, disease, and danger, were never of Satanic nature, while the kindliest divinities were disposed to punish, and that severely, any neglect of their ceremonies.

Moral dualism can only arise where the ideas of good and evil are not synonymous with those of pleasure and pain, for the conception of a wholly good or a wholly evil nature requires the use of these terms in their higher ethical sense. The various deities of the Indians, it may safely be said in conclusion, present no stronger antithesis in this respect than those of ancient Greece and Rome. Some gods favored man and others hurt him; some, like the forces they embodied, were beneficent to him, others injurious. But no ethical contrast, beyond what this would imply, existed to the native mind.

CHAPTER VIII

THE ORIGIN OF MAN

Usually man is the EARTH-BORN, both in language and myths.—The Earth-Mother.—Illustrations from the legends of the Caribs, Appalachians, Iroquois, Quichuas, Aztecs, and others.—The underworld.— Man the product of one of the primal creative powers, the Spirit or the Water, in the myths of the Athapascas, Eskimos, Moxos, and others. Not literally derived from an inferior species.

No man can escape the importunate question, Whence am I? The first replies framed to meet it possess an interest to the thoughtful mind, beyond that of mere fables. They illustrate the position in creation claimed by our race, and the early workings of self-consciousness. Often the oldest terms for man are synopses of these replies, and merit a more than passing contemplation.

The seed is hidden in the earth. Warmed by the sun, watered by the rain, presently it bursts its dark prison-house, unfolds its delicate leaves, blossoms, and matures its fruit. Its work done, the earth draws it to itself again, resolves the various structures into their original mould, and the unending round recommences.

This is the marvellous process that struck the primitive mind. Out of the Earth rises life, to it it returns. She it is who guards all germs, nourishes all beings. The Aztecs painted her as a woman with countless breasts, the Peruvians called her Mama Allpa, mother earth; the Caribs addressed her as Mama Nono, "the good mother from whom all things come." In the Algonkin dialects the word for earth, *ohke*, is derived from the same radical as mother and father, a verbal which means to come forth from. So in the creation myths of the Zuñis we read of the "Fourfold containing Mother Earth," and of "Earth with her fourfold Womb."

In the legends of the Dakotas, the female Unktahe, the invisible powers which conduct the motions of the world, dwell in the earth. It was they, indeed, who first lifted it to the surface of the primeval waters and fitted it for habitable land. They are still its vitalizers, and their cult is connected with that of the reproductive powers and the *lingam* symbol.

In the legends of the western Algonkins the earth is spoken of by the tender word Nokomis, my grandmother, and from her fertile womb issued all nations of the world.

It was a curious result of this myth of the Earth-Mother that led the Passes of Brazil to the surprising conclusion that the earth moves around the sun! It is a great creature, said they, the rivers and streams are its bloodvessels, and it turns itself, first one side then the other to the sun, that it may keep itself warm.

Distinctly related to the notion of the earth as the mother and matrix of men and animals was the reverse of the concept, to wit, that which regarded her as the tomb as well as the womb of all.

In the esoteric language of the Nagualists of Mexico which preserved in later days the national religion, the earth was invoked as Tonan, Our Mother, and as "the flower which contains all flowers," for from her prolific breast all come forth; but another and ominous one of her titles was, "The mouth which eats all mouths"; for she it is that at last eats all eaters.

Those of Tezcuco therefore painted her in their sacred books under the figure of a wild beast with mouths at every joint, dripping with blood; for, said they, she it is who eats and swallows all things. One of her names was Ilama, "The Old Woman," to whom a woman victim was sacrificed at night, with tears and grief, for the earth-mother will be the grave of all that breathes. How appropriate the name was to the native mind is seen in the Quichua language of Peru, where our expression, "to grow old," is rendered by *allpa-way*, "to become earthen," "to change to earth," and unwittingly, how correctly does it express that gradual increase of inorganic matter in the system which is the physiological cause of senile changes!

With almost the same imagery the Creeks in their national legend say that "the Earth ate up the children of the ancestors"; and they add that when the day of the final extinction of their nation shall arrive, they will disappear in "the navel of the earth," returning whence they came. In the Mayan theogony the earth is, indeed, the common ancestress of the race of men; but her usual name is Ix-mucane, "the woman who buries" all things.

From the womb of the earth, therefore, figuratively or literally, did man, in the primitive thought of many races, proceed and emerge. *Homo, Adam, chamaigenēs,* what do all these words mean but the earth-born, the son of the soil, repeated in the poetic language of Attica in *anthropos,* "he who springs up as a flower"?

The word that corresponds to the Latin *homo* in American languages has such singular uniformity in so many of them, that we might be tempted to regard it as a fragment of some ancient and common tongue, their parent stem. In the Eskimo it is *inuk, innuk,* plural *innuit;* in Athapasca it is *dinni, tenné;* in Pima, *tinot;* in Algonkin, *inini, lenni, inwi;* in Iroquois, *onwi, eniha;* in the Otomi of Mexico, *n-aniehe;* in Zapotec, *beni;* in the Maya, *inic, winic, winak;*—all in North America, and the number might be extended.

Of these only the last mentioned can plausibly be traced to a radical (unless the Iroquois *onwi* is from *onnha* life, *onnhe* to live). This Father Ximenes derives from *win,* meaning to grow, to gain, to increase, in which the analogy to vegetable life is not far off, an analogy strengthened by the myth of that stock, which relates that the first of men were formed of the flour of maize.

In many other instances religious legend carries out this idea. The mythical ancestor of the Caribs created his offspring by sowing the soil with stones or with the fruit of the Mauritius palm, which sprouted forth into men and women, while the Yurucares clothed this crude tenet in a somewhat more poetic form, fabling that at the beginning the first of men were pegged, Ariel-like, in the knotty entrails of an enormous bole, until the god Tiri—a second Prospero—released them by cleaving it in twain.[1]

As in oriental legends the origin of man from the earth was veiled under the story that he was the progeny of some mountain fecundated by the embrace of Mithras or Jupiter, so the Indians often pointed to some height or some cavern, as the spot whence the first of men issued, adult and armed, from the womb of the All-mother Earth. The oldest name of the Alleghany Mountains is Paemotinck or Pemolnick, an Algonkin word, the meaning of which is said to be "the origin of the Indians."

The Witchitas, who dwelt on the Red River among the mountains named after them, have a tradition that their progenitors issued from the rocks about their homes, the Blackfoot legends point for the origin of their class to Nina Stahu, "chief of mountains," a bold, square-topped peak of the Rocky Mountains near Lake Omaxeen, and many other tribes, the Tahkalis, Navajos, Coyoteros, and the Haitians, for instance, set up this claim to be autochthones.

Most writers have interpreted this simply to mean that they knew nothing at all about their origin, or that they coined these fables merely to strengthen the title to the territory they inhabited when they saw the whites eagerly snatching it away on every pretext. No doubt there is some truth in this, but if they be carefully sifted, there is sometimes a deep psychological significance in these myths, which has hitherto escaped the observation of students. An instance presents itself in our own country.

All those tribes, the Creeks, Seminoles, Choctaws, Chicasaws, and Natchez, who, according to tradition, were in remote times

[1] It is still a mooted point whence Shakespeare drew the plot of *The Tempest*. The coincidence mentioned in the text between some parts of it and South American mythology does not stand alone. Caliban, the savage and brutish native of the island, is undoubtedly the word Carib, often spelt Caribani, and Calibani in older writers; and his "dam's god Setebos" was the supreme divinity of the Patagonians when first visited by Magellan.

banded into one common confederacy under the headship of the last mentioned, unanimously located their earliest ancestry near an artificial eminence in the valley of the Big Black River, in the Natchez country, whence they pretended to have emerged.

Fortunately we have a description, though a brief one, of this interesting monument from the pen of an intelligent traveller. It is described as "an elevation of earth about half a mile square and fifteen or twenty feet high. From its northeast corner a wall of equal height extends for near half a mile to the high land."

This was the Nunne Chaha or Nunne Hamgeh, the High Hill, or the Bending Hill, famous in Choctaw stories, and which Captain Gregg found they have not yet forgotten in their western home. The legend was that in its centre was a cave, the house of the Master of Breath. Here he made the first men from the clay around him, and as at that time the waters covered the earth, he raised the wall to dry them on. When the soft mud had hardened into elastic flesh and firm bone, he banished the waters to their channels and beds, and gave the dry land to his creatures. The Muskokis call this mountain "King of Mountains," or "King of the Land," *rvne em mekko*.

It is at first sight astonishing with what uniformity the traditional lore of tribes widely sundered in North and South America repeat the story of the early men climbing up from the underworld; with what almost monotony their religions refer to the earth as the mother of living creatures as well as of the vegetable kingdom. But the explanation which would cite these similarities as examples of "borrowing," or of the "diffusion of myths," is not merely without historic support, but misses in this study the most precious fruit it brings to the science of man—the proof of his psychological unity.

It is easy to multiply examples. We may turn, for instance, to the legends of the Iroquois of the north. They with one consent, if we may credit the account of Cusic, looked to a mountain near the falls of the Oswego River in the State of New York, as the locality where their forefathers first saw the light of day, and that they had some such legend the name Oneida, people of the Stone, would seem to testify.

The cave of Pacari Tampu, the Lodgings of the Dawn, was five leagues distant from Cuzco, surrounded by a sacred grove and inclosed with temples of great antiquity. From its hallowed recesses the mythical civilizers of Peru, the first of men, emerged, and in it during the time of the flood, the remnants of the race escaped the fury of the waves. Viracocha himself is said to have dwelt there, though it hardly needed this evidence to render it certain that this consecrated cavern is but a localization of the general myth of the dawn rising from the deep. It refers us for its prototype to the Aymara allegory of the morning light flinging its beams like snow-white foam athwart the waves of Lake Titicaca.

An ancient legend of the Aztecs derived their nation from a place called Chicomoztoc, the Seven Caverns, located north of Mexico. Antiquaries have indulged in all sorts of speculations as to what this means. Sahagun explains it as a valley so named; Clavigero supposes it to have been a city; Hamilton Smith, and after him Schoolcraft, construed caverns to be a figure of speech for the *boats* in which the early Americans paddled across from Asia(!); the Abbé Brasseur confounds it with Aztlan, and very many have discovered in it a distinct reference to the fabulous "seven cities of Cibola" and the Casas Grandes, ruins of large buildings of unburnt brick in the valley of the River Gila. From this story arose the supposed sevenfold division of the Nahuas, a division which never existed except in the imagination of Europeans.

When Torquemada adds that *seven* hero gods ruled in Chicomoztoc and were the progenitors of all its inhabitants, when one of them turns out to be Xelhua, the giant who with six others escaped the flood by ascending the mountain of Tlaloc in the terrestrial paradise and afterwards built the pyramid of Cholula, and when we remember that in one of the flood-myths *seven* persons were said to have escaped the waters, the whole narrative acquires a fabulous aspect that shuts it out from history, and brands it as one of those fictions of the origin of man from the earth so common to the race.

Fictions yet truths; for caverns and hollow trees were in fact the houses and temples of our first parents, and from them they went forth to conquer and adorn the world; and from the inorganic constituents of the soil acted on by Light, touched by Divine Force, vivified by the Spirit, did in reality the first of men proceed.

This cavern, which thus dimly lingered in the memories of nations, frequently expanded to a nether world, imagined to underlie this of ours, and still inhabited by beings of our kind, who have never been lucky enough to discover its exit.

According to a myth extensively disseminated among the Caribs, Arawacks, Warraus, Carayas and other South American tribes, in the beginning of things sky and earth were as one, and man abode within the earth in a joyous realm, where death and disease were unknown, and even the trees never rotted but lived on forever. One day the ruler of that happy realm walking forth discovered the surface of the world as we know it, but returning warned his people that though sunlight was there, so also were decay and death. Some, however, went thither, and the present unhappy race of men are their descendants, while others still dwell in gladness far below.

The Mandans and Minnetarees on the Missouri River supposed this exit was near a certain hill in their territory, and as it had been, as it were, the womb of the earth, the same power was attributed to it that in ancient times endowed certain shrines with such charms; and thither the barren wives of their nation made frequent pilgrimages when they would become mothers.

The Mandans added the somewhat puerile fable that the means of ascent had been a grapevine, by which many ascended and descended, until one day an immoderately fat old lady, anxious to get a look at the upper earth, broke it with her weight, and prevented any further communication. Yet even this detail recurs with precise parallelism in the legends of the Warraus, who live a semi-aquatic life at the mouth of the Orinoco.

Such tales of an under-world are very frequent among the Indians, and are a very natural outgrowth of the literal belief that the race is earth-born.

Man is indeed like the grass that springs up and soon withers away; but he is also more than this. The quintessence of dust, he is a son of the gods as well as a son of the soil. He is a direct product of the great creative power; therefore the Northwest Coast Indians and the Athapascan tribes west of the Rocky Mountains—the Kenai, the Kolushes, and the Atnai—claim descent from a raven—from that same mighty cloudbird, Yetl, already referred to, who in the beginning of things seized the elements and brought the world from the abyss of the primitive ocean.

The Athabascans, situate more eastwardly, the Dogribs, the Chepewyans, the Hare Indians, and also the west coast Eskimos, and the natives of the Aleutian Isles, all believe that they have sprung from a dog. The latter animal, we have already seen, both in the old and new world was the fixed symbol of the water goddess. Therefore in these myths, which are found over so many thousand square leagues, we cannot be in error in perceiving a reflex of their cosmogonical traditions already discussed, in which from the winds and the waters, represented here under their emblems of the bird and the dog, all animate life proceeded.

Without this symbolic coloring, a tribe to the south of them, a band of the Minnetarees, had the crude tradition that their first progenitor emerged from the waters, bearing in his hand an ear of maize, very much as Viracocha and his companions rose from the sacred waves of Lake Titicaca, or as the Moxos imagined that they were descended from the lakes and river on whose banks their villages were situated.

These myths, and many others, hint of general conceptions of life and the world, wide-spread theories of things, such as we are not accustomed to expect among savage nations, such as may very excusably excite a doubt as to their native origin, but a doubt infallibly dispelled by a careful comparison of the best authorities. Is it that hitherto, in the pride of intellectual culture, we have never done justice to the thinking faculties of those whom we call barbarians? Or shall we accept the alternative, that these are the unappreciated heirlooms bequeathed a rude race by a period of higher civilization, long since extinguished by constant wars and ceaseless fear? Or that they have been passed from hand to hand to America from the famed and ancient centres of civilization in Asia and Egypt?[2]

With almost unanimous consent the latter has been accepted as the true solution, but rather from the preconceived theory of a state of primitive civilization from which man fell, than from ascertained facts. Let us rather prefer that explanation which has been previously urged in these pages, that the faculties of the races of men differ little, that in dealing with the problems of the unknown their resources were limited, and that often they reached the same conceptions about it, and embodied them under the same or similar figures of speech, myths and stories.

It would, perhaps, be pushing symbolism too far to explain as an emblem of the primitive waters the coyote, which, according to the Root-Diggers of California, brought their ancestors into the world; or to the wolf, which the Lenni Lenape pretended released mankind from the dark bowels of the earth by scratching away the soil. They should rather be interpreted by the curious custom of the Tonkaways, a wild people in Texas, of predatory and unruly disposition. They celebrate their origin by a grand annual dance. One of them, naked as he was born, is buried in the earth. The others, clothed in wolf skins, walk over him, snuff around him, howl in lupine style, and finally dig him

[2] I believe that most students who have long and deeply studied the psychology of the American aborigines of almost any tribe will agree with these words of H. R. Schoolcraft:—"There is a subtlety in some of their modes of thought and belief on life and the existence of spiritual and creative power, which would seem to have been eliminated from some intellectual crucible without the limits of their present sphere" (*Oneota*, p. 131). It is difficult for the civilized man to concede equal intellectual faculties to those whom he knows are beneath him in acquirements, so that it at first requires an effort to accept this statement.

up with their nails. The leading wolf then solemnly places a bow and arrow in his hands, and to his inquiry as to what he must do for a living, paternally advises him "to do as the wolves do—rob, kill, and murder, rove from place to place, and never cultivate the soil." Most wise and fatherly counsel!

But what is there new under the sun? Three thousand years ago the Hirpini, or Wolves, an ancient Sabine tribe, were wont to collect on Mount Soracte, and there go through certain rites in memory of an oracle which predicted their extinction when they ceased to gain their living as wolves by violence and plunder. Therefore they dressed in wolf-skins, ran with barks and howls over burning coals, and gnawed wolfishly whatever they could seize.

Though hasty writers have often said that the Indian tribes claim literal descent from different wild beasts, probably in many instances, as in these, this will prove, on examination, to be an error resting on a misapprehension arising from the habit of the natives of adopting as their totem or clan-mark the figure and name of some animal, or else, in an ignorance of the animate symbols employed with such marked preference by the red race, to express abstract ideas. The totemic animal is, to the native mind, by no means identical in traits with a member of the existing species.

In some cases, doubtless, the natives themselves came, in time, to confound the symbol with the idea, by that familiar process of personification and consequent debasement exemplified in the history of every religion; but I do not believe that a single example could be found where an Indian tribe had a tradition whose real purport was that man came by natural process of descent from an ancestor, a brute, regarded merely as such.

The reflecting mind will not be offended at the contradictions in these different myths, for a myth is, in one sense, a theory of natural phenomena expressed in the form of a narrative. Often several explanations seem equally satisfactory for the same fact, and the mind hesitates to choose, and rather accepts them all than rejects any. Then, again, an expression current as a metaphor by-and-by crystallizes into a dogma, and becomes the nucleus of a new mythological growth. These are familiar processes to one versed in such studies, and involve no logical contradiction, because they are never required to be reconciled.

CHAPTER IX

THE SOUL AND ITS DESTINY

Universality of the belief in a soul and a future state shown by the aboriginal tongues, by expressed opinions, and by sepulchral rites.—The seat of the soul.—The "name soul."—The future world never a place of rewards and punishments.—The house of the Sun the heaven of the red man.—The terrestrial paradise and the under-world.—Cupay.—Xibalba.—Mictlan.—Metempsychosis.—Preservation of Bones.—Mummies.—Belief in a resurrection of the dead almost universal.

The missionary Charlevoix wrote several excellent works on America toward the beginning of the last century, and he is often quoted by later authors; but probably no one of his sayings has been thus honored more frequently than this: "The belief the best established among our Americans is that of the immortality of the soul." His statement is emphatically supported by the expression of one of the acutest living students of American aboriginal thought when he says of the Indian: "He *knows* he will not die."

The tremendous stake that every one of us has on the truth of this dogma makes it quite a satisfaction to be persuaded that no man is willing to live wholly without it. Certainly exceptions are very rare, and most of those which materialistic philosophers have taken such pains to collect, rest on misunderstandings or superficial observation.

In the New World I know of only one well authenticated instance where the notion of a future state appears to have been entirely wanting, and this in quite a small clan, the Lower Pend d'Oreilles, of Oregon. This people had no burial ceremonies, no notion of a life hereafter, no word for soul, spiritual existence, or vital principle. They thought that when they died, that was the last of them. The Catholic missionaries who undertook the unpromising task of converting them to Christianity, were at first obliged to depend upon the imperfect translations of half-breed interpreters. These "made the idea of soul intelligible to their hearers by telling them they had a gut which never rotted, and that this was their living principle!" Yet even they were not destitute of religious notions. No tribe was more addicted to the observance of charms, omens, dreams, and guardian spirits, and they believed that illness and bad luck generally were the effects of the anger of a fabulous old woman.

The aborigines of the Californian peninsula were as near beasts as men ever become. The missionaries likened them to "herds of swine, who neither worshipped the true and only God, nor adored false deities." Yet they must have had some vague notion of an afterworld, for the writer who paints the darkest picture of their condition remarks, "I saw them frequently putting shoes on the feet of the dead, which seems to indicate that they entertain the idea of a journey after death."

Proof of Charlevoix's opinion may be derived from three independent sources. The aboriginal languages may be examined for terms corresponding to the word soul; the opinions of the Indians themselves may be quoted; and the significance of sepulchral rites as indicative of a belief in life after death may be determined.

The most satisfactory is the first of these. *We* call the soul a ghost or spirit, and often a shade. In these words the *breath* and the *shadow* are the sensuous perceptions transferred to represent the immaterial object of our thought. Why the former was chosen I have already explained; and for the latter, that it is man's intangible image, his constant companion, and is of a nature akin to darkness, earth, and night, are sufficiently obvious reasons.

These same tropes recur in American languages in the same connection. The New England tribes called the soul *chemung*, the

shadow, and in Quiché *natub*, in Eskimo *tarnak*, in Dakota *nagi*
express both these ideas. In Mohawk *atonritz*, the soul, is from
atonrion, to breathe, and other examples to the same purpose
have already been given.

Of course, no one need demand that a strict immateriality be
attached to these words. Such a colorless negative abstraction
never existed for them, neither does it for us, though we delude
ourselves into believing that it does. The soul was to them the
invisible man, material as ever, but lost to the appreciation of the
senses.

Nor let any one be astonished if its unity was doubted, and
several supposed to reside in one body. This is nothing more than
a somewhat gross form of a doctrine upheld by most creeds and
most philosophies. It seems the readiest solution of certain psychological enigmas, and may, for aught we know, be an instinct
of fact. The Rabbis taught a threefold division—*nephesh*, the
animal, *ruah*, the human, and *neshamah*, the divine soul, which
corresponds to that of Plato into *thumos*, *epithumia*, and *nous*.
And even Saint Paul seems to have recognized such inherent
plurality when he distinguishes between the bodily soul, the
intellectual soul, and the spiritual gift, in his Epistle to the
Romans.

No such refinements, of course, as these are to be expected
among the red men; but it may be looked upon either as the
rudiments of these teachings, or as a gradual debasement of them
to gross and material expression, that an old and wide-spread
notion was found among both Iroquois and Algonkins, that man
has two souls, one of a vegetative character, which gives bodily
life, and remains with the corpse after death, until it is called to
enter another body; another of more ethereal texture, which in
life can depart from the body in sleep or trance, and wander over
the world, and at death goes directly to the land of spirits.

The Sioux extended it to Plato's number, and are said to have
looked forward to one going to a cold place, another to a warm
and comfortable country, while the third was to watch the body.
Certainly a most impartial distribution of rewards and punish-

ments. Some other Dakota tribes shared their views on this point, but more commonly, doubtless owing to the sacredness of the number, imagined *four* souls, with separate destinies, one to wander about the world, one to watch the body, the third to hover around the village, and the highest to go to the spirit land.

Even this number is multiplied by certain Oregon tribes, who imagine one in every member; and by the Caribs of Martinique, who, wherever they could detect a pulsation, located a spirit, all subordinate, however, to a supreme one throned in the heart, which alone would be transported to the skies at death. For the heart that so constantly sympathizes with our emotions and actions, is, in most languages and most nations, regarded as the seat of life. In many of the native tongues the compound words formed with its name indicate that various emotions and feelings were supposed to arise from its conditions. And when the priests of bloody religions tore out the heart of the victim and offered it to the idol, it was an emblem of the life that was thus torn from the field of this world and consecrated to the rulers of the next.

The seat of the soul was, however, variously located. The Costa Rica Indians place the powers of thought and memory in the liver; and a Thlinkit legend relates that the first of all men came into being "when the liver came out from below," showing that this tribe also regarded that viscus as the seat of life. Frequently the head was regarded as the vital member. Roger Williams remarks of the New England Indians: "In the braine theire opinion is that the soule keeps her chiefe seate and residence." By an easy metonymy, exemplified in all the classical languages, the head represents the man, and in this meaning appears in the picture writing, in the usage of preserving heads and skulls, and in the custom of scalping which was encountered by the early explorers in both North and South America.

Between these various souls there was a clear distinction made by most of the aboriginal philosophers. In their meditations on the principle of personality, on the Ego, they had reached certain subtle distinctions not unworthy of a Hegelian dialectician, and which the most astute of students of their thoughts fails completely to grasp. For example, Dr. Washington Matthews, a most competent scholar, in explaining this doctrine as it exists among the Navajos, says that the personal soul is neither the vital force which animates the body, nor yet the mental power, but a *tertium quid*, "a sort of spiritual body," which has the uncomfortable habit of sometimes leaving its owner, or getting lost, much to his pain and peril. Just such an unstable ghost do the Chinook Indians believe belongs to every one; and the recognition of it was common in North and South America. Among the Nahuas it bore the name *tonal*, which is probably from a root meaning (divine) knowledge, or else light.

In many tribes this third soul, or "astral body," bore a relation to the private personal name. Among the Mayas and Nahuas, it was conferred or came into existence with the name, and for this reason the personal name was sacred and rarely uttered. It was part of the individuality, and through it this capricious element of the I could be injured.

What Miss Fletcher remarks of the Dakotas is true generally: "The personal name among Indians indicates the protecting presence of a deity, and must therefore partake of the ceremonial character of the Indian's religion."[1] From almost any part of the continent I might choose examples to illustrate this. Let us go to the east coast of Greenland, among people who a dozen years ago had never seen or heard of a white man. They believe that the person consists of three components, his living body, his thinking faculty and his name (*atekata*). This last enters the body when the child is named. It survives physical death, whereas the body and the thinking faculty die, the first certainly, the latter sometimes. After the death of a person, his private name is not mentioned, and if it is a common noun, the tribe devise some other term in its place.

In many of the invocations of the Shamans, we find the object to be the recovery or restitution to the individual of this soul, or, as Dr. Rink says of the Eskimo *angekoks*, the "repairing the soul." Father de la Serna cites a long prayer for this special

---

[1] *Rep. Peabody Museum*, 1884.

purpose and Dr. Matthews gives another. It is through their malevolent influence on this that the evil spirits and unfriendly sorcerers cast sickness or misfortune upon one, and they can go so far as to capture this soul or drive it away; wicked intentions, to be counteracted by the more potent spells of the friendly shaman summoned for the purpose.

Various motives impel the living to treat with respect the body from which life has departed. Lowest of them is a superstitious dread of death and the dead. The stoicism of the Indian, especially the northern tribes, in the face of death, has often been the topic of poets, and has been interpreted to be a fearlessness of that event. This is by no means true. Savages have an awful horror of death; it is to them the worst of ills; and for this very reason was it that they thought to meet it without flinching was the highest proof of courage.

Everything connected with the deceased was, in many tribes, shunned with superstitious terror. His name was not mentioned, his property left untouched, all reference to him was sedulously avoided. A Tupi tribe used to hurry the body at once to the nearest water, and toss it in; the Akanzas left it in the lodge and burned over it the dwelling and contents; and the Algonkins carried it forth by a hole cut opposite the door, and beat the walls with sticks to frighten away the lingering ghost. Burying places were always avoided, and every means taken to prevent the departed spirits exercising a malicious influence on those remaining behind.

These craven fears do but reveal the natural repugnance of the animal to a cessation of existence, and arise from the instinct of self-preservation essential to organic life. Other rites, undertaken avowedly for the behoof of the soul, prove and illustrate a simple but unshaken faith in its continued existence after the decay of the body.

None of these is more common or more natural than that which attributes to the emancipated spirit the same wants that it felt while on earth, and with loving foresight provides for their satisfaction. Clothing and utensils of war and the chase were, in ancient times, uniformly placed by the body, under the impression that they would be of service to the departed in his new home. Some few tribes in the far west still retain the custom, but most were soon ridiculed into its neglect, or were forced to omit it by the violation of tombs practised by depraved whites in hope of gain.

To these harmless offerings the northern tribes often added a dog slain on the grave; and doubtless the skeletons of these animals in so many tombs in Mexico and Peru point to similar customs there. It had no deeper meaning than to give a companion to the spirit in its long and lonesome journey to the far off land of shades. The peculiar appropriateness of the dog arose not only from the guardianship it exerts during life, but further from the symbolic signification it so often had as representative of the goddess of night and the grave.

Where a despotic form of government reduced the subject almost to the level of a slave and elevated the ruler almost to that of a superior being, not animals only, but men, women and children were frequently immolated at the tomb of the cacique.

The territory embraced in our own country was not without examples of this sad custom. On the lower Mississippi the Natchez Indians practised it in all its ghastliness. When a sun or chief died, one or several of his wives and his highest officers were knocked on the head and buried with him, and at such times the barbarous privilege was allowed to any of the lowest caste to at once gain admittance to the highest by the deliberate murder of their own children on the funeral pyre—a privilege of which respectable writers tell us human beings were found base enough to take advantage.

Oviedo relates that in the province of Guataro, in Guatemala, an actual rivalry prevailed among the people to be slain at the death of their cacique, for they had been taught that only such as went with him would ever find their way to the paradise of the departed. Theirs was therefore somewhat of a selfish motive, and only in certain parts of Peru, where polygamy prevailed, and the rule was that only one wife was to be sacrificed, does the deportment of husbands seem to have been so creditable that their widows actually disputed one with another for the pleasure of being buried alive with the dead body, and bearing their spouse company to the other world. Wives who have found few parallels since the famous matron of Ephesus!

The fire built nightly on the grave was to light the spirit on his journey. By a coincidence to be explained by the universal sacredness of the number, both Algonkins and Mexicans maintained it for *four* nights consecutively. The former related the tradition that one of their ancestors returned from the spirit land and informed their nation that the journey thither consumed just *four* days, and that collecting fuel every night added much to the toil and fatigue the soul encountered, all of which could be spared it by the relatives kindling nightly a fire on the grave. Or as Longfellow has told it:

> "Four days is the spirit's journey
> To the land of ghosts and shadows,
> Four its lonely night encampments.
> Therefore when the dead are buried,
> Let a fire as night approaches
> Four times on the grave be kindled,
> That the soul upon its journey
> May not grope about in darkness."

The same length of time, say the Navajos, does the departed soul wander over a gloomy marsh ere it can discover the ladder leading to the world below, where are the homes of the setting and the rising sun, a land of luxuriant plenty, stocked with game and covered with corn. To that land, say they, sink all lost seeds and germs which fall on the earth and do not sprout. There below they take root, bud, and ripen their fruit. The Nahuas held that the journey of the soul lasted four years before it reached its final resting-place.

After four days, once more, in the superstitions of the Greenland Eskimos, does the soul, for that term after death confined in the body, at last break from its prison-house and either rise in the sky to dance in the aurora borealis or descend into the pleasant land beneath the earth, according to the manner of death.

That there are logical contradictions in this belief and these ceremonies, that the fire is always in the same spot, that the weapons and utensils are not carried away by the departed, and that the food placed for his sustenance remains untouched, is very true. But those who would therefore argue that they were not intended for the benefit of the soul, and seek some more recondite meaning in them as "unconscious emblems of struggling faith or expression of inward emotions," are led astray by the very simplicity of their real intention. Where is the faith, where the science, that does not involve logical contradictions just as gross as these? They are tolerable to us merely because we are used to them. What value has the evidence of the senses anywhere against a religious faith? None whatever. A stumbling block though this be to the materialist, it is the universal truth, and as such it is well to accept it as an experimental fact.

The preconceived opinions that saw in the meteorological myths of the Indian a conflict between the Spirit of Good and the Spirit of Evil, have with like unconscious error falsified his doctrine of a future life, and almost without an exception drawn it more or less in the likeness of the Christian heaven, hell, and purgatory. Very faint traces of any such belief except where derived from the missionaries are visible in the New World. Nowhere was any well-defined doctrine that moral turpitude was judged and punished in the next world. No contrast is discoverable between a place of torments and a realm of joy; at the worst but a negative castigation awaited the liar, the coward, or the niggard.

The typical belief of the tribes of the United States was well expressed in the reply of Esau Hajo, great medal chief and speaker for the Creek nation in the National Council, to the question, Do the red people believe in a future state of rewards and punishments? "We have an opinion that those who have behaved well are taken under the care of Esaugetuh Emissee, and assisted;

and that those who have behaved ill are left to shift for themselves; and that there is no other punishment."

Neither the delights of a heaven on the one hand, nor the terrors of a hell on the other, were ever held out by priests or sages as an incentive to well-doing, or a warning to the evil-disposed. Different fates, indeed, awaited the departed souls, but these rarely, if ever, were decided by their conduct while in the flesh, but by the manner of death, the punctuality with which certain sepulchral rites were fulfilled by relatives, or other similar arbitrary circumstance beyond the power of the individual to control.

This view, which I am aware is at variance with that of all previous writers, may be shown to be that natural to the uncultivated intellect everywhere, and the real interpretation of the creeds of America.[2] Whether these arbitrary circumstances were not construed to signify the decision of the Divine Mind on the life of the man, is a deeper question, which there is no means at hand to solve.

Those who have complained of the hopeless confusion of American religions have but proven the insufficiency of their own means of analyzing them. The uniformity which they display in so many points is nowhere more fully illustrated than in the unanimity with which they all point to the *sun* as the land of the happy souls, the realm of the blessed, the scene of the joyous hunting-grounds of the hereafter.

Its perennial glory, its comfortable warmth, its daily analogy to the life of man, marked its abode as the pleasantest spot in the universe. It matters not whether the eastern Algonkins pointed to the south, others of their nation, with the Iroquois and Creeks, to the west, or many tribes to the east, as the direction taken by the spirit; all these myths but mean that its bourn is the home of the sun, which is perhaps in the Orient whence he comes forth, in the Occident where he makes his bed, or in the south whither he retires in the chilling winter.

Where the sun lives, they informed the earliest foreign visitors,

[2] These words of the first edition I retain, although now the opinion of the text is that of many scholars who have carefully studied the subject.

were the villages of the deceased, and the milky way which nightly spans the arch of heaven, was, in their opinion, the road that led thither, and was called the path of souls (*le chemin des âmes*). To *hueyu ku*, the mansion of the sun, said the Caribs, the soul passes when death overtakes the body. To the warm southwest, whence blows the wind which brings the sunny days and the ripening corn, said the New England natives to Roger Williams, will all souls go.

Our knowledge is scanty of the doctrines taught by the Incas concerning the soul, but this much we do know, that they looked to the sun, their recognized lord and protector, as he who would care for them at death, and admit them to his palaces. There—not indeed, exquisite joys—but a life of unruffled placidity, void of labor, vacant of strong emotions, a sort of material Nirvana, awaited them. For these reasons, they, with most other American nations, interred the corpse lying east and west, and not as the traveller Meyen has suggested, from the reminiscences of some ancient migration.

Beyond the Cordilleras, quite to the coast of Brazil, the innumerable hordes who wandered through the sombre tropical forests of that immense territory, also pointed to the west, to the region beyond the mountains, as the land where the souls of their ancestors lived in undisturbed serenity; or, in the more brilliant imaginations of the later generations, in a state of perennial inebriety, surrounded by infinite casks of rum, and with no white man to dole it out to them.

The natives of the extreme south, of the Pampas and Patagonia, suppose the stars are the souls of the departed. At night they wander about the sky, but the moment the sun rises they hasten to the cheerful light, and are seen no more until it disappears in the west. So the Eskimo of the distant north, in the long winter nights, when the aurora bridges the sky with its changing hues and arrowy shafts of light, believes he sees the spirits of his ancestors clothed in celestial raiment, disporting themselves in the absence of the sun, and calls the phenomenon *the dance of the dead.*

The home of the sun was the heaven of the red man; but to this joyous abode not every one without distinction, no miscellaneous crowd, could gain admittance. The conditions were as various as the national temperaments. As the fierce gods of the Northmen would admit no soul to the banquets of Walhalla but such as had met the "spear-death" in the bloody play of war, and shut out pitilessly all those who feebly breathed their last in the "straw-death" on the couch of sickness, so the warlike Aztec race in Nicaragua held that the shades of those who died in their beds went downward and to naught; but of those who fell in battle for their country to the east, "to the place whence comes the sun."

In ancient Mexico not only the warriors who were thus sacrificed on the altar of their country, but with a delicate and poetical sense of justice that speaks well for the refinement of the race, also those women who perished in child-birth, were admitted to the home of the sun. For are not they also heroines in the battle of life? Are they not also its victims? And do they not lay down their lives for country and kindred?

Every morning, it was imagined, the heroes came forth in battle array, and with shout and song and the ring of weapons, accompanied the sun to the zenith, where at every noon the souls of the mothers, the Cihuapipilti, received them with dances, music, and flowers, and bore them company to their western couch. Except these, none—unless it may be the victims sacrificed to the gods, and this is doubtful—was deemed worthy of the highest heaven.

A mild and unwarlike tribe of Guatemala, on the other hand, were persuaded that to die by any other than a natural death was to forfeit all hope of life hereafter, and therefore left the bodies of the slain to the beasts and vultures.

The Mexicans had another place of happiness for departed souls, not promising perpetual life as the home of the sun, but unalloyed pleasure for a certain term of years. This was Tlalocan, the realm of the god of rains and waters, the terrestrial paradise, whence flowed all the rivers of the earth, and all the nourishment of the race. The diseases of which persons died marked this destination. Such as were drowned, or struck by lightning, or succumbed to humoral complaints, as dropsies and leprosy, were by these tokens known to be chosen as the subjects of Tlaloc.

To such, said the natives, "death is the commencement of another life, it is as waking from a dream, and the soul is no more human but divine (*teotl*)." Therefore they addressed their dying in terms like these: "Sir, or lady, awake, awake; already does the dawn appear; even now is the light approaching; already do the birds of yellow plumage begin their songs to greet thee; already are the gayly-tinted butterflies flitting around thee."

Before proceeding to the more gloomy portion of the subject, to the destiny of those souls who were not chosen for the better part, I must advert to a curious coincidence in the religious reveries of many nations which finds its explanation in the belief that the house of the sun is the home of the blessed, and proves that this was the first conception of most natural religions.

It is seen in the events and obstacles of the journey to the happy land. We everywhere hear of a water which the soul must cross, and an opponent, either a dog or an evil spirit, which it has to contend with. We are all familiar with the dog Cerberus (called by Homer simply "the dog"), which disputed the passage of the River Styx, over which the souls must cross; and with the custom of the Vikings, to be buried in a boat so that they might cross the waters of Ginunga-gap to the inviting strands of Godheim.

Relics of this belief are found in the Koran which describes the bridge *el Sirat*, thin as a hair and sharp as a scimitar, stretched in a single span from heaven to earth; in the Persian legend, where the rainbow arch Chinevad is flung across the gloomy depths between this world and the home of the happy; and even in the current Christian allegory which represents the waters of the mythical Jordan rolling between us and the Celestial City.

How strange at first sight does it seem that the Hurons and Iroquois should have told the earliest missionaries that after death the soul must cross a deep and swift river on a bridge formed by a single slender tree most lightly supported, where it had to defend itself against the attacks of a dog? If only they had expressed this belief, it might have passed for a coincidence merely. But the Athapascas (Chepewyans) also told of a great water, which the soul must cross in a stone canoe; the Algonkins and Dakotas, of a stream bridged by an enormous snake, or a narrow and precipitous rock, and the Araucanians of Chili of a sea in the west, in crossing which the soul was required to pay toll to a malicious old woman. Were it unluckily impecunious, she deprived it of an eye.

With the Aztecs this water was called Chicunoapa, the Nine Rivers. It was guarded by a dog and a green dragon, to conciliate which the dead were furnished with slips of paper by way of toll. The Greenland Eskimos thought that the waters roared through an unfathomable abyss over which there was no other bridge than a wheel slippery with ice, forever revolving with fearful rapidity, or a path narrow as a cord with nothing to hold on by. On the other side sits a horrid old woman gnashing her teeth and tearing her hair with rage. As each soul approaches she burns a feather under its nose; if it faints she seizes it for her prisoner, but if the soul's guardian spirit can overcome her, it passes through in safety.

The similarity to the passage of the soul across the Styx, and the toll of the obolus to Charon is in the Aztec legend still more striking, when we remember that the Styx was the ninth head of Oceanus (omitting the Cocytus, often a branch of the Styx). The Nine Rivers probably refer to the nine Lords of the Night, ancient Aztec deities guarding the nocturnal hours, and introduced into their calendar. The Tupis and Caribs, the Mayas and Creeks, entertained very similar expectations.

We are to seek the explanation of these widespread theories of the soul's journey in the equally prevalent tenet that the sun is its destination, and that that luminary has his abode beyond the ocean stream, which in all primitive geographies rolls its waves around the habitable land. This ocean stream is the water which all have to attempt to pass, and woe to him whom the spirit of the waters, represented either as the old woman, the dragon, or the dog of Hecate, seizes and overcomes. In the lush fancy of the Orient, the spirit of the waters becomes the spirit of evil, the ocean stream the abyss of hell, and those who fail in the passage the damned, who are foredoomed to evil deeds and endless torture.

No such ethical bearing as this was ever assigned the myth by the red race before they were taught by Europeans. Father Brebeuf could only find that the souls of suicides and those killed in war were supposed to live apart from the others; "but as to the souls of scoundrels," he adds, "so far from being shut out, they are the welcome guests, though for that matter if it were not so, their paradise would be a total desert, as Huron and scoundrel (*Huron et larron*) are one and the same."

When the Minnetarees told Major Long and the Mannicicas of the La Plata the Jesuits, that the souls of the bad fell into the waters and were swept away, this was, beyond doubt, attributable either to a false interpretation, or to Christian instruction. No such distinction is probable among savages. The Brazilian natives divided their dead into classes, supposing that the drowned, those killed by violence, and those yielding to disease, lived in separate regions, but no ethical reason whatever seems to have been connected with this.

If the conception of a place of moral retribution was known at all to the race, it should be found easily recognizable in Mexico, Yucatan, or Peru. But the so-called "hells" of their religions have no such significance, and the spirits of evil, who were identified by early writers with Satan, no more deserve the name than does the Greek Pluto.

Çupay or Supay, the Shadow, in Peru was supposed to rule the land of shades in the centre of the earth. To him went all souls not destined to be the companions of the Sun. This is all we know of his attributes; and the assertion of Garcilasso de la Vega, that he was the analogue of the Christian devil, and that his name was never pronounced without spitting and muttering a curse on his head, may be invalidated by the testimony of an earlier and better authority on the religion of Peru, who calls him the god of rains, and adds that the famous Inca, Huyana Capac, was his high priest.

"The devil," says Cogolludo of the Mayas, "is called by them Xibilha, which means he who disappears or vanishes." In the legends of the Quichés, the name Xibalba is given as that of the under-world ruled by the grim lords One Death and Seven Deaths. The derivation of the name is from a root meaning to fear, from which comes the term in Maya dialects for a ghost or phantom.[3]

Under the influence of a century of Christian catechizing, the Quiché legends portray this really as a place of torment, and its rulers as malignant and powerful; but as I have before pointed out, they do so, protesting that such was not the ancient belief, and they let fall no word that shows that it was regarded as the destination of the morally bad. The original meaning of the name given by Cogolludo points unmistakably to the simple fact of disappearance from among men, and corresponds in harmlessness to the true sense of those words of fear, Scheol, Hades, Hell, all signifying hidden from sight, and only endowed with more grim associations by the imaginations of later generations.[4]

Mictlanteuctli, Lord of Mictlan, from a word meaning to kill, was the Mexican Pluto. Like Çupay, he dwelt in the subterranean regions, and his palace was named Tlalxicco, the navel of the earth. Yet he was also located in the far north, and that point of the compass and the north wind were named after him. Those who descended to him were oppressed by the darkness of his abode, but were subjected to no other trials; nor were they sent thither as a punishment, but merely from having died of diseases unfitting them for Tlalocan.

Doubtless in many instances the darkened abode of the dead was regarded with that natural fear and horror which every-where environ the fact of death. Among the Nahuas it bore the ominous name, "the valley of Ximohuayan," eternal oblivion, and

---

[3] The attempt of the Abbé Brasseur to make of Xibalba an ancient king-dom of renown, with Palenque as its capital, is so unsupported as to justify the humorous flings which have so often been cast at antiquaries.

[4] Scheol is from a Hebrew word, signifying to dig, to hide in the earth. Hades signifies the *unseen* world. Hell Jacob Grimm derives from *hilan*, to conceal in the earth, and it is cognate with *hole* and *hollow*.

Apochquiahuayan, "where there are neither tracks nor trails." Both with them, with the Mayas and with the Caribs of the South, its principal deity was represented by the bat, the ill-omened bird of darkness.

Mictlanteuctli was said to be the most powerful of the gods. For who is stronger than Death? And who dare defy the Grave? As the skald lets Odin say to Bragi: "Our lot is uncertain; even on the hosts of the gods gazes the gray Fenris wolf."

These various abodes to which the incorporeal man took flight were not always his everlasting home. It will be remembered that where a plurality of souls was believed, one of these, soon after death, entered another body to recommence life on earth. Acting under this persuasion, the Algonkin women who desired to become mothers, flocked to the couch of those about to die, in hope that the vital principle, as it passed from the body, would enter theirs, and fertilize their sterile wombs; and when, among the Seminoles of Florida, a mother died in childbirth, the infant was held over her face to receive her parting spirit, and thus acquire strength and knowledge for its future use.

So among the Takahlis, the priest is accustomed to lay his hand on the head of the nearest relative of the deceased, and to blow into him the soul of the departed, which is supposed to come to life in his next child. Probably, with a reference to the current tradition that ascribes the origin of man to the earth, and likens his life to that of the plant, the Mexicans were accustomed to say that at one time all men have been stones, and that at last they would all return to stones; and, acting literally on this conviction, they interred with the bones of the dead a small green stone, which was called the principle of life.

Whether any nations accepted the doctrine of metempsychosis, and thought that "the souls of their grandams might haply inhabit a partridge," we are without the means of knowing. La Hontan denies it positively of the Algonkins; but the natives of Popoyan refused to kill doves, says Coreal, because they believe them inspired by the souls of the departed. And Father Ignatius Chomé relates that he heard a woman of the Chiriquanes in

Buenos Ayres say of a fox: "May that not be the spirit of my
dead daughter?"

But before accepting such testimony as decisive, we must first
inquire whether these tribes believed in a multiplicity of souls,
whether these animals had a symbolical value, and if not, whether
the soul was not simply presumed to put on this shape in its
journey to the land of the hereafter: inquiries which are unan-
swered. Leaving, therefore, the question open, whether the sage
of Samos had any disciples in the new world, another and more
fruitful topic is presented by their well-ascertained notions of the
resurrection of the dead.

This seemingly extraordinary doctrine, which some have asserted was entirely unknown and impossible to the American
Indians, was in fact one of their most deeply-rooted and wide-
spread convictions, especially among the tribes of the eastern
United States. It is indissolubly connected with their highest
theories of a future life, their burial ceremonies, and their modes
of expression.

The Moravian Brethren give the grounds of this belief with
great clearness: "That they hold the soul to be immortal, and
perhaps think the body will rise again, they give not unclearly to
understand when they say, 'We Indians shall not forever die;
even the grains of corn we put under the earth, grow up and
become living things.' They conceive that when the soul has been
a while with God, it can, if it chooses, return to earth and be
born again."

This is the highest and typical creed of the aborigines. But
instead of simply being born again in the ordinary sense of the
word, they thought the soul would return to the bones, that these
would clothe themselves with flesh, and that the man would
rejoin his tribe. That this was the real, though often doubtless the
dimly understood reason of the custom of preserving the bones
of the deceased, can be shown by various arguments.

This practice was almost universal. East of the Mississippi
nearly every nation was accustomed, at stated periods—usually
once in eight or ten years—to collect and clean the osseous remains

of those of its number who had died in the intervening time, and inter them in one common sepulchre, lined with choice furs, and marked with a mound of wood, stone, and earth. Such is the origin of those immense tumuli filled with the mortal remains of nations and generations which the antiquary, with irreverent curiosity, has so frequently chanced upon in all portions of our territory.

Throughout Central America the same usage obtained in various localities, as early writers and existing monuments abundantly testify. Instead of interring the bones, were they those of some distinguished chieftain, they were deposited in the temples or the council-houses, usually in small chests of canes or splints. Such were the charnel-houses which the historians of De Soto's expedition so often mentioned, and these are the "arks" which Adair and other authors, who have sought to trace the descent of the Indians from the Jews, have likened to that which the ancient Israelites bore with them on their migrations. A widow among the Tahkalis was obliged to carry the bones of her deceased husband wherever she went for four years, preserving them in such a casket handsomely decorated with feathers.

The Caribs of the mainland adopted the custom for all without exception. About a year after death the bones were cleaned, bleached, painted, wrapped in odorous balsams, placed in a wicker basket, and kept suspended from the door of their dwellings. When the quantity of these heirlooms became burdensome, they were removed to some inaccessible cavern, and stowed away with reverential care. Such was the cave Ataruipe, a visit to which has been so eloquently described by Alexander von Humboldt in his "Views of Nature."

So great was the filial respect for these remains by the Indians, that on the Mississippi, in Peru, and elsewhere, no tyranny, no cruelty, so embittered the indigenes against the white explorers as the sacrilegious search for treasures perpetrated among the sepulchres of past generations. Unable to understand the meaning of such deep feeling, so foreign to the European who, without a second thought, turns a cemetery into a public square, or seeds it down in wheat, the Jesuit missionaries of Paraguay accused the natives of worshipping the skeletons of their forefathers, and the English of Virginia repeated it of the Powhatans.

In a certain sense this may be regarded as a development of the worship of ancestors. In America, however, ancestral worship in its true sense, as it has long existed in China, for example, was not prominent. The Knisteneaux on Nelson River were accustomed to strangle their parents when old; yet each master of a family, the deed performed, kept by him a bunch of feathers tied with a string, called it "his father's head," and regarded it with superstitious reverence.

The Aztecs celebrated a feast to the dead once in each year, at which time they gazed to the north and called upon their ancestors to "come soon, for we wait you." The Quichés of Guatemala had a similar annual festival when they recited the names of their deceased ancestors, and when also each person visited the spot where his or her navel-string had been buried. The Tupis worshipped Tamoin and the Incas Pacarina, alleged ancestors of their nation, but only in the recondite sense well explained by Mr. Markham, "as the forefathers of the clan idealized in the soul or essence of his descendants.[5]

In some of the gentes in various parts of the continent there prevailed a belief that the soul would somehow return to the eponymous ancestor; that is, that those of the buffalo gens, for example, would at death either enter buffaloes, or go where dwells the great original buffalo. For the totemic eponym, or original forefather of the gens, was not considered to be a brute merely, but one of the mighty primal spirits to whom was given or who had assumed the brute form.

The question has been debated and variously answered, whether the art of mummification was known and practised in America. Without entering into the discussion, it is certain that preservation of the corpse by a long and thorough process of exsiccation over a slow fire was nothing unusual, not only in Peru, Popoyan, the Carib countries, and Nicaragua, but among

[5] C. R. Markham, *Jour. Roy. Geog. Soc.*, 1871, p. 291.

many of the tribes north of the Gulf of Mexico, as I have elsewhere shown. The object was essentially the same as when the
bones alone were preserved; and in the case of rulers, the same
homage was often paid to their corpses as had been the just due
of their living bodies.

The opinion underlying all these customs was, that a part of
the soul, or one of the souls, dwelt in the bones; that these were
the seeds which, planted in the earth, or preserved unbroken in
safe places, would, in time, put on once again a garb of flesh, and
germinate into living human beings. Language illustrates this not
unusual theory. The Iroquois word for bone is *esken*—for soul,
atisken, literally that which is within the bone. In an Athapascan
dialect bone is *yani*, soul *i-yune*. The Hebrew Rabbis taught that
in the bone *lutz*, the coccyx, remained at death the germ of a
second life, which, at the proper time would develop into the
purified body, as the plant from the seed.

But mythology and superstitions add more decisive testimony.
One of the Aztec legends of the origin of man was, that after one
of the destructions of the world the gods took counsel together
how to renew the species. It was decided that one of their number, Xolotl, should descend to Mictlan, the realm of the dead, and
bring thence a bone of the perished race. The fragments of this
they sprinkled with blood, and on the fourth day it grew into a
youth, the father of the present race.

The profound mystical significance of this legend is reflected
in one told by the Quichés, in which the hero gods Hunahpu and
Xblanque succumb to the rulers of Xibalba, the darksome powers
of death. Their bodies are burned, but their bones are ground in a
mill and thrown in the waters, lest they should come to life. Even
this precaution is insufficient—"for these ashes did not go far;
they sank to the bottom of the stream, where, in the twinkling of
an eye, they were changed into handsome youths, and their very
same features appeared anew. On the fifth day they displayed
themselves anew, and were seen in the water by the people,"
whence they emerged to overcome and destroy the powers of
death and hell (Xibalba).

The strongest analogies to these myths are offered by the superstitious rites of distant tribes. Some of the Tupis of Brazil were wont on the death of a relative to dry and pulverize his bones and then mix them with their food, a nauseous practice they defended by asserting that the soul of the dead remained in the bones and lived again in the living. Even the lower animals were supposed to follow the same law. Hardly any of the hunting tribes, before their original manners were vitiated by foreign influence, permitted the bones of game slain in the chase to be broken, or left carelessly about the encampment. They were collected in heaps, or thrown into the water. Mrs. Eastman observes that even yet the Dakotas deem it an omen of ill luck in the hunt, if the dogs gnaw the bones or a woman inadvertently steps over them; and the Chipeway interpreter, John Tanner, speaks of the same fear among that tribe.

The Yurucares of Bolivia carried it to such an inconvenient extent, that they carefully put by even small fish bones, saying that unless this is done the fish and game will disappear from the country. The traveller on our western prairies often notices the buffalo skulls, countless numbers of which bleach on those vast plains, arranged in circles and symmetrical piles by the careful hands of the native hunters. The explanation they offer for this custom gives the key to the whole theory and practice of preserving the osseous relics of the dead, as well human as brute. They say that "the bones contain the spirits of the slain animals, and that some time in the future they will rise from the earth, re-clothe themselves with flesh, and stock the prairies anew."

This explanation, which comes to us from indisputable authority, sets forth in its true light the belief of the red race in a resurrection. It is not possible to trace it out in the subtleties with which theologians have surrounded it as a dogma. The very attempt would be absurd. They never occurred to the Indian. He thought that the soul now enjoying the delights of the happy hunting grounds would some time return to the bones, take on flesh, and live again.

Such is precisely the much discussed statement that Garcilasso de la Vega says he often heard from the native Peruvians. He adds that so careful were they lest any of the body should be lost that they preserved even the parings of their nails and clippings of the hair. In contradiction to this the writer Acosta has been quoted, who says that the Peruvians embalmed their dead because they "had no knowledge that the bodies should rise with the soul." But, rightly understood, this is a confirmation of La Vega's account. Acosta means that the Christian doctrine of the body rising from the dust being unknown to the Peruvians (which is perfectly true), they preserved the body just as it was, so that the soul when it returned to earth, as all expected, might not be at a loss for a house of flesh.

The notions thus entertained by the red race on the resurrection are peculiar to it, and stand apart from those of any other. They did not look for the second life to be either better or worse than the present one; they regarded it neither as a reward nor a punishment to be sent back to the world of the living; nor is there satisfactory evidence that it was ever distinctly connected with a moral or physical theory of the destiny of the universe, or even with their prevalent expectation of recurrent epochs in the course of nature.

It is true that a writer whose personal veracity is above all doubt, Mr. Adam Hodgson, relates an ancient tradition of the Choctaws, to the effect that the present world will be consumed by a general conflagration, after which it will be reformed pleasanter than it now is, and that then the spirits of the dead will return to the bones in the bone mounds, flesh will knit together their loose joints, and they shall again inhabit their ancient territory.

There was also a similar belief among the Eskimos. They said that in the course of time the waters will overwhelm the land, purify it of the blood of the dead, melt the icebergs, and wash away the steep rocks. A wind will then drive off the waters, and the new land will be peopled by reindeers and young seals. Then will He above blow once on the bones of the men and twice on those of the women, whereupon they will at once start into life, and lead thereafter a joyous existence.

But though there is nothing in these narratives alien to the course of thought in the native mind, yet as the date of the first is recent (1820), as they are not supported (so far as I know) by similar traditions elsewhere, and as they may have arisen from Christian doctrines of a millennium, I leave them for future investigation.

What strikes us the most in this analysis of the opinions entertained by the red race on a future life is the clear and positive hope of a hereafter, in such strong contrast to the feeble and vague notions of the ancient Israelites, Greeks and Romans, and yet the entire inertness of this hope in leading them to a purer moral life. It offers another proof that the fulfilment of duty is in its nature nowise connected with or derived from a consideration of ultimate personal consequences. It is another evidence that the religious is wholly distinct from the moral sentiment, and that the origin of ethics is not to be sought in connection with the ideas of divinity and responsibility.

CHAPTER XI

THE INFLUENCE OF THE NATIVE RELIGIONS
ON THE MORAL
AND SOCIAL LIFE OF THE RACE

Natural religions hitherto considered of Evil rather than of Good.—Distinctions to be drawn.—Morality not derived from religion.—The positive side of natural religions in incarnations of divinity.—Examples.—Prayers as indices of religious progress.—Religion and social advancement.—Conclusion.

Drawing toward the conclusion of my essay, I am sensible that the vast field of American mythology remains for the most part untouched—that I have but proved that it is not an absolute wilderness, pathless as the tropical jungles which now conceal the temples of the race; but that, go where we will, certain land-marks and guide-posts are visible, revealing uniformity of design and purpose, and refuting, by their presence, the oft-repeated charge of entire incoherence and aimlessness.

It remains to examine the subjective power of the native religions, their influence on those who held them, and the place they deserve in the history of the race. What are their merits, if merits they have? what their demerits? Did they purify the life and enlighten the mind, or the contrary? Are they in short of evil or of good?

The problem is complex—its solution most difficult. An author who some years ago studied profoundly the savage races of the globe, expressed the discouraging conviction: "Their religions have not acted as levers to raise them to civilization; they have rather worked, and that powerfully, to impede every step in advance, in the first place by ascribing everything unintelligible in nature to spiritual agency, and then by making the fate of man dependent on mysterious and capricious forces, not on his own skill and foresight."

It would ill accord with the theory of mythology which I have all along maintained if this verdict were final. But in fact these false doctrines brought with them their own antidotes, at least to some extent, and while we give full weight to their evil, let us also acknowledge their good. By substituting direct divine interference for law, belief for knowledge, a dogma for a fact, the highest stimulus to mental endeavor was taken away.

Nature, to the heathen, is no harmonious whole swayed by eternal principles, but a chaos of causeless effects, the meaningless play of capricious ghosts. He investigates not, because he doubts not. All events are to him miracles. Therefore his faith knows no bounds, and those who teach that doubt is sinful must contemplate him with admiration.

The damsels of Nicaragua destined to be thrown into the seething craters of volcanoes, went to their fate, says Pascual de Andagoya, "happy as if they were going to be saved," and doubtless believing so. The subjects of a Central American chieftain, remarks Oviedo, "look upon it as the crown of favors to be permitted to die with their cacique, and thus to acquire immortality." The terrible power exerted by the priests rested, as they themselves often saw, largely on the implicit acceptance of their dicta.

In some respects the contrast here offered to enlightened nations is not always in favor of the latter. Borrowing the pointed antithesis of the poet, the mind is often tempted to exclaim—

> "This is all
> The gain we reap from all the wisdom sown
> Through ages: Nothing doubted those first sons
> Of Time, while we, the schooled of centuries,
> Nothing believe."—*Lytton.*

But the complaint is unfounded. Faith is dearly bought at the cost of knowledge; nor in a better sense has it yet gone from among us. Far more sublime than any known to the barbarian is the faith of the astronomer, who spends the nights in marking the seemingly wayward motions of the stars, or of the anatomist, who studies with unwearied zeal the minute fibres of the organism, each upheld by the unshaken conviction that from least to greatest throughout this universe, purpose and order everywhere prevail.

Natural religions rarely offer more than this negative opposition to reason. They are tolerant to a degree. The savage, void of any clear conception of a supreme deity, sets up no claim that his is the only true church. If he is conquered in battle, he imagines that it is owing to the inferiority of his own gods to those of his victor, and he rarely therefore requires any other reasons to make him a convert.

Acting on this principle, the Incas, when they overcame a strange province, sent its most venerated idol for a time to the temple of the Sun at Cuzco, thus proving its inferiority to their own divinity, but took no more violent steps to propagate their creeds. So in the City of Mexico there was a temple appropriated to the idols of conquered nations in which they were shut up, both to prove their weakness and prevent them from doing mischief.

A nation, like an individual, was not inclined to patronize a deity who had manifested his incompetence by allowing his charge to be gradually worn away by constant disaster. As far as can now be seen, in matters intellectual, the religions of ancient Mexico and Peru were far more liberal than that introduced by the Spanish conquerors, which, claiming the monopoly of truth, sought to enforce its claim by inquisitions and censorships.

In this view of the relative powers of deities lay a potent corrective to the doctrine that the fate of man was dependent on the caprices of the gods. For no belief was more universal than that which assigned to each individual a guardian spirit. This invisible monitor was an ever present help in trouble. He suggested expedients, gave advice and warning in dreams, protected in danger, and stood ready to foil the machinations of enemies, divine or human.

With unlimited faith in this protector, attributing to him the devices suggested by his own quick wits and the fortunate chances of life, the savage escaped the oppressive thought that he was the slave of demoniac forces, and dared the dangers of the forest and the war path without anxiety.

By far the darkest side of such a religion is that which it presents to morality. The religious sense is by no means the voice of conscience. The Takahli Indian when sick makes a full and free confession of sins, but a murder, however unnatural and unprovoked, he does not mention, not counting it a crime. Scenes of licentiousness were approved and sustained throughout the continents as acts of worship; maidenhood was in many parts freely offered up or claimed by the priests as a right; in central America twins were slain for religious motives; human sacrifice was common throughout the tropics, and was not unusual in higher latitudes; cannibalism was often enjoined; and in Peru, Florida, and Central America it was not uncommon for parents to slay their own children at the behest of a priest.

The philosophical moralist, contemplating such spectacles, has thought to recognize in them one consoling trait. All history, it has been said, shows man living under an irritated God, and seeking to appease him by sacrifice of blood; the essence of all religion, it has been added, lies in that of which sacrifice is the symbol, namely, in the offering up of self, in the rendering up of our will to the will of God.[1]

---

[1] Joseph de Maistre, *Eclaircissement sur les Sacrifices;* Trench, *Hulsean Lectures,* p. 180. The famed Abbé Lammennais and Professor Sepp, of Munich, with these two writers, may be taken as the chief exponents of a school of mythologists, all of whom start from the theories first laid down by Count de Maistre in his *Soirées de St. Petersbourg.* To them the strongest proof of Christianity lies in the traditions and observances of heathendom. For these show the wants of the religious sense, and Christianity, they maintain, purifies and satisfies them all. The rites, symbols, and legends of every natural religion, they say, are true and not false; all that is required is to assign them their proper places and their real meaning. Therefore the strange resemblances in heathen myths to what is revealed in the Scriptures, as well as the ethical anticipations which have been found in ancient philosophies,

But sacrifice, when not a token of gratitude, cannot be thus explained. It is not a rendering up, but a *substitution* of our will for God's will. A deity is angered by neglect of his dues; he will revenge, certainly, terribly, we know not how or when. But as punishment is all he desires, if we punish ourselves he will be satisfied; and far better is such self-inflicted torture than a fearful looking for of judgment to come. Craven fear, not without some dim sense of the implacability of nature's laws, is at its root.

Looking only at this side of religion, the ancient philosopher averred that the gods existed solely in the apprehensions of their votaries, and the moderns have asserted that "fear is the father of religion, love her late-born daughter"; that "the first form of religious belief is nothing else but a horror of the unknown," and that "no natural religion appears to have been able to develop from a germ within itself anything whatever of real advantage to civilization."

Far be it from me to excuse the enormities thus committed under the garb of religion, or to ignore their disastrous consequences on human progress. Yet this question is a fair one—If the natural religious belief has in it no germ of anything better, whence comes the manifest and undeniable improvement occasionally witnessed—as, for example, among the Aztecs, the Peruvians, and the Mayas?

The reply is, by the influence of great men, who cultivated within themselves a purer faith, lived it in their lives, preached it successfully to their fellows, and, at their death, still survived in the memory of their nation, unforgotten models of noble qualities.

Where, in America, is any record of such men? We are pointed, in answer, to Quetzalcoatl, Viracocha, Itzamna, and their congeners. But these august figures I have shown to be wholly mythical, creations of the religious fancy, parts and parcels of the earliest religion itself. The entire theory falls to

---

all, so far from proving that Christianity is a natural product of the human mind, in fact, are confirmations of it, unconscious prophecies, and presentiments of the truth.

nothing, therefore, and we discover a positive side to natural religions—one that conceals a germ of endless progress, which vindicates their lofty origin, and proves that He "is not far from every one of us."

I have already analyzed these figures under their physical aspect. Let it be observed in what antithesis they stand to most other mythological creations. Let it be remembered that they primarily correspond to the stable, the regular, the cosmical phenomena, that they are always conceived under human form, not as giants, fairies, or strange beasts; that they were said at one time to have been visible leaders of their nations, that they did not suffer death, and that, though absent, they are ever present, favoring those who remain mindful of their precepts.

I touched but incidentally on their moral aspects. This was likewise in contrast to the majority of inferior deities. The worship of the latter was a tribute extorted by fear. The Indian deposits tobacco on the rocks of a rapid, that the spirit of the swift waters may not swallow his canoe; in a storm he throws overboard a dog to appease the siren of the angry waves. He used to tear the hearts from his captives to gain the favor of the god of war. He provides himself with talismans to bind hostile deities. He fees the conjurer to exorcise the demon of disease. He loves none of them, he respects none of them; he only fears their wayward tempers. They are to him mysterious, invisible, capricious goblins.

But in his highest divinity, he recognized a Father and a Preserver, a benign Intelligence, who provided for him the comforts of life—man, like himself, yet a god—God of All. "Go and do good," was the parting injunction of his father to Michabo in Algonkin legend; and in their ancient and uncorrupted stories such is ever his object. "The worship of Tamu," the culture hero of the Guaranis, says the traveller D'Orbigny, "is one of reverence, not of fear." They were ideals, summing up in themselves the best traits, the most approved virtues of whole nations, and were adored in a very different spirit from other divinities.

None of them has more humane and elevated traits than Quetzalcoatl. He was represented of majestic stature and dignified demeanor. In his train came skilled artificers and men of learning. He was chaste and temperate in life, wise in council, generous of gifts, conquering rather by arts of peace than of war; delighting in music, flowers, and brilliant colors, and so averse to human sacrifices that he shut his ears with both hands when they were even mentioned.

Such was the ideal man and supreme god of a people who even a Spanish monk of the sixteenth century felt constrained to confess were "a good people, attached to virtue, urbane and simple in social intercourse, shunning lies, skilful in arts, pious toward their gods." Is it likely, is it possible, that with such a model as this before their minds, they received no benefit from it? Was not this a lever, and a mighty one, lifting the race toward civilization and a purer faith?

Transfer the field of observation to Yucatan, and we find in Itzamna, to New Granada and in Nemqueteba, to Peru and in Viracocha, or his reflex Tonapa, the lineaments of Quetzalcoatl—modified, indeed, by difference of blood and temperament, but each combining in himself all the qualities most esteemed by their several nations.

They are credited with an ethical elevation in their teachings which needs not blush before the loftiest precepts of Old World moralists. According to the earliest and most truthworthy accounts, the doctrines of Tonapa were filled with the loving kindness and the deep sense of duty which characterized the purest Christianity. "Nothing was wanting in them," says an historian, "save the name of God and that of his son, Jesus Christ."

In the numerous ancient formulas or *huehuetlatolli*, collected by the first missionaries to Mexico, we perceive a constant tendency toward inculcating purity of life, kindness to companions, and control of the appetites, which would not be out of place in the most civilized communities.

The Iroquois sage, Hiawatha, probably an historical character, made it the noble aim of his influence and instruction to abolish war altogether and establish the reign of universal peace and brotherhood among men.

Were one or all of these proved to be historical personages, still the fact remains that the primitive religious sentiment, investing them with the best attributes of humanity, dwelling on them as its models, worshipping them as gods, contained a kernel of truth potent to encourage moral excellence. But if they were mythical, then this truth was of spontaneous growth, self-developed by the growing distinctness of the idea of God, a living witness that the religious sense, like every other faculty, has within itself a power of endless evolution.

If we inquire the secret of the happier influence of this element in natural worship, it is all contained in one word—its *humanity*. "The Ideal of Morality," says the contemplative Novalis, "has no more dangerous rival than the Ideal of the Greatest Strength, of the most vigorous life, the Brute Ideal (*das Thier-Ideal*)." Culture advances in proportion as man recognizes what faculties are peculiar to him *as man*, and devotes himself to their education.

The moral value of religions can be very precisely estimated by the human or the brutal character of their gods. The worship of Quetzalcoatl in the City of Mexico was subordinate to that of lower conceptions, and consequently the more sanguinary and immoral were the rites there practised. The Algonkins, who knew no other meaning for Michabo than the Great Hare, had lost, by a false etymology, the best part of their religion.

Looking around for other standards wherewith to measure the progress of the knowledge of divinity in the New World, *prayer* suggests itself as one of the least deceptive. "Prayer," to quote again the words of Novalis, "is in religion what thought is in philosophy. The religious sense prays, as the reason thinks." Guizot, carrying the analysis further, thinks that it is prompted by a painful conviction of the inability of our will to conform to the dictates of reason.

Originally it was connected with the belief that divine caprice, not divine law, governs the universe, and that material benefits rather than spiritual gifts are to be desired. The gradual recognition of its limitations and proper objects marks religious advancement. The Lord's Prayer contains seven petitions, only one of which is for a temporal advantage, and it the least that can be asked for.

What immeasurable interval between it and the prayer of the Nootka Indian on preparing for war!—

"Great Quahootze, let me live, not be sick, find the enemy, not fear him, find him asleep, and kill a great many of him."

Or again, between it and a petition of a Huron to a local god, heard by Father Brebeuf:—

"Oki, thou who livest in this spot, I offer thee tobacco. Help us, save us from shipwreck, defend us from our enemies, give us a good trade and bring us back safe and sound to our villages."

This is a fair specimen of the supplications of the lowest religions. Another equally authentic is given by Father Allouez. In 1670 he penetrated to an outlying Algonkin village, never before visited by a white man. The inhabitants, startled by his pale face and long black gown, took him for a divinity. They invited him to the council lodge, a circle of old men gathered around him, and one of them, approaching him with a double handful of tobacco, thus addressed him, the others grunting approval:—

"This, indeed, is well, Blackrobe, that thou dost visit us. Have mercy upon us. Thou art a Manito. We give thee to smoke.

"The Naudowessies and Iroquois are devouring us. Have mercy upon us.

"We are often sick; our children die; we are hungry. Have mercy upon us. Hear me, O Manito, I give thee to smoke.

"Let the earth yield us corn; the rivers give us fish; sickness not slay us; nor hunger so torment us. Hear us, O Manito, we give thee to smoke."

In this rude but touching petition, wrung from the heart of a miserable people, nothing but their wretchedness is visible. Not the faintest trace of an aspiration for spiritual enlightenment cheers the eye of the philanthropist, not the remotest conception that through suffering we are purified can be detected.

By the side of these examples we may place the prayers of Peru and Mexico, forms composed by the priests, written out, committed to memory, and repeated at certain seasons. They are not less authentic, having been collected and translated in the first generation after the conquest. One to Viracocha Pachacamac was as follows:

"O Pachacamac, thou who hast existed from the beginning and shalt exist unto the end, powerful and pitiful; who createdst man by saying, let man be; who defendest us from evil and preservest our life and health; art thou in the sky or in the earth, in the clouds or in the depths? Hear the voice of him who implores thee, and grant him his petitions. Give us life everlasting, preserve us, and accept this our sacrifice."[2]

In the voluminous specimens of Aztec prayers preserved by Sahagún, moral improvement, the "spiritual gift," is not generally the object desired, as it is not in many Christian liturgies. Health, harvests, propitious rains, release from pain, preservation from dangers, illness, and defeat, these are the almost unvarying themes.

But here and there we catch a glimpse of something better, some sense of the divine beauty of suffering, some glimmering of the grand truth so nobly expressed by the poet:—

> aus des Busens Tiefe strömt Gedeihn
> Der festen Duldung und entschlossner That.
> Nicht Schmerz ist Unglück, Glück nicht immer Freude;
> Wer sein Geschick erfüllt, Dem lächeln beide.

"Is it possible," says one of them, "that this scourge, this affliction, is sent to us not for our correction and improvement, but for our destruction and annihilation? O Merciful Lord, let this chastisement with which thou hast visited us, thy people, be as those which a father or mother inflicts on their children, not out

---

[2] Geronimo de Ore, *Symbolo Catholico Indiano*, chap. ix. De Ore was a native of Peru and held the position of Professor of Theology in Cuzco in the latter half of the sixteenth century. He was a man of great erudition, and there need be no hesitation in accepting this extraordinary prayer as genuine.

of anger, but to the end that they may be free from follies and vices."

Another formula, used when a chief was elected to some important position, reads: "O Lord, open his eyes and give him light, sharpen his ears and give him understanding, not that he may use them to his own advantage, but for the good of the people whom he rules. Lead him to know and to do thy will, let him be as a trumpet which sounds thy words. Keep him from the commission of injustice and oppression."[3]

At first, good and evil are identical with pleasure and pain, luck and ill-luck. "The good are good warriors and hunters," said a Pawnee chief, which would also be the opinion of a wolf, if he could express it. Gradually the eyes of the mind are opened, and it is perceived that "whom He loveth, He chastiseth," and physical give place to moral ideas of good and evil. Finally, as the idea of God rises more distinctly before the soul, as "the One by whom, in whom, and through whom all things are," evil is seen to be the negation, not the opposite of good, and itself "a porch oft opening on the sun."

The influence of these religions on art, science, and social life, must also be weighed in estimating their value.

Nearly all the remains of American plastic art, sculpture, and painting, were obviously designed for religious or, what is practically the same, divinatory purposes. Idols of stone, wood, or baked clay, were found in every Indian tribe, without exception, so far as I can judge; and in only a few directions do these arts seem to have been applied to secular purposes.

The most ambitious attempts of architecture, it is plain, were inspired by religious fervor. The great pyramid of Cholula, the enormous mounds of the Mississippi valley, the elaborate edifices on artificial hills in Yucatan, were miniature representations of the mountains hallowed by tradition, the "Hill of Heaven," the peak on which their ancestors escaped in the flood, or that in the terres-

---

[3] Many other examples of prayers might be quoted from the works of de la Serna, Dr. Washington Matthews, James Mooney, etc., but those in the text will be sufficient to illustrate their usual character.

trial paradise from which flow the rains. Their construction took men away from war and the chase, encouraged agriculture, peace, and a settled disposition, and fostered the love of property, of country, and of the gods.

The priests were also close observers of nature, and were the first to discover its simpler laws. The Aztec sages were as devoted star-gazers as the Chaldeans, and their civil calendar bears unmistakable marks of native growth, and of its original purpose to fix the annual festivals. Writing by means of pictures and symbols was cultivated chiefly for religious ends, and the word *hieroglyph* is a witness that the phonetic alphabet was discovered under the stimulus of the religious sentiment.

Most of the aboriginal literature was composed and taught by the priests, and most of it refers to matters connected with their superstitions. As the gifts of votaries and the erection of temples enriched the sacerdotal order individually and collectively, the terrors of religion were lent to the secular arm to enforce the rights of property. Music, poetic, scenic, and historical recitations formed parts of the ceremonies of the more civilized nations, and national unity was strengthened by a common shrine. An active barter in amulets, lucky stones, and charms existed all over the continent, to a much greater extent than we might think.

As experience demonstrates that nothing so efficiently promotes civilization as the free and peaceful intercourse of man with man, I lay particular stress on the common custom of making pilgrimages.

The temple on the island of Cozumel in Yucatan was visited every year by such multitudes from all parts of the peninsula, that roads, paved with cut stones, had been constructed from the neighboring shore to the principal cities of the interior. Each village of the Muyscas is said to have had a beaten path to Lake Guatavita, so numerous were the devotees who journeyed to the shine there located.

In Peru the temples of Pachacamà, Rimac, and other famous gods, were repaired to by countless numbers from all parts of the realm, and from other provinces within a radius of three hundred leagues around. Houses of entertainment were established on all the principal roads, and near the temples, for their accommodation; and when they made known the object of their journey, they were allowed a safe passage even through an enemy's territory.

The more carefully we study history, the more important in our eyes will become the religious sense. It is almost the only faculty peculiar to man. It concerns him nearer than aught else. It holds the key to his origin and destiny. As such it merits in all its developments the most earnest attention, an attention we shall find well repaid in the clearer conceptions we thus obtain of the forces which control the actions and fates of individuals and nations.

ABOUT THE AUTHORS

EDWARD DAHLBERG was born in Boston in 1900. He grew up in Kansas City, Missouri, and in Cleveland. After attending the University of California, Berkeley, he was graduated in philosophy from Columbia College. His first novel, *Bottom Dogs*, was published in London in 1929. Two more novels followed, *From Flushing to Calvary* and *Those Who Perish*. Throughout this time he was writing and publishing poetry as well. *Do These Bones Live* (1941), a volume of essays on American literature, began a series of nonfiction works, including the *Flea of Sodom*, *The Sorrows of Priapus*, and the *Carnal Myth*. In 1964 *Because I Was Flesh*, an autobiographical fiction, appeared; last year *The Confessions of Edward Dahlberg* was published.

PETER MARTYR D'ANGHERA, the first reporter of the first observations of the New World, was born in Arona, Italy, in 1457. An accomplished humanist, he was invited by Queen Isabella of Spain to become a court tutor. Under Charles V he was made a member of the Council of the Indies and sent on diplomatic missions to the Near East. By this time he had also become a priest and the Royal Chronicler. He knew personally most of the explorers who set forth from Spain and was a friend of Columbus. Peter Martyr died in Granada in 1526, but his *De Orbe Novo* was not published until 1530. Based mainly upon correspondence and conversation with the returned voyagers themselves, it was the first published account of the great discoveries.

BERNARDINO DE SAHAGÚN, Franciscan missionary, historian, linguist, and anthropologist was born in Léon, Spain, in 1499. After studies at the University of Salamanca, he sailed for Mexico in 1529. There he secured a mastery of Nahuatl, the language of Ancient Mexico and conceived a deep love for the Indian people. At the same time he maintained a scrupulously scientific attitude and methodology in the collection of primary sources for his *Historia General de las cosas de Nueva España*. Its twelve books on the history and language, the material and spiritual culture of the Mexican people before and at the time of the Conquest remain the most important documents of their kind. Sahagún, who may be called the father of American ethnography, died in Mexico City in 1590.

ADOLPH F. BANDELIER was born in Berne, Switzerland, in 1840, and brought up in Highland, Illinois. Trained as a historian and archeologist, he began his work through the Peabody Museum at Harvard. In 1892 he undertook extensive explorations of the coastal and highland areas of Peru. Later, he worked at the American Museum of Natural History in New York, and was a lecturer on Spanish-American literature at Columbia. With his second wife, Fanny (he had become almost totally blind), he produced his last book, *The Islands of Titicaca and Koati*. He died in 1914 while engaged in archival research in Seville. No American archeologist was so thoroughly grounded in history; no American historian was so accomplished in archeology.

DANIEL G. BRINTON was born at Thornburg, Pennsylvania, in 1837, was graduated from Yale College, and then took an M.D. For a time he practiced medicine in West Chester, Pennsylvania; during the first part of the Civil War he served as an Army surgeon. His most abiding passions had been ethnology and archeology, and by 1886 he was Professor of American Linguistics at the University of Pennsylvania. Brinton made the first systematic classification of both North and South American aboriginal languages. His *Library of Aboriginal American Literature* provided the first original texts and translations of the sources. The first volume of this library, "The Maya Chronicles," was a crucial document in American archeology. *The Myths of the North American Indians* is the summation of all of Brinton's vast lore on the subject up to the time of his death in 1899.